The Real D. H. Lawrence

The Real D. H. Lawrence

Caroline Roope

WHITE OWL

AN IMPRINT OF PEN & SWORD BOOKS LTD.
YORKSHIRE - PHILADELPHIA

First published in Great Britain in 2024 by
White Owl
An imprint of Pen & Sword Books Limited
Yorkshire – Philadelphia

ISBN 978 1 39905 816 2

Typeset by Mac Style
Printed in the UK by CPI Group (UK) Ltd, Croydon, CR0 4YY.

Pen & Sword Books Limited incorporates the imprints of After
the Battle, Atlas, Archaeology, Aviation, Discovery, Family History,
Fiction, History, Maritime, Military, Military Classics, Politics,
Select, Transport, True Crime, Air World, Frontline Publishing, Leo
Cooper, Remember When, Seaforth Publishing, The Praetorian Press,
Wharncliffe Local History, Wharncliffe Transport, Wharncliffe True
Crime and White Owl.

For a complete list of Pen & Sword titles please contact

PEN & SWORD BOOKS LIMITED
47 Church Street, Barnsley, South Yorkshire, S70 2AS, England
E-mail: enquiries@pen-and-sword.co.uk
Website: www.pen-and-sword.co.uk
or
PEN AND SWORD BOOKS
1950 Lawrence Rd, Havertown, PA 19083, USA
E-mail: uspen-and-sword@casematepublishers.com
Website: www.penandswordbooks.com

Contents

Preface		vi
Acknowledgements		viii
Introduction: The 'Lawrence myth'		ix
Chapter 1	Boyhood	1
Chapter 2	On the Path to Adulthood	14
Chapter 3	A Stranger in a Strange Land	29
Chapter 4	It is Finished	44
Chapter 5	Something of a Miasma	47
Chapter 6	Sons and Lovers	57
Chapter 7	Frieda	64
Chapter 8	Untying the Knot; Tying a New One	78
Chapter 9	The Lawrences at War	94
Chapter 10	Living on the Edge	103
Chapter 11	Exile	111
Chapter 12	The Savage Pilgrimage	116
Chapter 13	Affairs of Love and Literature	126
Chapter 14	'I look forwards, mustn't look back'	135
Chapter 15	Return to Taos	145
Chapter 16	Lawrence and the Lady	156
Chapter 17	Towards Darkness	164
Epilogue: Unconquered		172
Notes		175
Bibliography		188
Index		192

Preface

The Real D. H. Lawrence is something of a misnomer – for who can ever really know the real Lawrence? Lawrence spent a lifetime roaming the depths of his imagination trying to communicate the essence of who he really was – a quest that ultimately gifted the world 12 full-length novels, 8 plays, more than 800 poems, enough paintings to form an exhibition, travel essays, novellas and short story collections, and a vast catalogue of non-fiction ranging from topics as diverse as European history to psychoanalysis. He famously rejected the conventional path his ambitious, middle-class mother had mapped for him, that of the 'adoring, humble, high-minded' (in Lawrence's words) gentleman who would 'get on' in life – either as a schoolteacher or office clerk – and bring a modicum of respectability to a family whose existence was wholly reliant on the success of the local colliery.

Lydia Lawrence would fail to mould Lawrence, although mercifully, she didn't live long enough to see the man he would become – an impression that would have shattered her secret dreams, where the 'sleeve links were solid gold, and the socks were silk'. Lawrence lived much of his adult life in poverty, only really achieving financial success posthumously, and with the ever-present whiff of scandal attached to it – a fact that would be ironic, if it wasn't so tragic; although now knowing something of Lawrence's character, it wouldn't have changed the way he chose to live his life.

And that choice to live *vitally* and convey a sense of it through his work is what distinguishes Lawrence from other writers of his generation. He needed to feel something – *anything* – to be alive. To be able to render this 'divine otherness,' as Lawrence called it, artistically, was an intrinsic part of his complex and multi-faceted personality. To get to the root of the human soul and cross the boundaries of the conscious mind was a concept Lawrence returned to time and again, and his own ability to access this within himself was the well from which he drew his creative energy. 'Below what we think we are/ we are something else,/ we are almost anything' he composed shortly before his death. Being able to successfully communicate, these sensibilities to the world was his life's work, as well as being the biggest cause of his torment and frustration. But to live his life any other way would have been anathema to Lawrence – truth in all things was the maxim by which he defined his life, even when appraising his own work, which he confessed at times to be completely mediocre, despite his genius.

I confess to knowing little of Lawrence the man before I embarked on this project. To me, as to many other students of English literature, he was the disgraced writer of *Lady Chatterley's Lover* – that racy novel with those short but irresistibly rebellious words – 'fuck' and 'cunt' – in it, which I'd read as part of a short-lived teenage interest in sexually divergent novels, along with Nabokov's *Lolita* and Winterson's *Oranges Are Not the Only Fruit*. To my young, and at that point, uncorrupted mind I remember those expletives going off like little bombs in my head. But I knew nothing of the pariah Lawrence, and even less about his motivation to write something that still had the power to shock some seventy years later.

What we do know, of course, are the chronological facts of his life. But to merely lay these bare in the pages of a book is to do Lawrence and all he stood for an injustice. Because to capture the *real* Lawrence one must engage with the discourse he had with himself throughout his lifetime, and consequently, the discourse he has with us, the reader. And this can be found within his body of work, the introspection he so often invoked in his letters to others, and his lived experience – that of being D. H. Lawrence.

Acknowledgements

It would not have been possible to write this book had I not stood on the shoulders of many Lawrence scholars, past and present. Without drawing on the insight of writers such as John Worthen and Mark Kinkead-Weekes; the seven volumes of Lawrence's letters; the personal memoirs of some of Lawrence's closest friends and acquaintances such as Catherine Carswell, Dorothy Brett and Aldous Huxley; and of course his wife and frequent combatant Frieda Lawrence Ravagli, I'm not sure I would have 'found' the real Lawrence at all, much less understood him. This book represents just that – D. H. Lawrence as I find him. A man as complex and fascinating in death as he was in life.

Introduction:
The 'Lawrence myth'

'The book is to be deemed to be obscene if its effect...if taken as a whole, is such as to tend to deprave and corrupt persons who are likely, having regard to all relevant circumstances, to read...the matter contained...in it.'
The Obscene Publications Act, 1959.[1]

On 20 October 1960, thirty years after Lawrence took his final breath, Mr Francis Boyd cleared his throat in readiness to address Court Number One of the Old Bailey. As the Clerk of the Court, it was his responsibility to begin proceedings – and today the proceedings were to be like no other.

A hush came over the court – which was, fittingly, the largest in the building and where every major and infamous trial had taken place for a century – and then Mr Boyd began:

'Members of the Jury...the Prisoner at the Bar, Penguin Books Limited, is charged that on the 16th day of August last it published an obscene article, to wit, a book entitled Lady Chatterley's Lover by D. H. Lawrence. To this indictment it has pleaded not guilty, and it is your charge to say, having heard the evidence, whether it be guilty or not.'[2]

What followed was a landmark in British legal history.

The Trial of Lady Chatterley's Lover has become literary legend. It still resonates today. Indeed, when an annotated copy of the book used by the trial judge, Mr Justice Byrne, came up for auction at Sotheby's in 2019 it was sold to an overseas bidder for £56,250. But such was the cultural and historical (not to mention, literary) value of the item that arts minister, Michael Ellis, took immediate steps to ban its export from the UK and a crowdfunding campaign was launched to keep the book in the country.

The idea of putting a book, or more accurately, its publisher, on trial before a jury in the twenty-first century seems preposterous, but in the taboo-averse autumn of 1960, a favourable outcome for the publisher was by no means a fait accompli.

The acquittal of Penguin Books by a jury made up of nine men and three women was a victory for freedom of expression as well as a challenge to the establishment values that had placed it on trial in the first place. It also highlighted the disconnect between Lawrence's motivation for writing his final full-length work – what he hoped the reader would take from it – and how it was received on its initial publication in 1928 – by the 'establishment' at any rate. The public would have to wait until after the 1960 trial to read about Lady Constance Chatterley and her extra-marital affair with gamekeeper Oliver Mellors, as well as all the sexual activities and – *shock* – the blatant naming of those activities within the text.

When Lawrence first conceived the idea of Lady Chatterley and began to write her story, the reputation he had had unfairly foisted on him as a writer of obscene and pornographic material was already fully formed. Lawrence's earlier novel *The Rainbow* (1915) had caused a furore for its publishers, Methuen, when obscenity charges were brought against them for their decision to release 1,011 copies of the book. Methuen were given the opportunity to defend their decision at Bow Street Magistrates Court but offered no real argument. Instead, they placed the blame mostly on Lawrence, citing that he 'refused to do anything more'[3] to alter the 'obscene' text. The 'obscene' text contained none of the expletive language associated with its more famous literary sister, *Lady Chatterley's Lover*. Instead, the novel was criticised for containing 'obscenity of thought, idea, and action throughout', which was 'wrapped up in language which he supposed would be regarded in some quarters as an artistic and intellectual effort'.[4] Following the prosecution, all 1,011 copies of *The Rainbow* were seized and destroyed, and Methuen publicly stated that they regretted publishing it – which for Lawrence was a greater blow than the destruction of his work.

This suppression of his artistic licence would have profound consequences for Lawrence's attitude towards Britain and what he saw as the 'bourgeois world', as well as his ability to find a publisher for his future works, but in the short-term Lawrence was now conspicuous. He had brought himself to the world's attention, but not in the way that he intended – he was the author of licentious and immodest books. 'Orgies of sexiness'[5] was one description levied at Lawrence's works, along with criticism of his 'decadent mind'. He was 'indecent', and his prose, 'filthy', 'dirty' and 'depraved'. His writing would remain categorised in this way for many years after *The Rainbow* and *Lady Chatterley*, creating a myth around Lawrence that persisted for years after his death.

The world, as it was in Lawrence's lifetime, wasn't ready for him. And neither were they ready to be confronted with Lawrence's uncomfortable depictions of human interaction. 'To read a really new novel will *always* hurt, to some extent', Lawrence tells us in one of his many essays. 'There will always be resistance.'[6] For

Lawrence, that resistance took the form of a wholescale vilification, censorship and, at times, outright hostility.

The *Lady Chatterley* trial allowed Lawrence the man to become disentangled from Lawrence the myth. The process of separation began in the courtroom with the thirty-six expert witnesses who were called to defend the literary, ethical and spiritual qualities of the book. These witnesses – not just scholars and academics, but journalists, critics, authors and child education experts, as well as four Anglican clergymen – and their contention that the book had sufficient literary merit to be published for the public good, allowed this enlightenment to begin – and hypocrisy to begin to flounder.

'I think these passages [in *Lady Chatterley's Lover*]', stated Oxford academic Helen Gardner at the trial, 'do succeed, far beyond expectation, in doing something extraordinarily difficult, which very few other writers have really attempted with such courage and devotion, and that is to attempt to put into words experiences that are really very difficult to verbalize.'[7]

Dame Rebecca West was also quick to point out Lawrence's failings, suggesting that 'A lot of pages in this book are, to my point of view, ludicrous, but I would still say this is a book of undoubted literary merit…And though there are ugly things, though there is this unsuccessful attempt to handle the ugly words, this is still from that standard a good book in my opinion.'[8]

The trial was also notable for its absurdity. A long discussion about Lawrence's description of Connie's feelings in her womb and bowels, and whether it was possible to feel alive in one's womb and bowels was one memorable moment; as was the point at which the prosecution asked the Bishop of Woolwich whether it was his view that Christian's ought to read *Lady Chatterley's Lover*. 'Yes, I think it is [my view],' he replied 'Because I think what Lawrence was trying to do…'[9] But the courtroom never got to hear what the Bishop of Woolwich thought Lawrence was trying to do, because the prosecution interrupted with an objection – thus supplying perfect fodder for the evening papers, which were thrilled to be able to print the headline, 'A Book All Christians Should Read.'

And as for those ubiquitous four-letter words.

'How far are the four-letter words in the book either relevant or necessary to the theme or meaning of the book?'[10] asked the prosecution.

Well…despite the shock tactics they employed – metaphorically flinging words across the courtroom and straight into the jury's faces very early on in the proceedings (along with the number of times each one appeared) – the words lost their shock value remarkably quickly. Which, paradoxically, was exactly Lawrence's point. 'The word arse is clean enough', Lawrence once mused. 'We must accept the word arse as we accept the word face, since arses we have and always shall have', which sums up his position perfectly. Words were Lawrence's life, whether he was speaking of 'John Thomas, an' th' cunt',[11] or reflecting on the 'sweet honeyed scent' of the tree-heather in Tuscany. Being able to express himself using an exhaustive vocabulary was critical for him to effectively convey the full range of life's sensations and emotions in his work. 'The body feels real hunger, real thirst, real joy in the sun or the snow, real pleasure in the smell of roses or the look of a lilac bush; real anger, real sorrow, real love, real tenderness, real warmth, real passion, real hate, real grief', Lawrence wrote in his *Propos of Lady Chatterley's Lover* – his 1929 attempt to defend and explain his infamous novel. Without language – in all its guises – Lawrence would never have been able to get to the heart of what it means to be human. And if he couldn't express that, he would fail at awakening the reader's consciousness to the higher human emotions he believed to be dead in mankind: 'love in all its manifestations, from genuine desire to tender love, love of our fellow-men, and love of God: we mean love, joy, delight, hope, true indignant anger, passionate sense of justice and injustice, truth and untruth, honesty and dishonour, and real belief in *anything*: for belief is a profound emotion that has the mind's connivance.'[12]

Lawrence was, above all other things, an artist. His manifesto for life exists in the pages of his poetry and prose, his essays, his letters and his paintings, essentially that: 'our life *consists in* this achieving of a pure relationship between ourselves and the living universe about us.'[13] He lived in the here and now, in a perpetual state of spirited mindfulness that seems remarkably forward thinking for a man who lived through an era of intense pessimism following the Great War. Far from being an accidental consequence of his artistic output, Lawrence's doctrine provides the foundation on which he creates his extraordinary works of literary and artistic merit, and for some, works of genius. 'A work of art is not an arbitrary thing', argued Dame Rebecca West in 1960. 'A work of art is an analysis of an experience, and a synthesis of the findings of the analysis, that makes life a serious matter and makes the world seem beautiful.'[14]

It was Lawrence's gift for finding that beauty that endures.

Chapter 1

Boyhood

To me it seemed, and still seems, an extremely beautiful countryside, just between the red sandstone and the oak-trees of Nottingham, and the cold limestone, the ash-trees, the stone fences of Derbyshire.[1]

D. H. Lawrence

I hate the damn place.[2]

D. H. Lawrence

The ex-mining village of Eastwood, Nottinghamshire sits just on the Notts-Derby border, some eight miles northwest of Nottingham and ten miles northeast of Derby. Sandwiched between two county towns, in the heart of the industrial Midlands, it is a village with only a handful of notable features, although pleasant enough. Architectural historian John Charles Cox was thoroughly underwhelmed in the early twentieth century. When he compiled *The Churches of Nottinghamshire* he recorded Eastwood's primary church, St Mary's, in just one line: 'Entirely rebuilt, 1858.'[3]

Its historical narrative follows a similar pattern to hundreds of other villages in the coal-rich areas of the British Isles: a once thriving agricultural district of several hundred residents grows exponentially with the coming of industry – in Eastwood's case, via the man-made Erewash Canal, and then later the Great Northern Railway – coal pits are sunk, money is made, the pits close and everyone laments the ruined landscape and the lack of opportunities for the younger generation.

Visitors to the area are informed several miles out of Eastwood that they are entering 'Lawrence country'. The rolling landscape and vast swathes of green stretching in every direction confirms that yes indeed, this is the country Lawrence captured so eloquently in many of his works – the 'sleepy' fields and woods that he later found so disconnected from the modern world. An old, preserved pit headstock looms into view – Brinsley Colliery being one of ten within a one-mile walk of Eastwood, and famous for being the place in which Lawrence's father, Arthur, was employed as a miner. The spectral frame, which sits incongruously in the conservation area surrounding it, is the only visible evidence of the mine that claimed the life of Lawrence's uncle James and was immortalised as 'Beggarlee Colliery' in Lawrence's 1913 novel, *Sons and Lovers*. A memento mori to industry and the literature of Lawrence. Nature has reclaimed the rest, thanks to a dedicated band of voluntary workers – a sentiment Lawrence no doubt would have approved of immensely.

If you follow the line of Brinsley Brook – made easier by the busy A608 that tracks the same path (although in slightly noisier and more polluted fashion – Lawrence would certainly have had something to say about that – Eastwood comes into view. A blink-and-you'll-miss-it sign of tiny proportions directs visitors to the D. H. Lawrence Birthplace Museum, also known as 8a Victoria Street, an innocuous red-brick Victorian terrace – the place where David Herbert Lawrence was born. Fortunately, if you do miss the turning, the Lady Chatterley Wetherspoons pub and White Peacock Coffee Shop give a good indication that you're in the right place.

If Lawrence had a troubled relationship with his birthplace – as evidenced by the quotes that open this chapter – the feeling was most definitely mutual. For a time anyway.

Eastwood spent the forty years following Lawrence's death, and before to the creation of the museum in 1976, feeling rather incensed at Lawrence's liberal use of the local people as material for his novels – often unfavourably, and with little attempt to disguise their characters. If the Nottinghamshire landscape was to provide inspiration for the backdrop, Lawrence naturally needed to populate his novels with authentically drawn-from-life characters. Free use of the people he knew was part of his modus operandi, albeit one that didn't endear him to many of them, and the autobiographical nature of his early works demanded a level of truth in all things.

This betrayal cast a long shadow. The local council couldn't raise the money to buy 8a Victoria Street, where Lawrence was born; the promise of a Lawrence Memorial Hall for the community fell through due to 'lack of funds'; and the Phoenix headstone from his first grave in Vence, France, where he died in 1930, was consigned to a dusty attic in the council offices in 1957, where it languished, forgotten, for almost two decades, before being retrieved and placed on display in the new Eastwood Library in 1975. The Birthplace Museum finally gave it a permanent and more fitting residency in 2008.

Thanks to an enthusiast group of local people, the slightly grimy terraced house in Victoria Street was eventually purchased and now provides visitors with a glimpse into Lawrence's world circa 1885 – the year he was born. The Victorian age he was born into was dominated by empire – by the 1880s Britain was in the final stages of acquiring the last of its territories, and full of its own self-importance, was prepared to fight tooth and claw to ensure it got what it wanted; or at the very least negotiate around the diplomatic table with the other European nations when it came to the annexation of Africa.

The Lawrence family were just one tiny cog in the gigantic industrial machine that made up Great Britain and her colonies in the late nineteenth century. Their minute corner of the British empire, ordinary though it was, was the engine house driving that progress and, like many of the other colliery villages that boomed during the late eighteenth and nineteenth centuries, it was characterised by row upon row of two-up two-down workers' cottages – most likely constructed by the local colliery company – housing the estimated ninety-eight per cent of the population of Eastwood who depended on coal mining for their existence.[4] As Lawrence remembered, 'little local speculators already began to straggle dwellings in rows, always in rows, across the fields: nasty red-brick, flat-faced dwellings with dark slate roofs.'[5] In this 'queer jumble of the old England and the new',[6] sons were expected to become colliers, and daughters were expected to marry colliers. Several generations of colliers could be found at the same pit – or if not, in one nearby. A microcosm of dirt, back-breaking (not to mention, dangerous) labour, financial hardship and bleak prospects – for both sexes. Respectability was maintained, above all things, although the lure of the public house no doubt trumped that of the local church. Many a miner's wife spent pay-day wrestling what pittance she could from the grasp of her husband so she could keep the rest of the family afloat before he could drink his wages away in the local pub.

The same path through life was mapped for David Herbert 'Bert' Lawrence when he came into the world on 11 September 1885. Except Lawrence's mother, Lydia, was a Beardsall – and the Beardsalls were most certainly *not* colliers, or native to the colliery villages in and around Eastwood. Born in 1851 into a family whose roots were in Nottingham, but who spent Lydia's childhood moving to wherever her engine-fitter father could find work, by 1871 Lydia, along with two of her sisters, was a lace drawer – until she caught the eye of miner Arthur Lawrence. The two were wed in 1875, with Lydia's father promoting himself to 'Engineer' on her marriage certificate.

Lydia Lawrence made much of her pedigree, proudly telling her own children of the Beardsalls' well-to-do middle-class background, but this myth obscured the difficult truth. Her father suffered a life-changing accident in 1870 and was superannuated on the tiny sum of £18 a year; an amount that would have to support the entire family. Little wonder that Lydia and her sisters found themselves contributing to the family pot by becoming part of Nottingham's famous lace trade. The family had little option but to take a house in Sneinton – one of Nottingham's notorious slum suburbs where factory-workers lived cheek by jowl with each other in tenements that had little to no sanitation and even less privacy. The workhouse that loomed ominously over the district was within walking distance of the Beardsalls' house and would have served as a constant reminder to the family of the precariousness of their situation.

In terms of their employment status and financial prospects, Arthur Lawrence was an entirely suitable match for Lydia Beardsall at that time, despite her delusions of gentility. He offered her the chance to escape from her somewhat domineering and puritanical father, as well as a household budget that was substantially greater per week than George Beardsall's measly monthly pension. Arthur Lawrence was certainly not her match intellectually – Lydia was a keen reader of books, occasionally wrote poetry, and had been to school. She had even taught younger children alongside her own studies before the family fortunes took a downward turn – but what Arthur lacked in intelligence, he compensated for with a spirited nature and easy-going charm, as well as good looks and, surprisingly, a talent for dancing that was renowned in the district.[7]

The couple met in 1874 and were married a year later, living first at Brinsley in a house Arthur rented from his mother, before moving to Sutton-in-Ashfield, Old Radford and then finally settling in Eastwood where 'Bert' – who became known universally, and by his own choice, as D. H. Lawrence – was born in 1885. Lawrence was the fourth of five children, with elder siblings George Arthur, William Ernest and Emily, and younger sister, Lettice Ada.

It is no secret that Lawrence's third full-length novel, *Sons and Lovers* (1913), was largely autobiographical, and just as the union of Walter and Gertrude Morel floundered early on, so too did Arthur and Lydia Lawrence's. Having spent her earlier childhood sheltered from the heavy industry that was now on her doorstep, Lydia was unprepared for the realities of being a miner's wife. But she was resourceful. Their first Eastwood home included a shop window, and whether out of sheer boredom at the tedium of working-class life, a desire for some autonomy, or (more likely) because Arthur wasn't handing over enough of his wages to keep house, Lydia began to make and sell her own lace products from the front parlour of their house in Victoria Street. This did little to commend Lydia to the other local wives, however, who saw this distinction as further evidence of Lydia's 'airs and graces' – further compounded by her genteel Kentish accent from a spell living in Sheerness during her childhood.

Each pregnancy that Lydia endured strengthened the ties that bound her to her miserable existence. Arthur Lawrence's favourite haunt, along with much of the mining fraternity, was the local public house – an evening social activity Lydia came to resent when she was burdened with the responsibility of ensuring the children were warm, clothed and well fed, which was routinely made more difficult by Arthur's drinking habits. 'There was nothing else for the colliers to do', one Eastwood local commented in 1960. Just as Gertrude Morel in *Sons and*

Lovers felt 'wretched with the coming child', so too would the expectant Lydia. 'The world seemed a dreary place', writes Lawrence of Gertrude's predicament,

> *where nothing else would happen for her – at least until William grew up. But for herself, nothing but this dreary endurance – till the children grew up. And the children! She could not afford to have this third. She did not want it. The father was serving beer in a public house, swilling himself drunk. She despised him and was tied to him. This coming child was too much for her...she was sick of it, the struggle with poverty and ugliness and meanness...And looking ahead, the prospect of her life made her feel as if she were buried alive.*[8]

Lydia made no real secret of how miserable she was – an impression that was seared onto Lawrence's memory, providing both inspiration and a source of torment that lasted his lifetime. It seems likely that Lydia's final link to independence – her front parlour lace shop – was severed on the birth of Lawrence in 1885. By 1887 Lydia was expecting her last child, Lettice Ada (known as Ada), and a lack of space meant the family had to move to a larger house in Eastwood – this time to the end house on a row known as 'the Breach', which was cavernous in comparison to Victoria Street and had its own garden on three sides.

The Breach provided the inspiration for 'the Bottoms' in *Sons and Lovers* but by 1891, the Lawrences were on the move again, this time to Walker Street, which with its bay windows and sweeping views of Brinsley, High Park woods and the surrounding countryside made not only a perfect playground for the youngest Lawrence children but also allowed Lydia to believe they were 'getting on'. 'How nice we thought that Walker Street house', Ada wrote after Lawrence's death, 'with its comfortable kitchen which always looked so homelike.'[9] Lawrence captured something of this childhood idyll in his poem, 'Piano', although the memory is clearly painful for him:

> *Softly in the dusk, a woman is singing to me;*
> *Taking me back down the vista of years, till I see*
> *A child sitting under the piano, in the boom of the tingling strings*
> *And pressing the small, poised feet of a mother who smiles as she sings*
> *In spite of myself, the insidious mastery of song*
> *Betrays me back, till the heart of me weeps to belong*
> *To the old Sunday evenings at home, with winter outside*[10]

But behind Lydia's carefully constructed façade of chintz curtains and brass candlesticks, relations between the couple were at their lowest point. Lydia would purposefully wait for Arthur to arrive home from the pub, 'her rage seething, until on his arrival it boiled over in a torrent of biting truths which turned him from his slightly fuddled and pleasantly apologetic mood into a brutal and coarse beast'.[11] Elizabeth Thorp, a resident of Eastwood and whose parents knew the Lawrences, remembered her mother leaving their door unlocked at night so that Lydia could run in for protection when Arthur came home after drinking.[12] In *Sons and Lovers*, Lawrence describes the 'battle-pitch' between Gertrude and Walter Morel: 'Each forgot everything save the hatred of the other and the battle between them. She was fiery and furious as he.'[13] The Morels' argument famously climaxes when Walter thrusts Gertrude out of the door and into the cold night air – and bolts the door against her. This may be autobiographical – but irrespective of whether Arthur Lawrence did indeed lock Lydia out for the night, the children were aware of the ferocity of their arguments. 'With palpitating hearts we waited until he came to bed', Ada Lawrence wrote, 'knowing that not until then could we safely sleep.'[14] Lawrence summed up his feelings succinctly in a letter he wrote in 1910, describing the Lawrence's marriage as a 'carnal, bloody fight'.

The children idolised their mother, and she in turn doted on them, providing them with a 'wealth of love and a security past all understanding'.[15] But the children also recognised that her lack of tolerance for their father's drinking was also a contributing factor to the undercurrent of misery in the household. With little in common with his wife, Arthur Lawrence sought solace with his own kind where he felt more at ease and sure of himself. 'He was too different from her', D. H. Lawrence wrote in *Sons and Lovers*. 'His nature was purely sensuous, and she strove to make him moral, religious. She tried to force him to face things. He could not endure it – it drove him out of his mind.'[16] Lawrence wrote at length on the idea of 'sensuousness' and how it related to the mining community. The intimacy of the men in the pit was an intimacy borne out of the instinctiveness of the senses rather than of intellect. Working alongside each other, stripped to the waist, in the dark, remote corners of the subterranean world, with danger lurking in every tunnel, bred a powerful sense of togetherness and comradeship that the men failed to achieve on the surface. And so, 'the collier went to the pub and drank to continue his intimacy with his mates. They talked endlessly, but it was rather of wonders and marvels, even in politics, than of facts. It was hard facts, in the shape of wife, money, and nagging home necessities, which they fled away from, out of the house to the pub, and out of the house to the pit.'[17] Little wonder Arthur and Lydia were unable to find common ground. A local family who knew the Lawrences and were interviewed by *The Guardian* in 1960 reflected that, 'we had very little sympathy for Mrs Lawrence. She felt herself superior to her husband…Mr Lawrence, although he drank, was a very respected man.'[18]

Regardless of local sentiment, resentment in the Lawrence marriage festered on both sides – Arthur was a constant source of disappointment to his wife, and Lydia was no longer the thing of 'mystery and fascination'[19] that had so attracted Arthur in the first place. Instead, she was in a perpetual state of dissatisfaction and despair. She withdrew her love for him and made no secret of it.

Instead, Lydia poured all her love and effort into ensuring her children didn't follow the same path as their father: 'It was a mother's business to see that her sons "got on", and it was the man's business to provide the money',[20] Lawrence wrote just before his death. The couple's eldest son, George, left school shortly after the Lawrences moved to Walker Street and was able to secure a position as an errand boy in his uncle's picture framing business in Nottingham – a situation no doubt contrived by Lydia to keep him well away from the lure of the pits. Despite his promising start, George would go on to disappoint his mother by running away to join the army (for which Lydia had to spend £18 buying him out) and then had the temerity to get his girlfriend, Ada Wilson, pregnant. The young couple were hurried up the aisle in 1897, just months before their baby arrived. George and Ada's almost-illegitimate son, William Ernest Lawrence, would go on to become a Nottinghamshire dentist – a profession that Lydia would no doubt have approved.

It was the Lawrences' second son, Ernest, who Lydia was most devoted to, and whom D. H. Lawrence would revive as the character of William in *Sons and Lovers*. Ernest was, quite literally, Lydia's blue-eyed boy. After showing much academic promise, Ernest obtained employment as a clerk in the Shipley colliery offices, and then at the Cooperative Society's office at Langley Mill. As far as Lydia was concerned, he embodied what she meant by 'getting on' – his drive to better himself led him to attend night classes in his spare time so that he could become proficient in typewriting and shorthand. This allowed him to leave the mining community of Nottinghamshire for a position in London as a clerk in a busy shipping office. According to Ada Lawrence, he was 'the life and soul of the house' and his homecomings were the highlight of his siblings' lives, something of which Lawrence captures in *Sons and Lovers*: 'The children drew back with beating hearts. A great train, bound for Manchester, drew up. Two doors opened, and from one of them, William. They flew to him…. Everybody was mad with happiness in the family. Home was home, and they loved it with a passion of love, whatever the suffering had been…People came in to see William, to see what a difference London had made to him. And they all found him 'such a gentleman, and SUCH a fine fellow, my word!''[21]

Thus, the sickly D. H. Lawrence (Bert to his family) was something of a weakling in comparison to his 'fine fellow' of a brother Ernest, suffering bouts of poor health throughout his infancy and childhood. Being the second from youngest of the five Lawrence children, Bert was born into a marriage that had already failed beyond reconciliation, and although Arthur and Lydia never formally separated, they were separated in heart and mind. This polarisation extended to the children's relationship with their father, as Lydia sought to alienate Arthur and any remaining influence he had over the children. It was Lydia's family, the Beardsalls, who were held up as a paradigm of respectability. The Lawrences were not suitable role models, so Lydia would mould her children to be higher moral beings – just as her own family had been. They would go to school, take the teetotal pledge, and attend Sunday School and the Congregational Chapel in Eastwood. Lydia's effort – not just in terms of raising her children to strive for more, but her constant struggle to maintain them all on Arthur's meagre wages – was repaid with a fierce loyalty that burned bright in all the Lawrence children, but most particularly in Bert. The result of this was an almost visceral dislike of his father; an emotion Lawrence explored in depth through the autobiographical 'Paul' in Sons and Lovers.

'Paul hated his father so. The collier's small, mean head, with its black hair slightly soiled with grey, lay on the bare arms, and the face, dirty and inflamed, with a fleshy nose and thin, paltry brows, was turned sideways, asleep with beer and weariness and nasty temper.'[22] Lawrence once wrote in a letter that he 'shivered with horror'[23] whenever his father touched him.

This revulsion at his father was a sentiment he shared with the rest of the Lawrence family who, in varying degrees, seemed similarly appalled by Arthur's ability to upset the equilibrium of the household. Just as Walter Morel is described by Lawrence as an 'ugly irritant to their souls',[24] who takes a grim satisfaction in 'disgusting them, and driving them nearly mad',[25] so too did the loathed Arthur Lawrence. The strange family dynamics within the Lawrence household did not go unnoticed by others either. A contemporary of Lawrence's, May Chambers, was a frequent visitor to the family during his adolescent years, and observed that Lawrence,

> seemed to gather the gloom of the back yard into his being and crouch among the shabbiness like something sinister...Bert seemed to send out jagged waves of hate and loathing that made me shudder...I wanted to get away. The queer behaviour of mother and son made me tremble internally.[26]

Arthur was painfully aware that his children looked down on him; they were ashamed of his rough ways and lack of intellect, and therefore alienated him.

The unhappy result of this estrangement was that Arthur went out of his way to engender his children's low opinion of him even more. Lydia's constant characterisation of him as a drunken ne'er-do-well undermined the patriarchal authority he naturally expected to exert over his family – and without this, Arthur's role as husband and father was negligible; 'more or less a husk.'[27]

Lydia seemed to understand her youngest son Bert in a way no one else could. Likewise, Bert's perception of his mother's innermost thoughts and feelings was the cornerstone of not just Lawrence's childhood, but the rest of his life. In Lawrence's mind, they were bound together in their mutual antipathy for Arthur Lawrence. Just before Lydia's death he explained their bond as being like a 'husband and wife' love; it was instinctive. The 'peculiar fusion of soul' as Lawrence called it – the synergy of their emotions – sustained them both. One could not live without the other – a status quo which, that eventually broken, was to have profound consequences for Lawrence. Lawrence's deep sense of empathy for his mother and their shared pain haunts *Sons and Lovers* – it is there in the 'wide, dismayed eyes'[28] of Annie and William when they realise their father caused the cut on Gertrude's head; or in Paul's terror when his father comes home drunk after the children have gone to bed – a silent fear expressed through the noises he can hear below – the 'booming shouts', 'snarling' and fists banging on the table. 'He might hit their mother again', Lawrence wrote. 'There was a feeling of horror, a kind of bristling in the darkness, and a sense of blood. They lay with their hearts in the grip of an intense anguish.'[29] It is not until the children hear the kettle being filled that they can go to sleep peacefully – because the ordinary sound they have listened out for so intently through the shouting and banging signals that she is still alive and uninjured.

Lawrence's recreation of his childhood fear is drawn so acutely one can readily believe it was written from personal experience. Perhaps there is truth in it. A contemporary and close school friend of Lawrence's, George Neville, recalls a violent scene between father and son in his memoir of Lawrence – the cause of which was the expenditure on Bert Lawrence's new suit, and his father's annoyance that it was his 'money that "peed [paid] for it,"'

> 'Ere I ain't got a copper even ter get mesen a drink, an' 'e can 'ave owt 'e wants. What's 'e want wi' new suits? An' if 'e does why can't 'e goo out an' earn 'em? Not get you ter rob me for 'em.' He shouted this harangue in quite a loud voice, thumping the table at intervals, by way of punctuation.[30]

The result of Arthur Lawrence's fury, and his son's anger at him for shouting at his mother, is raised fists on both sides: 'he raised his right fist and stepped towards Bert', Neville recalls, 'who, taut and white with passion, raised his fist and stepped forward also. And there they stood, breast to breast, teeth exposed and all but snarling, glaring into each other's eyes, just as you have seen the untamed things of the wild.'[31] Neville claims to have intervened – fortunately, before any punches were thrown – and the two young lads make themselves scarce. This recollection came to light after Lawrence's death and was written more than twenty-five years after the incident – and so must be considered in this context.

Yet if Arthur Lawrence was violent towards Lydia or his children, there is no record of it in Ada Lawrence's account of their childhood. Indeed, Lawrence himself describes his father as being of 'sanguine temperament, warm and hearty', although he also points to his lack of principles and capacity to lie. Arthur certainly enjoyed drinking and was probably drunk on numerous occasions but not to the point of alcoholism. His wages did fund his drinking but did not compromise the welfare of his family. He was a hard worker, although Ada admits he 'probably told them [the colliery owners] to go to Hell from time to time'.[32] There was also regret. 'He was never really intolerable,' Ada writes, 'and if, instead of wanting the impossible from him, we had tried to interest ourselves in the things for which he really cared, we should have been spared many unhappy and sordid scenes.'[33]

What is more likely is that Lawrence's characterisation of Walter Morel in *Sons and Lovers* used elements of not just his father's character, but that of his uncle (coincidentally called Walter), his father's friends and the wider mining community. Walter embodies Lawrence's fears of what he could have become if not for the influence of his mother: a brutish, unpredictable and narrow-minded shell of a man. And in a wider sense, he personifies Lawrence's dread of what the mining community represented – a 'vile' man-made England where industry would gradually erode the countryside he so loved. He reflected on this later in life, commenting angrily on those who perpetrated 'the ugliness of my native village…scrabbling over the face of England with miles and square miles of red-brick "homes", like horrible scabs.'[34]

The rural Nottinghamshire of Lawrence's childhood was to provide the panacea he so desperately needed to the torments he suffered at home, and it is wholly unsurprising that some of Lawrence's best writing is of the bucolic scenes of the open countryside described in his works. His childhood was pockmarked by intermittent episodes of crying for which he could not explain the cause, and by his ferocious temper, a trait he famously carried with him into adulthood. 'These fits were not often', Lawrence writes of his alter-ego Paul in *Sons and Lovers*, 'but they caused a shadow in Mrs Morel's heart, and her treatment of Paul was different from that of the other children.'[35] But Lawrence found emotional freedom in outdoor exploration, and later his roaming would also take him to Haggs Farm and Jessie Chambers – where Lawrence would form another intense and influential bond. But first, he would have to go to school.

Lawrence started at the local board school, Beauvale, when he was just three years and eight months, but was withdrawn again soon after his fourth birthday.[36] There is no written record of why, although some historians have speculated that the first bout of pneumonia he suffered during his childhood may have been the reason. Coupled with his sensitive emotional disposition, and attachment to his mother, it seems likely that Lawrence was intensely unhappy at school. He did, however, return at the age of 7 – by now a 'dirty-nosed child' who was, 'very fond of the girls',[37] according to one Eastwood local.

Beauvale Board School still stands, imposingly, just a short walk from Lawrence's birthplace in Victoria Street. Now in a state of disrepair, the three-winged Grade II listed building was erected in 1878 – the first by Greasley School Board that, acting on the 1870 Education Act, levied local rates to fund the £6,000 build. The school could accommodate 550 children but was oversubscribed from the start – a problem compounded by the 1880 Education Act, which made school attendance compulsory for all children up to the age of 10. Lawrence first attended the infant wing in 1889 and one can imagine the anguish he probably suffered on finding himself removed from the comfort of his mother and his home to attend a draughty, overcrowded school with hundreds of other children from mining families. When Lawrence returned to the school in 1893 after his unexplained absence, it was to the boys' wing. A group photograph of Lawrence with his peers taken soon after he restarted shows a smartly dressed lad – only one of a handful wearing a neat silk tie, and the only one with a handkerchief in his breast pocket. These small details marked Lawrence out; he was not 'one of them', despite Lawrence's assertion in later life that he was 'just like anybody else of the miners' children'.[38] His childhood school friend George Neville described him as:

a thin, pale, weakly lad always scrupulously clean, neat and tidy, with no energy for our oft-times over-robust games, and no apparent inclination to attempt to join us. A book and a quiet corner were always his delight and he would much more often be found with girl companions than with boys.[39]

'He was very studious', commented a former pupil in 1960. 'Whenever you saw him he was always going somewhere with books or papers under his arm.'[40] 'Delicate', seems to have been a word strongly attached to Lawrence. Yet his lack of robustness for the rough and tumble of the playground provided the perfect breeding ground for his genius to flourish; his escape into those 'quiet corners' giving him the opportunity to capitalise on his schooling.

Despite sharing a classroom with more than seventy other children, Lawrence was exceptional enough to be selected for the examination to gain a scholarship to Nottingham High School; one of his former teachers describing him as 'a brilliant boy'.[41] Headmaster William Whitehead tutored Lawrence himself and in the spring of 1898, Lawrence was successful – only the second miners' son ever to obtain a place at the prestigious day school. His friend George Neville would follow him a year later.

Lawrence understood that as a scholarship boy he was considered 'a class apart' and although he made a couple of friends, he 'recoiled away from the bourgeoisie, regular sort'. He didn't fit the stereotype of a miner's son, yet he didn't fit the persona of a public schoolboy either. He was neither working class, nor middle class. He was intellectual, yet from a largely unintellectual community. Delicate, yet strong in mind and conviction. Highly sensitive yet capable of downright insensitivity. This narrative of contradiction was the metaphorical seam that ran through Lawrence's life – a seam that he not only mined for the purposes of his writing but also on which his entire personality seemed to rest. For without contradiction, Lawrence wouldn't have been Lawrence. And Lawrence may have been brilliant in many areas, but after a good start, his performance at high school dwindled significantly.

This may be explained by a tragic family event that occurred in March 1900 involving his Uncle Walter and Lawrence's 15-year-old cousin, also called Walter, at their home in Ilkeston, Derbyshire. In a scene that is reminiscent of the violence threatened by Walter Morel towards Paul in *Sons and Lovers*, the real Walter lost his temper with his young son, and in a fit of rage threw a sharpening steel at his head. Just as in the novel, the squabble started over who had the most claim on the food in the larder, with the young Walter antagonising his father by insinuating that he didn't deserve the food because of his laziness. Despite several warnings by Walter senior that he would throw something at the lad if he 'didn't give over',[42] and his mother's plea to 'hold your noise',[43] the youngster continued to taunt his father. Walter senior then picked up the steel and hurled it at his son, claiming in court that he was 'not intending to hurt him'.[44] Unfortunately, the steel struck his son on his left ear, penetrated his brain, and caused a two-and-a-half-inch-long skull fracture. The youngster clung on to life for three days but succumbed to his injuries. The incident was a sensation locally, with one newspaper relishing the opportunity to regale its readers with the news that a man had been charged with 'feloniously killing and slaying his son'.[45] Walter Lawrence was tried that summer at the Derby Assizes and pleaded 'not guilty' to manslaughter, despite his wife and youngest son witnessing the entire episode and the testimony of the local doctor. He had already served fifteen weeks in jail, and although he was found guilty by the jury, the judge allowed him to go. 'The decision was greeted with loud applause in court',[46] reported the *Nottinghamshire Guardian*. Walter's release may not be palatable by today's standards but the loss of the main wage earner due to a prison sentence would have been disastrous for the Ilkeston Lawrences – whether he had killed his son or not.

There is no record of what the Eastwood Lawrences thought about what occurred over in Ilkeston, but with Bert Lawrence also aged 15 at the time, and with the Lawrence family name being dragged through all the local papers, one can assume it made for some awkward questions.

The remainder of Lawrence's time at Nottingham High School was uneventful, save for a handful of termly prizes in maths, French and German. But another family disaster – this time much closer to home – would not only upset the fragile progress Lawrence had made towards climbing the class ladder but also make for a tragic end to Lawrence's childhood.

Chapter 2

On the Path to Adulthood

She stood in her white apron on the open road, watching him as he crossed the field. He had a small, compact body that looked full of life. She felt, as she saw him trudging over the field, that where he determined to go he would get... Now she had two sons in the world. She could think of two places, great centres of industry, and feel that she had put a man into each of them, that these men would work out what she *wanted; they were derived from her and their works also would be hers.* [1]

Lawrence left Nottingham High School in 1901 at the age of 16. There was no fanfare for the miner's son, whose school career had been remarkably undistinguished thus far; his 'quite satisfactory' school report from 1898 certainly giving no indication of the greatness to come.

Leaving school as a 'quite satisfactory' boy, rather than an outstanding one – albeit one who had at least been liberated from a future in the pit – meant Lawrence's options were limited. With the help of his brother Ernest, Lawrence applied in the autumn of 1901 for a post as a junior clerk with a manufacturer of surgical goods, Messrs. Haywood, in Nottingham. His meticulously crafted letter, which the more worldly Ernest had clearly assisted with, was successful in gaining Lawrence the position and he began his new role that same autumn at thirteen shillings a week.[2] Lawrence didn't record his own feelings at being launched into the world of business – except those that he described in his alter-ego Paul when he realises he has been summoned to an interview by Thomas Jordan, Manufacturer of Surgical Appliances: 'Paul looked at the picture of a wooden leg, adorned with elastic stockings and other appliances, that figured on Mr. Jordan's notepaper, and he felt alarmed. He had not known that elastic stockings existed. And he seemed to feel the business world, with its regulated system of values, and its impersonality, and he dreaded it. It seemed monstrous also that a business could be run on wooden legs.'[3]

His first impressions of life at Haywood's were recreated in *Sons and Lovers*; from climbing the 'dismal stairs',[4] to his assessment that the factory was 'an insanitary, ancient place'.[5] He also recreates the young women he worked with – some of whom, according to Lawrence's contemporaries, took a great deal of pleasure in enlightening him on the 'ways of the world', and 'searing his youthful innocence'.[6] But the factory girls would turn out to be the least of Lawrence's troubles. The autumn and winter of 1901 became one of the most difficult periods of Lawrence's life due to a family tragedy that was to have profound consequences for both him and his mother.

Lawrence's elder brother Ernest was certainly 'getting on' in London. Besides his steady job at a solicitor's firm on £120 a year, he was studying short-hand and teaching himself to type in his spare time. The 23-year-old was also engaged to a girl he had met in London called Louise Lily Western Dennis – who, like him, was also working in an office. Ernest seemed to have fallen on his feet, and buoyed by his mother's pride, was set to go even further. Despite boarding full time in London, Ernest regularly made the trip back to Eastwood, where – just like the fictional version, William – he would regale the family with tales of the city and they in turn would admire how refined and cultivated he now was. 'Quite the fairy prince of the family', was one remark levied in Ernest's direction after one of his visits.[7] But one weekend in early October 1901, Ernest returned to London, and after spending the day at work he collapsed at his Catford lodgings on the Monday evening and was dead by Friday. Lydia was present at his death, having been summoned by Ernest's landlady when he first fell ill, but by the time she arrived she barely recognised his inflamed, disfigured face, and he was insensible of her presence there. His sudden death from pneumonia caused by erysipelas (an inflammatory disease) was a huge blow to not just the family, but the people of Eastwood.

'The sad news of his death produced a very sorrowful sensation locally, deceased being well-known',[8] noted the writer of his obituary in the *Eastwood and Kimberley Advertiser*. 'As one of his close associates I cannot let this man pass without recording a little of his past life. The memory of his associations amongst us is yet quite fresh in our minds…His knowledge for a young man was considerable, London's gaiety could not wrest from him his love for work and his keen desire to get on…To undertake so much was too much, but his large mind, his keen desire for hard work, his ambition to make himself thoroughly fitting to fill a high post, to get on and be useful in the world was so great'.

Arthur joined Lydia in London and arranged for Ernest to be brought back to the family home in Eastwood the following day, Saturday. He was interred on the Monday at Eastwood Cemetery, just a week after his family waved him off on his return train journey to London.

In one of the most poignant episodes in *Sons and Lovers*, Lawrence depicts William's return to the family home with a mixture of morbid fascination and shock at the spectacle of the coffin being brought into the family home:

The coffin swayed, the men began to mount the three steps with their load.
Annie's candle flickered, and she whimpered as the first men appeared, and the
limbs and bowed heads of six men struggled to climb into the room, bearing the
coffin that rode like sorrow on their living flesh.

'Oh, my son – my son!' Mrs Morel sang softly, and each time the coffin swung
to the unequal climbing of the men: 'Oh, my son – my son – my son!'[9]

For Lawrence, Ernest's death – and that of his fictional equivalent, William –
only served to strengthen Lawrence's distrust of the bourgeois world. Ernest's
efforts to 'get on' and climb the ladder into middle-classdom culminated in
the tragedy of his death. In many respects, Ernest was as much adrift in the
world as Lawrence – he may have been following the path expected of a young
man with his charm, intelligence and determination; it was certainly the path
expected by his mother – but at what cost? 'To undertake so much was too much',
reads his obituary. It is as much a tribute to Ernest's short life as a cautionary
tale. His gravestone bears the words from Psalm 21:4, 'He asked life of thee,
and thou gavest it him'; which not only conveys Lydia's conviction that Ernest
would live on in eternal righteousness but also provided a fitting tribute to the
'promising young man'[10] who grasped all of life's opportunities (as well as a nod
towards the woman who quite literally gave him life and facilitated his rise up
the social ladder).

Lydia's shock at losing the son she had pinned so much hope on caused her
to cut herself off from the rest of the Lawrence family. She internalised her
feelings, becoming mute in her grief and seemingly oblivious to the needs of
her other children. 'She remained shut off', is how Lawrence framed the period
following Ernest's death in *Sons and Lovers*, 'his [Paul's] mother sat looking
blankly in front of her, her mouth shut tight'.[11] Lawrence didn't just lose his
brother in the autumn of 1901, but his mother too.

Lydia's brooding over Ernest's untimely death was cut short in dramatic
fashion by Lawrence himself. The long hours at Haywood's factory, coupled
with his own grief over the loss of Ernest and the withdrawal of his mother, left
Lawrence vulnerable in both mind and body. By Christmas, Lawrence too was
dangerously ill – this time with pneumonia – but it was the jolt Lydia needed
to bring her back to the land of the living. While Lawrence recuperated at
home – perilously close to death himself – so began one of the most important
relationships of Lawrence's life. It was as though Lydia hadn't really *known* her
youngest son until that point – the shared experience of grief followed swiftly by
Lawrence's critical illness fostered an interdependence in mother and son that
would last Lydia's lifetime and haunt what remained of Lawrence's. Ernest was
dead but Lawrence was alive; and he would go on living through the strength

of Lydia's will. Henceforth, Lydia would pour all her energy into Lawrence – ensuring that he trod a similar path to that of his dead brother.

Such aspirations inevitably came with some pitfalls. The intensity of Lydia's love and the weight of her expectation burdened Lawrence, and although the relationship was symbiotic on many levels, the sensitivity they had towards each other was also stifling to the point of suffocation: 'It has been rather terrible', Lawrence commented in a letter following her death, 'and has made me, in some respects, abnormal'.[12] Lawrence identified with his mother, and she with him. 'Nobody can have the soul of me', Lawrence wrote in 1910. 'My mother has had it, and nobody can have it again. Nobody can come into my very self again, and breathe me like an atmosphere'.[13]

During Lawrence's last year at Nottingham High School the Lawrence family became acquainted with another local family. The Chambers lived at Haggs Farm, two miles north of Eastwood, and attended the same chapel as the Lawrence family – where Mrs Ann Chambers had struck up a friendship with Lydia Lawrence; the two women no doubt finding mutual comfort in the fact that they were both outsiders to Eastwood. Lawrence's countryside roaming – particularly during his convalescence in the spring and summer of 1902– often took him in the direction of the farm, whether by accident or design, and the relationships he formed there, particularly with Alan the eldest son, and Jessie who was a year younger than Lawrence, became instrumental in his emergence as a fully fledged writer.

Haggs Farm offered Lawrence a kind of escape. With its old-fashioned bucolic setting and rustic way of life, it charmed Lawrence time and again, and he visited with increasing regularity. It also offered inspiration; Lawrence would recreate Haggs Farm in several of his prose works over the years – if he couldn't return to it in person then it was drawn from his memory and rebuilt on paper instead. With its long, low farmhouse and outbuildings, apple trees, haystacks, the gate opening straight onto the woods, and fields in all directions, it represented everything that Eastwood was not. 'As soon as the skies brightened and plum blossom was out, Paul drove off in the milkman's heavy float up to Willey Farm', Lawrence writes of Paul Morel's first outing to Willey Farm (Haggs Farm in *Sons and Lovers*) after his near-fatal episode of pneumonia,

White clouds went on their way, crowding to the back of the hills that were rousing in the springtime. The water of Nethermere lay below, very blue against the seared meadows and the thorn-trees.

*   It was four and a half miles' drive. Tiny buds on the hedges, vivid as copper-green, were opening into rosettes; and thrushes called, and blackbirds shrieked and scolded. It was a new, glamorous world.*[14]

Ada Lawrence described a childhood idyll in her recollections, remembering how they would climb the apple trees, play see-saw, and have endless games of hide and seek in the grain. Lawrence helped to milk the cows, as well as helping with the haymaking from sunset to sundown.

Farm life with the Chambers seemed to suit Lawrence – gone was the frail, vulnerable child, forever in the metaphorical lap of his mother. Instead, he drew strength from being in nature; its power and elemental vitality were transformative. This awakening coincided with Lawrence's new awareness of his spiritual and creative consciousness – an understanding he shared with the Chambers' second daughter, Jessie. Because it wasn't just the surroundings that Lawrence grew to love – it was the Chambers family themselves. And they, in turn, delighted in his company. May Chambers, the eldest girl of the seven Chambers children, recalled in her memories of Lawrence that: 'Bert's genius for making friends soon won the entire family, and if he was late, someone looking in would ask: "Isn't Bert here yet?" And on the rare occasion when he didn't come, there was real disappointment, for each separate member looked for some special pleasure he could give.'[15]

Both Jessie Chambers and Lawrence recalled in later years those heady days of their adolescence when Haggs Farm and its inhabitants were beginning to cast their spell over Lawrence. For Jessie, the memory of Lawrence's first visit was potent enough for her to recall it vividly over thirty years later:

> *It was on a day in early summer when the small, vigorous woman* [Lydia Lawrence] *and the slender boy she called Bertie, came into the farmyard, so still in the afternoon sunshine…Lawrence and I went into the field beyond the stackyard. He stood quite still there, as if fascinated with the view of the Annesley Hills and High Park wood, with the reservoir gleaming below.*[16]

For Lawrence, it was Jessie's aloofness at their first meeting that he remembered most of all: 'In the doorway suddenly appeared a girl in a dirty apron. She was about fourteen years old, had a dark rosy face, a bunch of short, black curls, very fine and free, and dark eyes; shy, questioning, a little resentful of strangers, she disappeared.'[17]

The pull of Haggs Farm was strong, and the Chambers family became a second, alternative family to young Lawrence. Where the Lawrence family home was full of intense emotions – be they love or hate – that often went unexpressed, except through the undercurrent of tension that permeated the house, the Haggs provided an atmosphere of free discussion, where everyone said exactly what they were thinking in plain terms, and other, deeper ways of considering life and everything in it was encouraged.

Alongside Lawrence's existential awakening, he also awakened in himself a new appreciation for the physicality of life on the farm, as Jessie recalled in her memoir:

> *Lawrence would spend whole days working with my father and brothers in the fields at Greasley. These fields lay four miles away, and we used to pack a big basket of provisions to last all day, so that hay harvest had a picnic flavour. Father enjoyed Lawrence's company quite as much as the rest of us. There was for years a fine understanding between them, a sympathy and recognition of what was best in each other. I heard father say to mother:*
>   *'Work goes like fun when Bert's there, it's no trouble at all to keep them going.'*[18]

Being immersed in nature – touching and *feeling* it physically and emotionally, heightened Lawrence's sense of knowingness that there was some greater force at play in the universe. It was the release that Lawrence needed from the stifling and emotionally charged atmosphere of his own home. And ultimately, it was the release he needed to become a writer.

Naturally, spending time on the farm also opened his eyes to the baser aspects of animal husbandry – often with slightly comical results. Reproduction of any kind was a taboo subject in the Lawrence household, so being exposed to the more 'visceral' qualities of farm life was always going to be a challenge for the innocently minded Lawrence. Lawrence's childhood friend George Neville recalled one such episode in which Lawrence had been to the Haggs and come back 'mightily disturbed' after Mr Chambers had instructed his son Alan to take one of the cows on a visit to the neighbouring farmer's prize bull the following day:

> *Poor Lawrence! I can imagine what a tingling of the skin he would experience as his blushes came. He blushed very readily in those days… But what had amazed him most of all was that Alan had simply answered 'Righto, father!', the mother had continued with what she was doing, Jessie had carried on her conversation with him, while the rest of the children had taken absolutely no notice at all…*

No subject was off limits for the Chambers, and matters relating to the farm were often discussed *en famille* around the table at teatime – and it was this unreserved approach to family life that Lawrence was so attracted to. As Lawrence historian Professor John Worthen speculates: 'The Chambers family probably felt more emotionally secure to Lawrence *because* of their constant quarrels, their overt affections, their singing and boisterous intimacy, their jokes and laughter…'[19]

Away from the comforting rural microcosm of the Haggs, Lawrence was still joylessly climbing the class ladder. Following his recovery from pneumonia in the spring of 1902, it was decided that Lawrence was not going to return to Haywood's factory. It needs little imagination to spot the hand of Lydia Lawrence in this turn of events – she felt a keen sense of guilt that she had pushed Lawrence too hard too soon, and the memory of Ernest and his tragic fate was still painfully raw. Still, Lawrence would still need to do *something*, else he might – shudder – end up working in the pit. After spending a month of convalescence at his Aunt Nellie's boarding house in Skegness, and with the heady days of the summer of 1902 fast fading, Lawrence took up a position as a pupil-teacher at the British School in Eastwood. Being just ten minutes from the family home, this suited Lydia – as well as sparing Lawrence the journey to Haywood's Factory in Nottingham, which had had such disastrous consequences for his health. Given his fragile constitution, it is ironic that Lawrence spent much of his adult life on the move, travelling widely and settling for years at a time in some of the remotest places on the planet. It is part of the 'Lawrence paradox' that he found comfort in both the landscape of his native country, and from being as far away from it as possible.

While teaching was a far cry from the world of business Lydia had hoped Lawrence would enter, it was at least respectable – although entry into the teaching world at the turn of the twentieth century was by no means assured, even with Lawrence's aptitude for academia. The financial advantages of being a scholarship boy did not extend past Nottingham High School, which meant that the higher education Lawrence needed to become a qualified teacher would have to be self-funded. The only route into the profession available for him was to become a pupil-teacher, or 'uncertified teacher' at a local school, and attending a teacher training centre in Ilkeston. Initially, his training was directed by the British School headmaster, George Holderness, but in 1903 he was drafted over to the Ilkeston Centre for his studies.

Lawrence was happy and worked conscientiously, and despite now teaching the 'rough and fierce' sons of the colliery workers – the kind of boys who had despised the young Lawrence for his effeminacy and indifference – he seemed to find a sense of rhythm in his life that he had previously lacked. A former pupil of Lawrence's at the British School recalled later that he 'taught very well',[20] and took centre-stage at the debating society that met in the school on a Monday evening – a pastime that would have unequivocally played to Lawrence's strengths.

And Lawrence did not neglect Jessie Chambers during this time either. His visits to the Haggs were to become a source of enrichment for both sides – not only did Lawrence help Jessie with her lessons (she was also attending the

Ilkeston Centre, but a year behind Lawrence) but also the two shared a common passion in reading and writing. They both read voraciously – devouring works by the Brontes, George Eliot, Thackeray, Dickens and Flaubert – which they would then discuss at length, taking pleasure in dissecting the nuances of each novel, its writer and the fictional world they had created. They could express themselves freely together, transcending from the ordinary to a higher intellectual plane in which they could enlighten each other. 'Right from infancy I had been aware of a world that glimmered beyond the surrounding world of fact', Jessie wrote in her memoir, 'and I dreaded lest the circumstances of my life should shut me out, compel me to live, as it were, in the dark, and prevent me from ever becoming a sharer in the feast of the human spirit'.[21]

In Lawrence, Jessie had met a kindred spirit. So often side-lined in her own family, particularly by her siblings ('I quarrelled continually with my brothers, who tried to order me about'[22]), Lawrence was not only an intimate friend with whom she could converse on an equal footing but also a mentor. In turn, Jessie gave Lawrence the opportunity to tentatively discuss what he really intended on doing with his life:

> We were in the field that ran alongside the Warren when he [Lawrence] said quietly:
> 'Have you ever thought of writing?'
> 'Oh yes,' I replied at once, 'I've thought of it all my life. Have you?'
> 'Yes, I have,' he said in the same quiet tone. 'Well, let's make a start. I'm sure we could do something if we tried.'[23]

The start the two young intellectuals made was on poetry, rather than prose – the decision that led Lawrence to utter the now oft-quoted words, 'A collier's son, a poet!'[24] The idea was met with derision by his wider family and friends, however, as his close friend George Neville recounts:

> The Little Woman [Lydia Lawrence] had sniffed, Ada had 'pshawed and rubbished' times without number, 'Injun Topknot' [his sister, Emily] had talked of prospective disappointments, 'Beat' [a neighbour, Beatrice Hall] had angered him, as usual, by ruffling his hair and clinging on to him while she said, 'Why David lad, tha' knows it's nobbut rubbish'...[25]

Little wonder Lawrence found solace in Jessie – the only person at the time who seemed to understand him. 'She thought it all wonderful', Lawrence wrote of Jessie just before his death, referring to himself in the third person '-else, probably he would never have written – His own family strictly "natural" looked on such performance as writing as "affectation". Therefore wrote in secret at home'.[26]

Lawrence juggled his two worlds – that of the working academic, and the budding literary genius, masterfully. In December 1904 he sat the King's Scholarship examination, which would secure his place in a training college for teachers. He passed with flying colours, earning a place in the first division of Class 1. Of the 2,500 students who took the exam that year, only 37 – including Lawrence – achieved the highest grade.

The next step was to achieve his teaching certificate, which he would do via a matriculation exam in June 1905, which allowed him to enter the day-training department of Nottingham University College. But Lydia Lawrence had bigger plans – why stop at a teaching certificate? If her son was to rise to greatness, he would need a BA degree. So, to fund this next step on the ladder, it was agreed that Lawrence would work full-time as an uncertificated teacher at the British School in Eastwood where he had been a pupil-teacher on a salary of £50 for the school year 1905–1906. Away from the demands of his studies and the classroom, the pressure of which was no doubt exacerbated by the expectations of his mother, Lawrence somehow found the time to retreat into the world of his writing. In many respects it represented not just the first step in his writing career, but the first step in the process of emotional separation from his mother. Here was something that was his, and his alone – he wasn't doing it at the behest of his mother, or trying to live up to her impossible expectations of how he *should* be spending his time. With his creativity unleashed, he could tentatively break away from the ordered, carefully planned future his mother had mapped for him. Keeping his writing secret didn't just protect him from the naysayers around him – and himself, since he still couldn't separate being a writer from the perceived pretentiousness that came with the label – but it also enabled him to nurture his craft without outside scrutiny. And, of course, it protected him from the embarrassment of failure should he prove to be unsuccessful.

For the most part, this was easy. Lawrence could disguise his poetry as 'academic work' if he was at home, and when he was at the Haggs there was no need for him to be surreptitious since he had a willing audience in Jessie, and she too in him. Yet it transpired to be the worst-kept secret of his formative years. His close friend George Neville remembered finding Lawrence and Jessie with their 'heads close together and the crumpled papers spread out in front of them',[27] which would disappear as soon as Neville arrived. May Chambers, Jessie's elder sister, recalled in her memoir that Jessie and Lawrence would 'pore over their books at a side table',[28] – ostensibly because Lawrence was tutoring Jessie in French and maths, but it is highly likely that alongside the academic study, the two would have used that time to share any writing they had done.

His mother knew of the growing closeness between Lawrence and Jessie – a fact she resented – and probably guessed that they were writing something at some point during 1905-1906. But for now, it was just Lawrence and Jessie cohabiting a literary world of their own creation. She described it as sitting 'in a world apart' where their feelings and thoughts were intensified. The door was closed for everyone else – and that included his mother Lydia Lawrence.

Unsurprisingly, Lydia felt shut out – and her reaction to this was to direct the blame onto Jessie Chambers. This resentment was couched in practical terms – Lawrence was on the cusp of a brilliant academic career and Jessie was an unhealthy distraction; not to mention the fact that by monopolising Jessie's time and friendship, he was denying her the opportunity to meet other men and jeopardising her chances of marriage.

'She could feel Paul being drawn away by this girl…', is how Lawrence depicts Gertrude Morel's anxiety over the relationship between Paul and Miriam (Jessie Chambers' fictional counterpart). '…So, while he was away with Miriam, Mrs. Morel grew more and more worked up'.[29] Still, Paul finds himself torn between his love for his mother and his emotional intimacy with Miriam. But his mother wins out – as she nearly always would, in fiction and reality. 'He could not harden his heart to ignore his mother…He kissed her forehead that he knew so well: the deep marks between the brows, the rising of the fine hair, greying now, and the proud setting of the temples. His hand lingered on her shoulder after his kiss. Then he went slowly to bed. He had forgotten Miriam; he only saw how his mother's hair was lifted back from her warm, broad brow. And somehow, she was hurt'.[30]

Back in the reality of Lawrence's adolescence, Lydia Lawrence's influence cast a long and permanent shadow between young Lawrence and Jessie. Yet she had her way. Jessie relates a pivotal conversation in her memoir in which Lawrence grapples with the best way to begin distancing himself from Jessie because he is worried she might be "getting to care too much," i.e. falling in love with him. According to Jessie, Lawrence had already tried to broach the subject rather clumsily one Christmas by reading Shakespeare's *Coriolanus* with her, but what Jessie didn't grasp were the parallels Lawrence was attempting to draw between Coriolanus's over-protective mother and his own – a relationship that in the play, drives a wedge between Coriolanus and his wife. 'You see it's the mother who counts', Lawrence explained, 'the wife hardly at all. The mother is everything to him'.[31]

Lawrence was testing the water. The two youngsters had grown up together, moved in the same circles, shared the same friends and Lawrence had singled Jessie out as a confidante and intellectual soulmate. It was understood implicitly – if not by the two of them, then by their respective friends and family – that one day they would officially 'court' each other. But although by Jessie's admission they were drawn to one another, the idea of romantic love was foreign to them in the earlier years of their relationship. It was something that glimmered tantalisingly on the horizon – at least for Jessie, who felt that there was a feeling of something 'rare and precious' between them.

When they did confront the inevitable in 1906, Jessie found, to her dismay, that they were less emotionally in tune with each other than she thought. Lawrence had not only deferred to his mother on the matter of their relationship but also had decided that Jessie held no real attraction to him as a wife. He then delivered the line that came to haunt their relationship for the remainder of their acquaintance: 'I've looked into my heart and I cannot find that I love you as a husband should love his wife'.[32] To add insult to injury, Lawrence then said that 'perhaps he might' given time, and that if Jessie loved him then they'd get engaged regardless of how he felt. Jessie was deeply humiliated but had enough self-respect to suggest they end their friendship completely, but despite his aversion to becoming intimate with her, Lawrence was reluctant to give Jessie up and so they carried on as before, albeit without spending time alone together. The crushing blow that Lawrence delivered to Jessie that day stayed with her for the rest of her life. It was the first of many tiny fractures to open in their relationship; a pivotal moment that Jessie would not forget, or indeed forgive easily.

Still, they were friends enough to be able to holiday together, which they did as part of a larger party – spending two weeks in Mablethorpe, Lincolnshire, in the summer of 1906. But Lawrence was clearly troubled. Jessie recalled how the two had set off on a moonlight walk together, but gradually a 'dark power' began to possess Lawrence, for which Jessie was somehow to blame. The strange episode culminated in a torrent of passionate words – some harsh, which were directed at Jessie, before Lawrence was able to admit it was all his fault. Jessie describes similar scenes on subsequent holidays, in which her presence seems to be the catalyst for his agitation. Jessie, with her intense capacity to love and her need to experience the world bodily (Lawrence was highly critical of Jessie's lack of detachment), was a constant reminder of his own reticence to submit himself to those very same feelings. Jessie recalled that Lawrence was like a 'strange wild' creature. His restraint was hurting her, but he was also hurting himself in the process.

Yet, Lawrence was able to capture this turmoil of feelings and use them to fuel his creativity. In the same year, Lawrence began writing 'Laetitia' – the novel that would become, four and a half years later, *The White Peacock*. Lawrence the prose writer had been born. It was a statement of intent, but also of rebellion, for Lawrence was due to start at the University College in Nottingham and begin his studies. Again, writing a novel that was all his and nothing to do with his mother. But there was still one person he wanted to share his progress with, and that was Jessie. Lawrence needed Jessie, just as much as she needed him – but the balance of power was all Lawrence's, and it was under his terms that the relationship continued.

It was perhaps fortuitous for Lawrence that his studies would take him away from Eastwood and the pull of Haggs Farm for most of the week. The physical distance created by his new role as a full-time student would, he no doubt hoped, provide some emotional distance from Jessie. It was a chance to recalibrate their relationship and let the intensity of it dissipate. Lawrence had high hopes for the rigours of academic life; his intellect would be stretched and challenged as never before, and he hoped that this enlightenment would lead to a new sense of fulfilment – of being 'vitally alive'.

During his first year, Lawrence was all set to study for a degree, but to do this he needed to learn Latin. He arranged for his classics professor to give him some tuition, and he 'slogged' away ('how I suffer',[33] he wrote to a friend) and after a term, Lawrence claimed to Jessie that he had 'broken the back' of the Latin. But his efforts were wasted. Soon after he had uttered these words, the professor who had been teaching him cancelled their arrangement due to a lack of time. This no doubt made Lawrence cross, but he was also secretly relieved, for now he would have extra time to concentrate on 'Laetitia'. He was already finding college tedious, even without the Latin lessons, and his real interest lay in his writing and not his studies.

By the close of his first year at college in the summer of 1907, Lawrence had completed 'Laetitia', and was also writing poems – all of which he shared with Jessie. She too was training to be a teacher, but via a vocational route that allowed her to teach in school all day and then study at home in the evenings. It shows something of Lawrence's need to be around Jessie that he suggested she attend a course of Saturday morning lectures at the college, which he too would be attending. This gave him the opportunity to speak to Jessie alone and ask her opinion of the writing he was secretly sharing with her. By April 1908, Lawrence had completely rewritten 'Laetitia', as well as many poems that Jessie remembered he wrote in a notebook with the college arms on the cover, which must have given him a great deal of satisfaction. But the secrecy wasn't to last. Lawrence's social circle had widened during his two years at the University College and now encompassed a broader spectrum of intellectuals, free-thinkers and like-minded companions. He began to align himself with socialist ideals – although this was less about politics for Lawrence at this time, and more an instinctive reaction to what he saw as a collective responsibility for humankind. It was also an act of rebellion – a way to assert the values that would come to define him, such as his sense of despair at the 'enslavement' of society. He became a founder member of a socialist group at his college called the 'Society for the Study of Social Reform', and took to reading the *New Age* – a weekly magazine for socialist sympathisers. Lawrence's world view is at times baffling and full of conflicting perspectives, but the idea of humankind blindly accepting the status quo is one that he returned to frequently – he would use this theme in a later poem, 'The North Country':

> *Out of the sleep, from the gloom of motion, soundlessly somnambule*
> *Moans and booms the soul of a people imprisoned, asleep in the rule*
> *Of the strong machine that runs mesmeric, booming the spell of its word*
> *Upon them and moving them helpless, mechanic, their will to its will deferred.*[34]

Lawrence also began to question organised religion during his college years. Jessie Chambers vividly recalls one such outburst from Lawrence regarding his stance on the Christian dogma that was the backbone of the mining villages at the time:

> *On one of our walks home he gave my brother and me a vivid description of the nebular theory of the universe, and he was troubled by the discrepancy between such a hypothesis of the origin of things and the God postulated by the Congregational chapel. He resented the tone of authority adopted by the conventionally religious people, including his mother...He used to complain that in chapel one had to sit still and seem to agree with all that the minister said. He would have liked to be at liberty to stand up and challenge his statements.*[35]

Lawrence resented the Church's monopoly on the 'right way of living'. One can almost imagine Lawrence sitting in the Congregational chapel in Eastwood listening, with arms crossed, in frustrated silence to the sermon – no doubt trying to quell the counterargument that would have been festering inside him all the while. Around the same time, Lawrence began to meet with notorious local socialists Willie and Sallie Hopkin, who had set up a rival cultural society to the one offered by the chapel and run by the Congregational minister, Reverend Robert Reid. Eastwood's 'official' cultural offering was provided by the Congregational Literary Society and for a shilling's membership, consisted of regular Monday evening lectures, delivered by members of the clergy and Reverend Reid, on religious subjects and occasionally more mainstream literature. To counter this, the Hopkins formed a debating society, and along with other local socialists – notably chemist Harry Dax and his wife Alice, Lawrence, and sometimes Alan and Jessie Chambers too – it provided an alternative cultural platform for other like-minded Eastwood locals.

The chapel and its minister symbolised everything Lawrence was beginning to rail against; the small-minded thinking of the mining community, the beliefs and values his mother held so dear, the assumed deference to not just the authority of the church, but the 'Chapel Men' (the traders and shopkeepers of Eastwood) whom Lydia held in such high esteem.

As the Congregational minister of Eastwood, the Reverend Robert Reid found himself in Lawrence's firing line – his frustration manifesting itself in a series of outbursts, both written and verbal, in which he questioned where God was in the scenes of poverty and deprivation he himself had witnessed. How could an omnipotent God allow such suffering and disease?

Lawrence also struggled with the idea of conversion – that God would one day speak to and inhabit him personally, prompting a spiritual turning point in which God would begin to touch every area of his life, thus allowing Lawrence to live out his Christianity. He wrote to Reverend Reid in December 1907: 'I believe that a man is converted when first he hears the low, vast murmur of life, of human life, troubling his hitherto unconscious self.' For Lawrence, religious conversion meant a dawning consciousness of the pain and sorrow of humanity. It could be shaped and reformed, gathered and added to, through his own lived experience. And it was an infinite process. The values and beliefs of Lawrence's alternative 'religion' (i.e. his own personal doctrine) were never fixed – unlike organised religion. Socialism was thus a natural fit. He argued that 'true Socialism' was religion, and that living 'earnestly and unselfishly' *was* religion. Lawrence would mould his own version of religion over the course of his life; one that recognised the human experience of life and love.

When Lawrence left the University College in the summer of 1908, he was not the same Lawrence who entered it – not least because of his newly formed religious opinions, which he could back up with rigorous intellect, but because he was now a published writer – albeit under Jessie's name. In the autumn of 1907, Lawrence had begun to write short stories as a response to a competition in the *Nottinghamshire Guardian* – the criteria for which were that the stories had to be set at Christmas and have a local setting. The prize was three guineas and Lawrence was determined to submit three – which meant roping in not only Jessie to submit a story for him but also another friend, Louie Burrows, to do the same.

Jessie recalled the incident in her memoir: 'As luck would have it the story I sent was accepted and came out under my name', she wrote. 'It was a sentimental little story called *A Prelude to a Happy Christmas*, and was Lawrence's first appearance in print. A cheque for three guineas came, so I signed and my father cashed Lawrence's first cheque. As he gave the money to him, father remarked: "Well Bert, it's the first, but I hope it won't be the last." The story Lawrence submitted himself, 'Ruby Glass' (under the pseudonym Herbert Richards), would eventually morph into 'A Fragment of Stained Glass' and was destined for greater things because it was published in the *English Review* in 1911. Louie's story was an early version of 'The White Stocking' – a story in which the character of a young girl, who was probably based on his mother, goes to a dance, and thinks she is pulling a handkerchief out of her pocket, but it is in fact a white stocking that she has picked up in error.

Although Lawrence continued to live at home during his college years, intellectually and emotionally, he was moving further and further away from the stifling influence of his mother and the constraints of village life. In 1908, with his college career over, he was on the cusp of leaving Eastwood for the south London suburbs – and he was also on the brink of yet another break with the Haggs and all that he found comforting there – including Jessie. Lawrence was about to travel further than ever before. He was bound for the uninspiring manufacturing landscape of Croydon, 170 miles south of Eastwood.

Chapter 3

A Stranger in a Strange Land

On his second day in Croydon Lawrence sent me a letter that gave me a shock. It was like a howl of terror. People were kind, he said, but everything was strange, and how could he live away from us all?[1]

Lawrence was an outsider in Eastwood and all it embodied, but he was no more comfortable in Croydon. He felt like 'a stranger in a strange land', but in the autumn of 1908 his options were limited. He had already failed to find a post during July or August, which would have secured him a job for the beginning of the new academic year in September, despite leaving college with the best marks of any man in his final year – B A B B in Teaching, Reading, Drawing and Music, respectively – although as Lawrence biographer John Worthen points out, he still marked lower than some of the best women students, some of whom achieved straight As.[2]

He was interviewed for teaching posts in both Stockport and Manchester, which he found to be 'vile, hateful' and 'filthy places', for which he was mercifully, given his opinion of them, unsuccessful. He was then interviewed for the post of assistant master at the Davidson Road Boys' School in Croydon – taking a week's sojourn in London, which he described as a 'pompous, magnificent capital of commercialdom, a place of stately individualistic ideas', where he felt 'remarkably at home' and 'cheerful and delighted' – no doubt feeling that as the centre of the literary world, he had found somewhere he belonged.

And as it was only thirty minutes by train from Croydon, the opportunities for an aspiring young writer would no doubt be numerous – or so Lawrence hoped. His writing, as always, would have been at the forefront of his thoughts, rather than readying himself for a future in teaching.

He was offered the post at Davidson Road Boys' School on a salary of £95 per annum, with an expected start date of 12 October. The school itself was only a year old, having opened the previous October in response to the needs of a booming population and a lack of educational facilities in the Lower Addiscombe area of Croydon. The boys' section of the school, in which Lawrence was to teach, accommodated students between the ages of 7 and 15 – all from a wide range of backgrounds including orphans, boys from the local home for actors' children, children from some of the poorest families in the area, as well as some from the more prosperous lower-middle-class homes in the South Norwood vicinity.[3] 'I looked at the boys, dressed in mouldering garments of remote men',[4] was how Lawrence portrayed his students in 'Lessford's Rabbits', a short story written in 1908, told through the eyes of a school teacher, about the spirit of enterprise in the working classes. In its companion piece, 'A Lesson on a Tortoise', Lawrence provides further descriptive clues as to the sort of children he was expected to teach: 'A difficult, mixed class, they were, consisting of six London Home boys, five boys from a fairly well-to-do Home for the children of actors and a set of commoners varying from poor lads who hobbled to school, crippled by broken enormous boots'.[5]

Both stories include stealing and dishonesty as a theme, as well as providing an insight into the plight of the working classes and the difficulties in teaching them. Lawrence knew all too well how the working classes suffered – and his fictional teacher-narrator is left 'very tired, and very sick', at the close of 'A Lesson on a Tortoise' from dealing with the poor behaviour of his students – the effects of their impoverished background and upbringing inevitably spilling into the classroom: 'The night had come up, the clouds were moving darkly, and the sordid streets near the school felt like disease in the lamplight'.[6]

Some of the boys at the Davidson Road Boys' School were certainly among the poorest in Croydon – that much is fact. Of the 208 students who made up the first cohort in 1907, 102 had to be given free breakfasts[7] – a policy implemented under the Education (Provision of Meals) Act of 1906 to ensure poorer children had access to healthy meals. However, not all families were keen on the idea of 'charity'. As the narrator of 'Lessford's Rabbits' comments,

> We could never get many boys to give their names for free meals. I used to ask the Kellet's, who were pinched and pared thin with poverty:
>
> 'Are you sure you don't want either dinners or breakfasts, Kellet?'
>
> He would look at me curiously, and say, with a peculiar small movement of his thin lips.
>
> 'No Sir.'
>
> 'But have you plenty – quite plenty?'
>
> 'Yes Sir' – he was very quiet, flushing at my questions. None – or very few – of the boys could endure to accept the meals. Not many parents would submit to the indignity of the officer's inquirer and the boys, the most foolishly sensitive animals in the world, would, many of them, prefer to go short rather than partake of charity meals of which all their school mates were aware.[8]

Lawrence was conflicted when he finally left Eastwood to take up his position in Croydon – on the one hand he was glad to be free of the influence of the chapel and his mother, but the nostalgic pull of 'the country and my own folks' and the valley where the Haggs was situated would consistently trouble him during his years in Croydon, and indeed throughout his life. For Jessie, their parting was one of the most painful episodes she remembers:

> *When he had to leave us to take up his post in Croydon he looked like a man under sentence of exile…He came to say good-bye to us. He was pale and his eyes looked dark with pain…I walked with him to the last gate, where we stopped. He leaned towards me.*
>
> *'La derniére fois,'* [the last time] *he said, inclining his head towards the farm and the wood. I burst into tears, and he put his arms round me. He kissed me and stroked my cheek, murmuring:*
>
> *'I'm so sorry, so sorry, so sorry.'*
>
> *His words scalded me. I drew away and dried my tears.*[9]

Jessie also records how Lawrence's mother reacted to his imminent departure. Lydia's entire life was dedicated to ensuring her children 'climbed the ladder' out of the mining district and into a bourgeoisie life – yet now the moment had come, it seemed a step too far. Lydia lived for Lawrence – he was her reason for being, and so his absence would leave her days empty. Little matter that she still had her other children living locally, as well as a growing brood of grandchildren. 'What shall *I* do when he's gone?' Lydia lamented to Jessie. With her purpose in life removed, she might just as well not live at all.

Despite his 'howl of terror' to Jessie, Lawrence's letters to his other friends and associates in the first two weeks at the school are, on the face of it, upbeat. In a letter written on 15 October to his old Eastwood friend Mabel Limb, he described Croydon as being 'clean and open', and that he had found accommodation with 'exceedingly nice people'. He complained that school was wearisome ('so much red tape, and so little discipline') but he fully expected to get used to it in time. He was clearly fond of the Jones family whose house he was lodging, in but found the headteacher of Davidson Road a 'weak kneed windy fool – he shifts every grain of responsibility off his own shoulders'.[10] Yet two days later, and just fourteen days after arriving at the school, disillusionment sets in as the reality of his situation hits home. Writing to his friend Blanche Jennings, Lawrence revealed that he was having trouble disciplining his students and that he was never born to command.

He did eventually instil some discipline into his unruly class of forty-five boys and by November he felt that things were better, but the dire circumstances of some of his pupils clearly played on his mind. 'Poor devils', he writes to Jessie's sister May Holbrook at the beginning of December 1908, 'they make me jolly mad, but I am sorry for them'.[11] It was not until the end of February 1909 that Lawrence felt as though he had some kind of control over the 'wild beasts' and he could finally boast that he had 'conquered my turbulent subjects, and can teach in ease and comfort'.[12]

This new-found harmony facilitated a renewed interest in all the things he held dear – reading, writing, and flexing his intellectual muscles, as well as exploring the locale and making regular excursions in both directions: north into London and south into Surrey. All would feed into his works, and of course his letters, of which there were many. London was a source of constant wonderment with its 'domes high for the magnification of the voices below' and 'pillared temples'. Surrey was equally enthralling with its 'gorgeous foliage' and 'rich folk riding horseback through the lanes'. He found Surrey to be clean, glorious, and much like Derbyshire, 'but softer, sweeter'.

Lawrence found day-to-day life at the school to be irksome, and he was ambivalent towards many of his colleagues, although he did eventually form a close professional relationship with the 'weak kneed windy fool' of a headmaster, Philip Smith, whom Lawrence would later describe as 'discerning' and 'kindly'. Of the rest of the staff, the 23-year-old Arthur McLeod made the biggest impression on Lawrence. He was academic (McLeod held a BA in Greek), well-read, and through his own personal library, introduced Lawrence to the modern fictional works of Joseph Conrad, H. G. Wells, George Gissing and Leo Tolstoy – all whose work he critiqued and applauded in his letters, while imploring the recipient to read them and judge for themselves. Crucially, it was during his time in Croydon that Lawrence became more acquainted with German philosopher Friedrich Nietzsche, whose theories he would draw upon in his works – notably in *Women in Love* (1920) through the character of Rupert Birkin, the alienated intellectual who articulates many of Lawrence's own perspectives and opinions. Lawrence was keen to share his ideas whenever he returned to Eastwood, particularly Jessie and the Eastwood intelligentsia, but his esoteric worldview no doubt irritated his Croydon colleagues – many of whom would have been more concerned with keeping boxes ticked and pupils in order, rather than bothering with the likes of Nietzsche. Yet it is entirely possible that Lawrence's ongoing intellectual curiosity was informing his teaching style and feeding into his lessons. He famously astonished a visiting school inspector in 1910 when the official interrupted Lawrence's lesson on *The Tempest*, in which he encouraged the children to act the part of the sea chorus by reciting their lines from behind the black board. It was a similar story when he taught *As You Like It* – an episode that Lawrence relayed with humour in a letter to fellow teacher and friend Louie Burrows in March 1911, where he describes how the boys 'caper round in a dance while Rosalind delivers the epilogue', and 'act as if the front of the class were a stage'.

Lawrence more than lived up to the testimonial given to the school by his former professor at the University College, Amos Henderson. 'He adopts intelligent methods', wrote Henderson, 'and his handling of a subject displays both originality and resource'.[13]

History lessons were also acted out for the apparent amusement of all, and his art lessons were singled out for praise in the inspector's report, for the unusually 'bold and vigorous' treatment in brush drawing witnessed by the school inspector. On several occasions his experiences of school life clearly bring him an immense amount of joy, and he relates these with humour.

His unorthodox approach was also an opportunity for a small act of rebellion against the regimen and dullness of life in a boys' school. Not just for himself but for his students too. He wanted to inspire rather than rule, and it seems he was successful; during Lawrence's time at the school and following its inspection, it was deemed a well-performing, above-average school. So why did Lawrence loathe it so much? 'School trammels me and makes me feel as if I can't breathe', he wrote in September 1911, and he found teaching to be 'the cruellest and most humiliating sport'. Lawrence was an intelligent and high-performing individual, and as such he naturally did well – or at the very least what was expected of him. But as an institution, Davidson Road Boys' symbolised 'the system' – the very ideology that Lawrence came to despise. And he was very much a square peg trying to fit into a round hole.

Despite (or perhaps because of) this, Lawrence turned to his writing as a source of escape – feverishly reading, re-reading and reworking 'Laetitia', and immersing himself in the landscape of the Haggs (or at least its fictional equivalent) yet again. 'Everything that I am now, all of me, so far, is in that. I think a man puts everything he is into a book – a real book',[14] he wrote to Jessie Chambers – and he meant it.

Lawrence was a tireless editor as well as writer and he poured out his anxieties over the direction of the novel and the quality of his writing regularly to his correspondents. 'Laetitia' was 'a sickness of mine', and Lawrence was convinced it was of poor quality and that he would have it to start it again. But he also knew it was his ticket out of teaching – because if he wasn't going to teach, he had to do *something*. Not least because he had his mother to appease: 'I am poor – and my mother looks to me – and I shall either have to wear motley all my days and be an elementary school teacher, or be an elementary school-teacher without motley – a lamentable figure I should cut – unless I can do something with that damned damnation of a Laetitia...'[15]

This period of Lawrence's life also saw a shift in who he was confident sharing his work with. Away from the Haggs, Jessie was no longer the sole editorial custodian of Lawrence's work in progress, and he was beginning to form other relationships. As well as his socialist friend Blanche Jennings, with whom Lawrence had shared his initial drafts of 'Laetitia' in 1908, Lawrence began to share the manuscript with several other contemporaries, some of whom would have a profound impact on the book's final incarnation as *The White Peacock* – and provide material for future novels.

Two teachers – the attractive Agnes Holt and the studious intellectual Helen Corke, were two such significant figures in Lawrence's life. Helen, especially, became someone with whom Lawrence could not only share his interests – for she was also passionate about literature and art – but also his writing.

By March 1909 he was still rewriting 'Laetitia', and had decided to rename the manuscript 'Nethermere'. He also showed it to a male friend for the first time – the trusted Arthur McLeod – whose opinion he sought as to whether the novel was any good. Jessie had already decided the novel was 'story-bookish' and 'unreal', but recognised the genuine thread of romance running through the story: 'something in the atmosphere was alive', she wrote.

Lawrence's rose-tinted nostalgia for the rural world of the Haggs, which was probably exacerbated by the suburban surroundings of Croydon, bore a considerable influence on Lawrence's early drafts of *The White Peacock*. His original plot saw the heroic farmer George reconciled with the heroine Lettie, with a new life in Canada hinted at. But the final published version was stripped back to a realism that was resonant of his own lived experience. Instead, Lettie marries the upper-class Leslie, despite her attraction to George – and George, having been spurned by the woman he loves, marries the conventional Meg and becomes a miserable alcoholic. It became an unromantic tale of mismatched lovers and unfulfilled desires, played out on a romantic Hardy-esque landscape.

The one constant throughout is the narrator, Cyril Beardsall, Lettie's brother – a thinly disguised version of Lawrence, whose purpose is not just to tell the story, but to provide a disinterested commentary on the middle-class world the characters inhabit. For Helen Corke, Cyril *was* Lawrence at that time. She wrote:

I saw him then as he appears in his first novel, Nethermere, *published as* The White Peacock *– Cyril, the narrator, an almost bodiless intelligence, passing in and out of the lives of family and friends; a keen observer, intently interested in their personal relations, yet seeing them as much a part of the landscape as the figures of a Watteau picture.*[16]

Lawrence was continually unsure of the direction of 'Nethermere', which explains its many rewritings. He didn't really know what he wanted to achieve with it, aside from it being a creative outlet and a test of his artistic skills. And he was still struggling to understand himself at this time; his desires, feelings and impulses. He was also no closer to being a published writer.

That was to change in 1909. The previous year Lawrence introduced the Chambers family to the *English Review*, Ford Madox Hueffer's (later Ford Madox Ford) new literary journal devoted to 'the arts, to letters, to ideas', to which they enthusiastically subscribed. The first issue, published in December 1908, was a who's who of the literary greats, including works by Thomas Hardy, Henry James, Joseph Conrad, H. G. Wells and Tolstoy. It was Jessie who noticed that the journal was interested in publishing new talent, but when she encouraged Lawrence to send in his work, he unequivocally refused. But…he would allow Jessie to send his work under a pseudonym.

Jessie duly sent a selection of Lawrence's poems, stating that the author was a young man who had been writing for several years, and that should his work be published, it should appear under the pseudonym Richard Greasley. Contrary to his dismissive attitude at the time, Lawrence was far from disinterested in the outcome of Jessie's efforts. 'Did you send those poems to the English?' he asked Jessie the next time they met, adding immediately, 'They'll never print them.' Lawrence was clearly trying to manage his own expectations – an abject fear of failure was never far from his thoughts. After all, he was Bert Lawrence the miner's son from the Midlands – and the thought of laying himself bare to be crucified in the font of literary greatness was just too much. He described how he felt exposed – 'quiveringly vulnerable in print' – when his work was finally published – a fear common to most, if not all writers. But his outward lack of concern for becoming published and attitude of self-deprecation disguised a sort of inner arrogance and belief in his own abilities. Pretending not to care whether he was published was a coping mechanism in case he *did* fail. If there's one thing Lawrence couldn't bear, it was humiliation – and he would rather remain unpublished but a successful writer in his own mind than have to face the crushing reality of being both unpublished and deemed *unpublishable* by the literary world.

As it turns out he would be neither. In August 1909, Jessie received a response from Hueffer. The Lawrences were on holiday in Shanklin on the Isle of Wight, and so she kept the letter from Lawrence until they had returned. Hueffer wanted to see him in London – 'perhaps something might be done', he had written. Jessie handed Lawrence the letter when he returned to Eastwood:

'Oh, I've got a letter for you.'
He looked at me quickly, then his eyes narrowed:
*   'From the English? About the poems? Show it me.'*
*   I gave him the letter, and his face became tense.*
*   'You are my luck,' he murmured. Then he said with suppressed excitement,*
"Let me take it to show mother.' And I never saw it again.[17]

In fact, Hueffer was so sure of Lawrence's talent that he was keen to share the name of his prodigy before Lawrence knew he was going to be published in the *English Review.* As Hueffer relates in his memoir, when Lawrence's short story, *Odour of Chrysanthemums,* appeared at Hueffer's editorial office (his drawing room) it was the final manuscript he read that day. Laying it in the 'Accepted' basket his secretary commented, 'You've got another genius?', to which Hueffer answered, 'It's a big one this time', before leaving the room to dress for dinner. Over dinner – with H. G. Wells, Hilaire Belloc, Maurice Baring and G. K. Chesterton, none the less – Hueffer remarked to H. G. Wells that he had discovered another genius:

D. H. Lawrence by name; and, to carry on the good work, Mr. Wells exclaimed
– to someone at Lady Londonderry's table:
*   "Hurray, Fordie's discovered another genius! Called D. H. Lawrence!"*
*   Before the evening was finished I had had two publishers asking me for the*
first refusal of D. H. Lawrence's first novel and, by that accident, Lawrence's
name was already known in London before he even knew that any of his work
had been submitted to an editor.[18]

With no idea that his name was already on the lips of some of the literary greats, Lawrence returned to Croydon for the new academic year and met Hueffer in September. He wrote to Jessie on 11 September – his twenty-fourth birthday – that Hueffer was 'fairish, fat, about forty, and the kindest man on earth'. Hueffer's first impressions of Lawrence were mixed: 'suddenly, leaning against the wall beside the doorway, there was, bewilderingly ... a fox. A fox going to make a raid on the hen-roost before him... that was really his attitude of mind. He had come, like the fox, with his overflood of energy – his abounding vitality of passionate determination that seemed always too big for his frail body – to get something – the hypnotic two thousand a year; from somewhere'.[19] Hueffer would later decide that he found something in Lawrence 'disturbing': 'I cannot say that I liked Lawrence much. He remained too disturbing even when I got to know him well'.[20]

Yet despite Hueffer's misgivings, he did have something that Lawrence desperately needed for his writing career to progress – a sphere of influence that stretched far and wide. As the grandson of Pre-Raphaelite painter Ford Madox Brown, his artistic and literary pedigree preceded him, and he could count several internationally acclaimed authors among his close friends. As the gate keeper to the London literary circles Lawrence was keen to enter, it was imperative the meeting went well. And it did. Hueffer accepted five poems for publication in the November 1909 issue with an assurance that he would be glad to read any of Lawrence's work. Lawrence's relationship with the *English Review*, established that autumn of 1909, endured for fourteen years across thirty-five issues, and two editors.

But for now, the opportunity had presented itself, which meant Lawrence needed to get 'Nethermere' into an acceptable state for Hueffer to read. Fortunately, two friends – the older but reliable Agnes Mason, who was also a teacher at Davidson Road School, and the more flighty but attractive teacher acquaintance, Agnes Holt – with whom he struck up a mutual attraction – helped him to copy his many drafts into something resembling a cohesive manuscript and the result was duly sent to Hueffer in early November 1909. The final version was substantially altered: Lawrence had added a third part in which Lettie and Leslie were married – as were George and Meg. The fictional Lawrence, under the guise of Cyril Beardsall in *The White Peacock*, remained unmarried, but the real Lawrence was, surprisingly, considering marriage. He rather flippantly (and with his customary lack of tact) wrote to Jessie Chambers, 'I ought to be out on Wimbledon Common with a girl, a teacher here…I have almost made up my mind to marry her as soon as I get some money. I think I shall. I am almost sure I shall'.[21] The girl was Agnes Holt – a fellow schoolteacher who was tall, auburn-haired and had a pleasant demeanour. Lawrence made the rather ill-judged and insensitive decision to introduce the heart-broken Jessie to Agnes when she went to visit him in London in late November 1909, and so we have Jessie to thank for the description of her – although what she really felt about the girl whom Lawrence had fallen in love with, she is careful to conceal. Very little is known of Agnes Holt, except that she exits Lawrence's life just as swiftly as she enters it, but her appearance does signify another shift in the trajectory of Lawrence's life. Buoyed by Hueffer's interest, and with access to the literati he had so often dreamed of meeting, his confidence in himself was renewed. Hueffer was able to introduce him to a whole gamut of contemporaries: Violent Hunt (a leading novelist of the day, and Hueffer's mistress), American poet Ezra Pound, Welsh-English writers Ernest and Grace Rhys among many others. It was also around this time that Lawrence was first referred to as a genius by Hueffer, who would introduce him as such – no doubt to explain what the awkward, slightly shabby miner's son was doing in his company. The word wasn't just used to praise Lawrence's talent, but it acted as a sort of consolation to his lack of literary pedigree. Lawrence recalled later in life the moment when Hueffer said, 'you've got GENIUS':

> *This made me want to laugh, it sounded so comical. In the early days they were always telling me I had got genius, as if to console me for not having their own incomparable advantages.*[22]

Lawrence later decided that he didn't like the label 'genius'. He saw it as tokenistic and most frequently used by the fortunate to patronise those who were less fortunate but had managed, through hard work, to improve their prospects.

But it was Lawrence's genius that helped Hueffer get him an introduction at one of the foremost publishers of the day – William Heinemann. Hueffer was reading 'Nethermere' by November 1909 and had told Lawrence he thought it was good. Lawrence, meanwhile, was attempting to find his feet among his new circle of friends. He dined with Ezra Pound, and other 'literary folk', and 'poetry people'.

In late 1909, Lawrence was still new to literary circles, as well as the associated poetry readings, drinking, dining and rubbing shoulders with celebrities (Lawrence met actress and singer Ellaline Terriss, as well as American singer Grace Crawford and Australian singer Florence Schmidt). 'I am no Society man', he commented to Louie Burrows, overwhelmed by his new literary world.

Ernest Rhys recalled that on one occasion Lawrence was invited to read his poetry to a gathering of intellectuals in Hampstead in the winter of 1909, when Lawrence was new to the scene – but he had no idea when to stop reading, and so Rhys had to rescue him.[23] Things did not improve with experience, and over time Lawrence became reconciled to his existence as a sort of societal nomad. He didn't fit in with the working classes, but neither did the middle-classes feel like his sort of people. And as for the elite – literary or otherwise – they were completely outside of Lawrence's sphere of experience, although initially he was in their thrall ('How that glittering taketh me',[24] he commented to Jessie on one occasion). Ironically, Lawrence had friends across every class of society – he just couldn't relate to a specific class or group of people en masse, and felt as though he couldn't get on very well with the world: 'whether I am a worldly success or not I really don't know. But I feel, somehow, not much of a human success',[25] he wrote.

There is a sad poignancy to Lawrence's words – that Lawrence, the great explorer of human connection, found himself entirely disconnected from the world around him.

Nevertheless, at the beginning of 1910 Lawrence was establishing new relationships and ending old ones. Heinemann had offered to publish 'Nethermere' – practically on spec barring four lines that he was asked to alter – and after almost four years, an abundance of drafts and two title changes, Lawrence was offered £50 plus royalties for his first novel. But January 1910 also marked the end of Lawrence's relationship with the woman he thought he might marry – Agnes Holt. 'I don't like her', he wrote to Blanche Jennings. It is difficult to ascertain exactly what happened between Lawrence and Agnes, since Lawrence wraps his account up in a veil of euphemisms, and Agnes left no account of her own – but in the same letter, Lawrence reveals he has a 'new girl'. The 'girl' was Helen Corke – but Lawrence's relationship with Jessie Chambers was moving in a new direction too, and the point at which the two women's lives would intersect with Lawrence's would mark the beginning of a friendship that would endure for a lifetime.

Having broken with Agnes, Lawrence was clearly conflicted. Jessie's visit to him in London in late 1909 seemed to reignite a new appreciation of his childhood friend – a sentiment he expresses in the poem 'Aware', which he sent to Jessie after her visit. The poem speaks of realisation, and a dawning recognition of feeling: 'Emerging white and exquisite; and I in amaze/ See in the sky before me, a woman I did not know/ I loved, but there she goes and her beauty hurts my heart;/ I follow her down the night, begging her not to depart'.[26] Jessie knew not to put too much stock in Lawrence's words, but that Christmas he declared, after eight years of platonic friendship (from his perspective at least), that he had been mistaken. He had loved Jessie after all, he just hadn't realised it, and he wanted to marry her. In Jessie's words, Lawrence explained that 'the years of our friendship had been simply a preparation for this…and he hadn't known before. But we wouldn't speak of it to anyone yet. They would make such a fuss and ask so many questions. It should be our secret for the present'.[27]

Jessie herself was sceptical – she recalls hearing 'the old forced note' in his voice and she was right to be on her guard – as the events of 1910 would eventually prove. But her eight years of loyalty and yearning for Lawrence made objectivity almost impossible.

At the same time, Lawrence was attempting to make sense of the romantic feelings for fellow teacher Helen Corke. The two had met at the house of their mutual friend, Agnes Mason – and although the meeting was brief, Helen was able to recall years later what transpired:

…he was sitting on a hassock in the midst of a family circle, pretending to tell fortunes. He rose and greeted me with momentary full concentration and returned to his game. I carried away an impression of deep-set grey eyes under

heavy brows, a white face, the skin opaque and stretched over the cheekbones –
a face suggesting strength – with thick, boyish fair hair and a body too slender
for its clothing.[28]

Lawrence was nothing if not honest in his approach to both Jessie and Helen
– both knew of the other's existence, and both were aware of his inner conflict
in trying to unpick the feelings he was experiencing. 'I have muddled my love
affairs most ridiculously and most maddeningly',[29] he later wrote in a letter.

Helen herself had her own set of challenging emotions to mentally untangle.
The previous summer, before she had become acquainted with Lawrence, she
had been involved with a married music teacher and violinist named Herbert
Macartney. The two lovers had holidayed together on the Isle of Wight (by
coincidence, at the same time as the Lawrence family and their friends, but their
paths didn't cross) and Helen had spent five tumultuous days veering from one
extreme of emotion to another. The lovers returned to south London – and for
Macartney, his wife and family – but two days later he killed himself. Helen
was paralysed with grief, writing later that she had been, 'Unable to see any
solution in death, I had continued to live only in my memories, without will,
purpose, or wish for the future'.[30] To deal with the pain of Herbert's tragic death,
Helen turned to writing, just as Lawrence so often did, and she was still in the
process of recovering from her ordeal when she became acquainted with him.
Her work, *The Freshwater Diary*, and its accompanying letter to her dead lover
chronicled her final five days with Macartney. In the memoir she subsequently
wrote of her years in Croydon. Helen relates how she shared the diary with
Lawrence – an intimate act that drew them together.

But for Lawrence it was more than that. Helen's pain became a source
of inspiration and he found himself imagining the situation from the male
perspective. With her consent, Lawrence took the material from the diary and
used it to conceive his own version of the story, which he called 'The Saga of
Siegmund' (published eventually as *The Trespasser* in 1912). Lawrence wrote
in a kind of frenzy – as he so often did when inspiration struck – cramming
his writing time into the short periods of free time he had during the school
day and in the evenings. He remarked in 1911, when he was still juggling
his writing around his teaching responsibilities, that he was 'supposed to be
marking Composition – such a stack of blue exercise books at my elbow…it
is awful: it'll be the death of me one of these days. Damn – there's the bell'.[31]
Jessie also recalled that he wrote apparently 'very much disturbed', and that he
was compelled to write the story of Siegmund. He then begged Jessie to go to
Croydon so that he could introduce her to Helen.

As was so often Lawrence's modus operandi when writing, he seemed to inhabit the novel; and the novel inhabited him – so much so, that fact quickly merged into fiction, not just because Lawrence had used a real-life drama as a plot for his next novel, but he felt himself *becoming* Siegmund. For Lawrence, the manuscript had become a 'work of fiction on a framework of fact',[32] but the boundaries between the two quickly became blurred during the writing process, as real identities merged with fictional ones. Helen inevitably found herself becoming drawn to Lawrence; the writing of the 'Saga' demanded an intimacy between the two, not just because Helen provided the inspiration for the plot, but because, as Helen later recalled, 'romance and reality join hands… Into what kind of a relationship are we drifting?'[33]

Helen was conscious not just of her feelings of affection towards Lawrence, but also a feeling of wonder and awe at his literary and imaginative talent. She was also aware that Lawrence's frame of mind while he was writing 'The Saga of Siegmund' was likely to be a temporary state because he was putting himself in the place of her dead lover. 'The conditions are…abnormal',[34] she reassures herself in a thoroughly understated manner in her memoir. 'I must not confuse the man with the artist'.[35] But Helen, still mentally fragile, was also desperate to *feel* something of Macartney in the corporeal world. Lawrence could make him come alive again on paper, but Helen needed proof that his spirit was still with her. 'During the months since his death I have half-hoped for some intimate sign from him: it has not come',[36] she confides to herself. 'Eleven months of separation have virtually convinced me that the dissolution of what I have known as the personality of H.B.M. [Herbert Baldwin Macartney] is complete, yet the idea, born of the *revenant* tales and ballads, that our island may retain some emanation of his being discernible by my consciousness persists…'[37]

Helen's grief and inability to move on from Macartney's death formed an emotional barrier that Lawrence couldn't penetrate, and during the writing of the 'Saga' it became clear that any permanent romantic relationship between the them was impossible. Lawrence's poems from this time say something of his frustration, both sexual and emotional. In 'The Appeal,' he urges Helen to 'put your mouth to mine and drink of me', but is frustrated by her disinterest: 'Helen, you let my kisses steam/ Wasteful into the night's black nostrils'.[38] 'Coldness in Love' conveys strikingly the emotional distance between them, despite the intimacy they had found in creating the 'Saga': 'Then I longed for you with your mantle of love to fold/ Me over, and drive from out of my body the deep/ Cold that had sunk to my soul, and there kept hold./ But still to me all evening long you were cold'.[39] Lawrence felt Helen was just out of reach – tantalisingly close but beyond the influence of his own emotions, which he seemed to be grappling with daily. 'How gladly will I bend and follow you if you will lead', he wrote to her in June 1910. 'But you will not. Nor will you walk with me, en camarade. You hang away somewhere to the left'.[40] Always just out of reach…

And what of Jessie Chambers? Despite the charm Lawrence injects into his short missives to Jessie in early March 1910, telling her that he could not rest 'without you next to me', a matter of weeks later he is complaining to Helen of his 'lethargy' at the thought of Jessie and the commitment he has made to her. His devotion to Helen and the 'Saga' led Lawrence to tell Jessie not to attempt to 'hold him', – in other words, he wanted Jessie to make no demands on him. In the interim, he needed Helen, but he reassured Jessie he would return to her if she would always 'leave him free'.

Tragically for Jessie, Lawrence was not true to his word, and her earlier scepticism was proved correct. Jessie's private memoir confirms that she and Lawrence entered a brief and thoroughly unfulfilling sexual relationship in May 1910 – the exact number of occasions in which they physically united could, according to Jessie, be easily counted on one hand.[41] Then, without a hint of what was to come, Lawrence abruptly broke his engagement with Jessie in August of that year – yet was still hopeful they could remain friends (again),

> I stood, as always, for complete union or a complete break. I could not move from my old standpoint of all or nothing, even when Lawrence said: "Then I am afraid it must be nothing."We agreed not even to correspond.[42]

Unsurprisingly, Lawrence was incapable of sticking to the agreement not to write and within a week of their break, he wrote to Jessie urging her to read a book that he thought would help to explain the situation.

Yet, despite everything, Helen and Jessie became intimate friends – their relationship outlasted their respective relationships with Lawrence and outlived his death in 1930. Lawrence revealed his troubled relationship with Jessie to Helen once he had completed the 'Saga' with his usual candidacy, explaining that he did not want to marry Jessie and he would rather they were just friends. On the same occasion, he also showed Helen a short story in which he refers to Jessie as 'Muriel' – a pet name that all parties would come to use in their future correspondence – and asks would Helen like to meet 'Muriel'? The arrangement was made, and Helen set out with misgivings, and was even prepared to dislike Jessie because of her previous claim on Lawrence.

That the two women would become kindred spirits probably surprised them all. 'Muriel belongs to my world', Helen recalled later, 'she may enter it in her own right.'They did not need Lawrence to give his blessing or permission. Yet Lawrence's behaviour immediately following Helen's first meeting with Jessie speaks volumes as to his feelings on the matter. According to Helen, he was in a cynical mood, and began a 'slashing criticism of a book of modern verse'. Yet she was also increasingly aware of his sexual desire towards her – a desire she couldn't bring herself to reciprocate. This was the basis on which any future relationship between them would have to take shape.

Thus, it was into this strange mix of romance, repulsion, grief, friendship and conflicting personalities – both real and imagined – that 'The Saga of Siegmund' was born. Little wonder that Ford Madox Hueffer was both perplexed and bemused by the manuscript when it finally landed on his desk in the autumn of 1910. Hueffer reflected on the episode twenty-six years after its publication, as *The Trespasser*, in his memoir – an occasion that was to become a watershed moment for both men:

> *One day he brought me half the MS [manuscript] of* The Trespassers [sic] *– and that was the end. It was a* Trespassers [sic] *much – oh, but much! – more phallic than is the book as it stands and much more moral in the inverted-puritanic sense... So that the whole effect was the rather dreary one of a schoolboy larking among placket-holes, dialoguing with a Wesleyan minister who has been converted to Ibsen...As it was it had the making of a thoroughly bad hybrid book and I told him so.*[43]

And with that, Lawrence and Hueffer parted professional ways, although the two did meet again on friendly terms during the Great War. 'Nethermere' – now *The White Peacock* – was well into its publication schedule in the autumn of 1910, but any excitement Lawrence was feeling at the time was destined to be completely overshadowed by grief: his greatest love, Lydia Lawrence, was dying.

Chapter 4

It is Finished

As he went along the ten miles of highroad, he felt as if he were walking out of life, between the black levels of the sky and the earth. But at the end was only the sick-room. If he walked and walked for ever, there was only that place to come to.[1]

Within two weeks of Lawrence's rather dishonourable treatment of Jessie Chambers, Lydia Lawrence fell ill. It was mid-August 1910, and during a holiday with her sister, Ada Krenkow, who lived in Leicester, Lydia had taken to her bed and was diagnosed with a cancerous tumour in her abdomen.

Lawrence was gallivanting in Blackpool with his friend George Neville at the time – an experience that he would relive on paper in *Sons and Lovers*. Lawrence's immediate relief at his break with Jessie is palpable in Neville's descriptions of their adventures, which according to him included a 'rush around the town on the Saturday night',[2] with some 'promiscuous dancing' on Central Pier and some 'love-making foolery' with a widow from Yorkshire called Clara – who despite her best efforts (she allegedly asked Lawrence one night to help her to 'lower the level of the whisky bottle' in her room) wasn't able to entice Lawrence completely. Lawrence also kept the hotel guests in a constant state of mirth and enjoyment – displaying some of the old humorous charm that had made him such a favourite at the Haggs.

But Lawrence's carefree summer was short-lived. After his break in Blackpool with Neville, Lawrence was supposed to travel to Leicester, where he would meet his mother and accompany her home to Eastwood, but she was too ill to be moved. The new school term was due to start at the end of August, so Lawrence had no option but to travel back to Croydon and try to return to the Midlands to see his mother at weekends. Fortunately, one of Lawrence's teacher friends, Louie Burrows – with whom he had kept up a constant correspondence with since their college days – lived close enough to Leicester to be able to visit Lydia and pass news between mother and son. Louie was also a conduit for Lawrence's work. Lawrence was acutely aware that the time he had left with his mother was diminishing and was hoping she would live long enough to see a bound copy of *The White Peacock*, but in the interim he sent his spare proofs up to his mother in Leicester and Louie was charged with reading them to her.

Lawrence feared that he'd never be able to place a copy of *The White Peacock* into the hands of his mother. But when a copy did finally arrive on 2 December – sent early especially for Lawrence to show his mother – she could merely look at it. She was too ill to read any of it – even Lawrence's dedication, which read, 'To my Mother, with love, D. H. Lawrence.' Lawrence was crushed. Jessie recalls the strain he was under at that time: 'I saw him several times, and although he was superficially interested in things one could not help feeling how utterly alone he was in his grief. Love was unavailing, no matter how sincere or how selfless. In his presence one felt only the horror of sheer hopelessness.'[3] Such hopelessness also provoked a sense of impulsivity, and Lawrence railed against the impending death of his mother with a sort of 'devil may care' attitude towards his relationship with Louie. The day after he presented *The White Peacock* to his mother, he suddenly asked Louie to marry him – whether out of genuine affection for his old friend, or as a spur-of-the-moment counter reaction to all that was horrible in his life at the time – only Lawrence knew. When he broke the news to Jessie Chambers, his uncertainty was clear. Lawrence said,

> *I suddenly asked her* [Louie] *to marry me. I never meant to. But she accepted me and I shall stick to it. I've written to her father. . . I'll go over the old ground again, if you like, and explain. Do you want me to say little, or nothing, or much? I'll say anything you like, only I can't help it, I'm made this way.*[4]

Perhaps he meant to soften the blow by stating that he 'never meant to', but his declaration that he 'can't help it, I'm made this way' was a convenient excuse that would have provided little comfort to an already aggrieved Jessie.

One thing he couldn't do was tell his mother. To do so in her final days would have been the ultimate betrayal: 'Nobody can have the soul of me', he wrote just days before her passing. His mother had his soul and he had no intention of giving it to anyone else.

The days and nights in which Lawrence watched his mother die were agonising – it is a credit to Lawrence's writing talent that he was later able to convey those moments through the character of Paul in *Sons and Lovers*, with a lyricism that transcends the awful business of death:

> *He stood looking out of the window. The whole country was bleak and pallid under the snow. Then he felt her pulse. There was a strong stroke and a weak one, like a sound and its echo. That was supposed to betoken the end. She let him feel her wrist, knowing what he wanted.*
>
> *Sometimes they looked into each other's eyes. They almost seemed to make an agreement. It was almost as if he were agreeing to die also. But she did not consent to die; she would not. Her body was wasted to a fragment of ash. Her eyes were dark and full of torture.*[5]

Mercifully, Lawrence was given leave from his teaching role in Croydon at the end of November so that he could return to Eastwood and be with his mother in her final weeks. In the liminal space between life and death, time seemed to stand still. Lawrence felt as though he had 'died since', and that his mother's death was part of 'an old life, dreamy'. In a sense, Lawrence was right. His old life was slipping away with the life of his mother, and he would never be the same again.

Lydia's death and the weeks preceding it were fictionalised in 'Paul Morel' – the manuscript that became *Sons and Lovers*. Lawrence portrays Gertrude Morel's stubborn refusal to die – 'She's got such a will, it seems as if she would never go – never!'[6] Paul tells Clara Dawes – which was probably closely allied to Lydia Lawrence's ability to cling on well into December. 'I wish she'd die!'[7] Paul says, echoing Lawrence's own hopes that, 'I wish she could die tonight.'[8] Lawrence shared the nursing of his mother with his sister, Ada, now 22 and a teacher herself. In desperation the two siblings agreed to give her an overdose of the morphia the doctor had given them in her nightly milk,[9] an episode Lawrence describes in *Sons and Lovers*. But just as Gertrude Morel lingers on, so too did Lydia. Despite the morphia, Lydia Lawrence survived until the following morning, finally passing away on Friday, 9 December 1910.

Lawrence felt empty. Like a leaf blown in the wind',[10] he commented to Jessie. His stark description of the sick room immediately after the death of Gertrude Morel in *Sons and Lovers* depicts something of that sense of abandonment:

> *The room was cold, that had been warm for so long. Flowers, bottles, plates, all sick room litter was taken away; everything was harsh and austere. She lay raised on the bed, the sweep of the sheet from the raised feet was like a clean curve of snow, so silent.*[11]

Lawrence poured his anguish into his poems; his writing provided him with an outlet for his grief and the poems he wrote immediately after Lydia's death gave him the opportunity to explore his emotions freely, in a way he couldn't do before. They veer from bleak ('I own that some of me is dead tonight'[12]) to a dawning realisation that he must say his last goodbyes ('Let the last word be uttered,/ Oh grant the farewell is said!/ Spare me the strength to leave you./ Now you are dead'.[13])

The Lawrence family buried Lydia the following Monday in Eastwood cemetery, beside her son Ernest on a typically gloomy December day. The gravestone inscription simply read, 'It is finished.' Her final struggle with life referenced through Christ's last words on the cross.

Chapter 5

Something of a Miasma

'It was midnight, full of sick thoughts,' says the author somewhere. In 'The White Peacock' the sick thoughts are always there, though the day be spring and the clouds high. We have said that it is clever; which is, perhaps, all the author wished said.[1]

Lydia Lawrence's death undoubtedly marred what should have been Lawrence's grand arrival onto the literary stage. *The White Peacock* was published in January 1911, but rather than the fanfare Lawrence was hoping for, the novel slipped quietly into the lists with nothing of note to commend it as the work of a 'genius'. Comments ranged from the promising ('...a very remarkable work in many ways'[2]) to the outraged ('...an instrument of deep depression, an unrelenting record of sordidness'[3]). Lawrence would have to wait a bit longer to be publicly hailed a 'genius' of the literary world. Only his contemporary, fellow Heinemann author and Hueffer's mistress, Violent Hunt, really understood what Lawrence was trying to achieve with *The White Peacock*. 'This novel, by a new writer, is really an important contribution to literature', Hunt stated in *The Daily Chronicle*. 'It should be read by all those superior persons who say that they have no time to read novels because they are engaged in public works...because from its pages they will learn something of the mind of the classes who really returned them to the top of the polls, or turned them down'.[4] Hunt had the benefit of knowing Lawrence personally, and so her opinion – however freely given – was always going to be prejudiced by their friendship. For Jessie Chambers it was 'a kind of anticlimax to the writing of it', but Lawrence did at least recognise her input: 'I its creator, you its nurse',[5] he wrote to Jessie on its publication.

It mattered little. Lawrence was in no mood for cheerfulness, irrespective of the success of his novel or not. 'Something of a miasma belongs to the novel', one review noted, '...the sick thoughts are always there.'[6] The sentiment was reflected in Lawrence's daily life as he attempted to dispel his own 'sick thoughts' over the death of his mother, the monotony of his teaching role and his impulsive engagement to Louie Burrows.

Haunted by images of his dying mother, and frustrated by the knowledge that to get married to Louie he would need to find a better-paid job – and the tedium of paperwork and interviews that would entail – it was inevitable that Lawrence would succumb to morosity. The couple decided that they could not marry without a lump sum of at least £100 and would need an annual income of £120 to support themselves. Louie expected to resign from her own role as a headteacher at Gaddesby in Leicestershire, either on marriage to Lawrence or very soon afterwards – as was customary – and so the financial responsibility was all Lawrence's. In late December 1910, he suggested Cornwall as a suitable location to Louie. A school was advertising a post for £115 per annum, but Lawrence's dithering over whether to send off for the application forms suggests a lack of commitment to the idea on his part – which was also exacerbated by Louie's lack of enthusiasm for moving so far away. He decided to send for the forms anyway – by this time there were two posts available in Cornwall. But he ripped one of the applications up and didn't fill in the second one.

During this time, the earning potential of Lawrence's writing took on a new importance – and his attitude changed to how well *The White Peacock* would fare now it was out in the world for all to read. 'I shall be very sorry if I get no success', he confided to Louie. The reality of their financial situation weighed heavy on Lawrence, particularly as he could see no discernible way to improve matters quickly.

But, until his writing paid what he needed it to, Lawrence was beholden to the Croydon School Board for his annual salary – despite Ford Maddox Hueffer's attempts to persuade him to 'get out'. 'It was quite obvious to me that here was a young fellow who ought to write, who, indeed would write, so the sooner he got to it the better',[7] Hueffer wrote in his autobiography.

There were other minor irritations for Lawrence in early 1911, both back in Eastwood. His sister Ada, who was still living at home, was having difficulties with their father. Rather than hand over most of his weekly earnings to his daughter to run the household, Arthur Lawrence was keeping nearly a quarter of it for himself and spending most of it on alcohol. It was the same issue of old – and the arguments Arthur was having with Ada no doubt mirrored those he had had with his wife repeatedly over the years.

The other annoyance was the Eastwood reception of *The White Peacock*. His family circle were clearly delighted to have a published author in the family, and soon after its publication, Lawrence requested several copies of the novel directly from the publisher so that he could distribute them to 'three rapacious relatives'. But the Eastwood community at large was less enthusiastic about the book – specifically with regard to its portrayal of the characters. It was the first of several disputes he would have with residents of his hometown, who recognising themselves in his works – often by name, as well as description – took umbrage at his characterisation of them. So much so, that Lawrence's betrayal of them, and the town in which he was born, remained a topic of local conversation for decades after his death. Back in February 1911 though, the issue was solely with the Hall family, and Lawrence's depiction of a friend from his youth – Alice Hall, renamed Alice Gall for the purposes of *The White Peacock*. Lawrence was, predictably, indignant when he found out how angry they were, suggesting that Alice 'ought to be flattered', and that if they felt their dignity had been impaired, he would change the name to 'Margaret Undine Widmerpuddle, or any such fantasy they shall choose' – whatever was furthest away from the sound of Hall or Gall.

The real Alice was now married to White Holdich – a 'snuffing idiot' according to Lawrence – who had threatened him with a lawsuit, and whom Lawrence was inclined to 'have a whack at'. But before it came to that, Lawrence hoped that Eastwood politician Willie Hopkin, as a person of local influence, could intervene on his behalf and smooth things over. Which he did, and fortunately within a couple of weeks the incident had blown over with no 'whacks' exchanged. Willie Hopkin would also find himself immortalised by Lawrence, but he 'took it in his stride',[8] according to his second wife when she was interviewed after his death. He is generally accepted to be the model for the socialist Mr Goddard in *Mr Noon* and for market orator Willie Houghton in *Touch and Go*.

It wouldn't be the last time that Lawrence would fall foul of Eastwood's residents. His old school friend George Neville – who incidentally was thought to be the template for Leslie Tempest in *The White Peacock* – attempted to remonstrate with him in March 1912, the year *The Trespasser* was published. But Lawrence was unmoved. 'Lawrence would not hear of any argument, and, knowing him so well, I knew it was quite useless to attempt to convince him',[9] Neville recalled.

While Lawrence was inadvertently upsetting the great and good of Eastwood, he was also heavily preoccupied with one of his other creative pursuits – painting. Lawrence had enjoyed sketching and painting since boyhood, and regularly gifted his works to friends and family. Immediately following his mother's death, a period in which Lawrence found writing particularly challenging, he found some solace in producing art. Similarly, when his writing flowed, he found he couldn't paint.

As early as 1908, Lawrence had been fascinated by 'An Idyll', a painting of 1891 by Maurice Greiffenhagen depicting the physical intimacy between a shepherd and young lady as he pulls her to him in a passionate embrace. The image was sent to him by his suffragette friend Blanche Jennings, on receipt of which Lawrence declared, 'it moves me almost as much as if I were fallen in love myself.' This visceral, emotional response to the painting meant it stayed with him – becoming almost like a talisman; something he could return to time and again when he felt untethered from the world around him. Perhaps he recognised some crucial element of his own personality in the painting, and it provided a means for him to express who he was, for he referenced it not only in *The White Peacock* when Lettie and George are looking through a book of art (and indeed the focus of the novel is the relationship between working-class farmer George and middle-class Lettie) but he also painted four copies of his own. One of these was begun the night his mother died, which was gifted to Ada; one was given as a wedding present to Agnes Holt; and one was sent to Arthur McLeod, when Lawrence was convalescing from pneumonia in the winter of 1911. The largest version was painted for Louie Burrows – a gift that was perhaps Lawrence's not-so-subtle way of conveying to her the importance of a physical expression of love – something that would be denied to him until they married.

The vitality of love, expressed through the painting's passionate embrace, was something Lawrence returned to frequently in his own artistic output. But he was also searching for the same experience in life, and he began to doubt whether Louie was the woman who could provide it. Louie embodied ordinary life – marrying her was the first step on the path to conventionality, professionalism and the ideology of 'the system', something Lawrence despised. The death of his mother had left him 'rudderless' and Louie could steer him in a direction that his mother would have approved of. The problem was, the direction his mother would have wished him to take as her son didn't appeal to Lawrence the man. He would be living a life that ignored those very qualities that marked him out as extraordinary – his unconventionality, his tendency for rebellion, his passionate outbursts, his intellect and, of course, his intensity.

Thus, his attraction to Louie was not enough – evidenced by his continuing intimacy with Helen Corke and the fact he was still writing poetry about the other women in his life. The poems covered themes that he dared not share with Louie, despite her request to see them. As well as poems that referenced his relationship with Louie, he had also written about his attraction to Helen, Alice Dax, and making love to Jessie Chambers. Lawrence's reticence about sharing them would have been worthy of Louie's suspicions – after all, she had previously copied Lawrence's poems for him, and so being denied access to the verses would have jarred. The 'Saga' was also off limits to Louie because its themes were a manifestation of how he felt about Helen. As a consolation, he offered to show Louie 'the first two hundred pages of Paul Morel'.

Whatever feelings Lawrence had committed to paper regarding Helen, 1911 did mark a cooling in their relationship. Following the intensity of the period in which they worked on the 'Saga' together, there came a lull over the winter of Lydia Lawrence's death in 1910. Nevertheless, the intimacy had been established, although Helen's perception of what existed between them was strikingly different to Lawrence's. To Helen, their relationship mirrored that of a brother and sister, but Lawrence wanted more.

Things came to a head in March 1911. Louie spent a weekend with Lawrence, staying as a guest of the family he lodged with, just as Jessie Chambers had the previous year. But the stay wasn't all that successful. Lawrence wrote to Louie after she had left to try to convey how much he desired a physical relationship with her – no doubt having been rebuffed during her stay – explaining that 'I go straight, like a bullet, towards my aim. I cannot loiter by the way'.[10] He was clearly impatient. Yet on the same day he wrote to Jessie revealing that being alone with Louie made him want to run away. As in everything, Lawrence was incapable of being anything other than contradictory.

The day after his letters to Louie and Jessie, he wrote to Helen Corke. The letter revealed that at some point before Louie's stay in Croydon, Lawrence had asked Helen to sleep with him. Unsurprisingly, Helen had declined his request. Irritated, Lawrence suggested that Helen had led him on and that her innocent physical interactions with him such as 'taking his arm' were akin to a sexual approach. He went on to explain that he believed it was the 'natural' course of their relationship and that he genuinely believed he 'was *not* wrong' in what he asked her.

Lawrence's moral compass was decidedly off-kilter in his dealings with the women in his life in 1911. He was telling half-truths to keep them all on-side – particularly Jessie Chambers – and he was pressurising both Louie and Helen to engage in physical relationships that they had made clear they did not want. In fact, he makes it all too easy for us to cry misogyny, as many researchers of Lawrence did fifty years ago. Yet to do so is to do Lawrence himself an injustice. As ever, he was emotionally conflicted, and this feeling of mental confusion was reflected in all his relationships. The death of his mother was the catalyst for a transition in Lawrence's life. He had to adjust to life without Lydia, which made him lose his sense of direction. He was liberated from her and so could make his own choices, but having been defined by the expectations of his mother for so long, he didn't know what he wanted, or indeed, how to get it. He *could* marry Louie, but then the opportunity for him to forge his own path would be lost forever.

He was also trying to reconcile himself to who he was, and who he wanted to be. Was he a teacher? Or a writer?...A genius? Or an imposter?...Literary? Or a realist?...Civilised or elemental?...Middle-class and urbane, or working-class and parochial? These were questions that no doubt plagued Lawrence during 1911. He couldn't just *be* himself because he didn't *know* himself. But the biggest question mark hung over his writing career, and whether he would have one.

With *The White Peacock* published, and a handful of mixed reviews, Lawrence's thoughts turned to his other material. An air of uncertainty hung over the 'Saga' following Hueffer's dismissal of it (and Lawrence's recognition that it was 'execrably bad art'), and there was no interest from any other publishers either. His career had already stalled, and any early momentum he had gained was already leeching away. He'd also come to a standstill on 'Paul Morel' and was stuck at the hundredth page for four months. 'I've no heart to tackle a serious work just now', he admitted. And it wasn't just the grief of losing his mother, or the chaotic nature of his personal relationships that were affecting Lawrence's writing. Having distanced himself from Jessie Chambers and the Haggs, he had lost an important source of inspiration, as well as his literary guide and critic.

Jessie's way of coping with their estrangement was to write about the incident that had caused their long-standing impasse. She felt that their long conflict had dated from the time when, as a boy of 20, Lawrence had told her fatefully that he had looked into his heart and could not find that he loved Jessie 'as a husband should love his wife'. So in an act of catharsis, Jessie wrote her thoughts in the form of a short story and sent the manuscript to Lawrence sometime in the spring of 1911. It was also an opportunity for Jessie to communicate to Lawrence just how hurtful he had been, which she knew would upset him, but she believed that the only way they could both move on was to confront the pain of the situation head on. Lawrence wrote back to Jessie and told her that he didn't think that anyone would publish it because it was 'too subtle', but then his detachment falters and he tells her, 'They tore me from you, the love of my life…It was the slaughter of the foetus in the womb.'[11]

Reading past the overly dramatic tone, Jessie had clearly hit a nerve, but whether it had the desired effect on Lawrence's state of mind, or the state of their relationship, is debatable. What is certain is that Lawrence continued in the same gloomy frame of mind that he'd been in since the beginning of the year, which meant that he was struggling to do anything other than painfully chip away at 'Paul Morel' while continuing to hold down his teaching role at Davidson Road. With things still unresolved with Jessie, he sent extracts to Louie, commenting that he thought it 'very rummy'.

Lawrence's lack of interest in working on anything other than his 'great but terrible' novel became a problem in June 1911 when up-and-coming young publisher, Martin Secker, wrote an extremely favourable letter to Lawrence expressing how much he had enjoyed *The White Peacock* and one of Lawrence's short stories, which had just been published in the *English Review*. On this basis, Secker proposed that Lawrence send him a volume of short stories as soon as he had sufficient material.

'I have not troubled to write any', Lawrence replied about the short stories. 'Because nobody wanted the things.' As well as being in the middle of a novel (Paul Morel) he was 'bejungled' in work – the signs of the conflict between writing and school already in evidence. Secker was undeterred, responding that he was prepared to wait until the following spring so that he could make Lawrence an offer of publication. It was yet another reminder of Lawrence's lack of direction. He desperately wanted to commit himself to writing, but progress on Paul Morel was glacial, and thanks to Hueffer, the 'Saga' had gone missing in action, along with two plays. Hueffer had left the *English Review* and gone abroad to become a German citizen, so that he could attempt to obtain a divorce from his wife, Elsie, who refused to divorce him in England. Lawrence's contact at the *Review* was now Austin Harrison – who was willing to publish Lawrences short stories, but only with some heavy editing. He needed to finish Paul Morel, and he needed to do so quickly. 'It's the third [novel] that counts', he had told Jessie on the publication of his first novel, *The White Peacock.*

To compound his problems, he had argued with Louie, this time over money. Lawrence was paid £10 by the *Review* for his short story 'Odour of Chrysanthemums', but almost immediately after receiving it he had spent most of it on a half-day trip to Dover, rather than save it for his forthcoming marriage to Louie. Dumbfounded by this act, Louie had questioned whether he was trying to save the money for their marriage, which was the same as questioning whether he wanted to get married. However, Louie was unaware that Lawrence had travelled to Dover because he was in a temper with Helen because she had rejected his sexual advances. On his return to Croydon, he wrote to Helen, telling her that he couldn't contain his feelings of desire and the temptation was becoming too much.

A holiday in Prestatyn, Wales in July with Louie and his sister Ada did nothing to distract him from these feelings. If anything, it made it worse, and he insisted on being accompanied by Ada whenever he was with Louie – presumably so that he could keep himself in check and keep her chastity safe from his desirous intentions. Social and moral proprieties had to be maintained at all costs. Although not present on the holiday, Jessie heard second-hand that, 'Lawrence was never still for a minute, that he ran up and down the crags like a man possessed; that he absolutely refused to be left alone with Louie and insisted on Ada accompanying them wherever they went'.[12]

But his time in Wales didn't seem to provide the inspiration he needed to continue writing at pace. And the start of the autumn term at school was looming. Two days into term and Lawrence was 'pretty rotten', but he was plodding on, nonetheless. Crucially at this time, Lawrence made the acquaintance of Edward Garnett (1868–1937), reader and adviser for Heinemann, who was also in the process of sourcing new material for the American magazine *Century*. It was an opportunity Lawrence couldn't afford to turn down and in early September he sent Garnett two stories, which he hoped Garnett would be able to place. These, unfortunately, were not suitable for the 'stupid American taste' of the magazine as Lawrence wrote later, but it did prompt Garnett to invite Lawrence to London for a lunchtime meeting. The outcome of the meeting was positive – Garnett invited Lawrence to stay with him at his house, the Cearne, in Edenbridge, Kent.

Lawrence's attitude towards his publisher, Heinemann's, was also changing at this time. He was concerned he had 'mortally offended' them – no doubt because he had insisted on the return of 'the Saga', and had yet produced no other completed manuscripts. But he was also fed up with Frederick Atkinson, Heinemann's editor and reader, whom he referred to as a 'sneering, affected little fellow'.

Meeting Garnett in the autumn of 1911 was fortuitous. Not only was Garnett known for discovering and developing young literary talent (he was known to have discovered Joseph Conrad in the late nineteenth century) – and being well connected in the literary world – but he also gave Lawrence a reason to re-absorb himself in his fictional worlds, and the material he had become increasingly disconnected from. But it was more than that. As well as assisting Lawrence with practical matters such as introducing him to the right sort of literary people, and getting his work read by publishers, he also nurtured Lawrence using just the right balance of criticism and support. He enhanced Lawrence's ability to edit his work and was able to make him see where the weaknesses in his writing were, without resorting to literary annihilation: 'Thanks for the advice concerning *Intimacy*', Lawrence wrote to Garnett in late September 1911. 'I myself felt the drag of the tale, and its slowness in accumulating.' It must have been a relief to Lawrence to be able to share his work with another literary-minded person after the hiatus his estrangement from Jessie had imposed on him.

Garnett was not appreciated in all quarters, however. Ford Madox Hueffer was on the receiving end of Garnett's 'teasing' on several occasions, but he took umbrage at Garnett's criticism of the *Review*, writing to him after the incident that, 'I think I ought to tell you that I resent – and resent intensely – yr [your] telling people that I can't write. It does not matter before intimates but when it comes to a table of comparative strangers I really think it is in distinctly bad taste.'[13] He was also the subject of a remarkably scathing attack from Hueffer's sub-editor, Douglas Goldring, who jumped to Hueffer's defence claiming that Garnett was 'boorish', 'patronising' and would not have 'achieved his reputation as a publisher's reader had he not been in a position to pick the brains of his betters'.[14]

Irrespective of the bad feeling that may have existed between them, Hueffer conceded that 'there are very few writers of any real worth that do not owe something to his support'.[15] Garnett certainly knew how to handle Lawrence and described him with genuine affection in his introduction to *A Collier's Friday Night*, recalling his 'loveableness, cheekiness, intensity and pride',[16] when he first knew him, and he visited the Cearne.

Garnett was able to offer Lawrence advice with regard to managing his relationship with Heinemann, as well as advise him on financial matters, and what it was reasonable for Lawrence to expect in terms of payments from his publisher.

Lawrence was clearly under Garnett's spell, although Garnett's success at placing Lawrence's short stories wasn't immediate. Nevertheless, Lawrence was enraptured by Garnett; his home in the Kent countryside, the Cearne; their literary chats; and everything Garnett's world embodied.

Garnett's unconventional relationship with his wife Constance – they chose to live primarily separate lives – and his liberal attitudes towards sex and sexuality ensured the two men had common ground. As a scholar of D. H. Lawrence, Analise Grice, points out: 'Garnett's notorious battle with censorship, his high standards for literature, his attempts to become a creative writer, his anti-institutional sentiments, unconventional marital arrangements and his advocacy of the rights of women to claim their sexual independence help us to understand how it was that he and Lawrence got on so well'.[17]

Lawrence was in no doubt that his future lay with Garnett, but how would he find the time he needed to immerse himself properly in the literary world? Things were reaching a climax in the autumn of 1911, as Lawrence tried to juggle his fledgling writing career with the demands of his role as a schoolteacher.

'I am very busy indeed with one thing and another – so busy, that I have only time to think about work and the things I've got to do tomorrow'.[18] This was Lawrence's refrain throughout October and into November.

Lawrence may have become reacquainted with his literary self, but it was to the detriment of his health. He desperately wanted to write – particularly now he had the steadying hand of Edward Garnett to guide him – but he was still teaching full time to support himself, which meant his writing had to be crammed in either before or after school. Jessie Chambers and Helen Corke – now close friends – bumped into Lawrence and his brother George (who was visiting him) at the theatre in October and although they did not sit together they chatted during the interval. The pressure Lawrence was under was obvious: 'He looked frail and insubstantial', Jessie commented. She had an insight into Lawrence's state of mind like no one else, recognising that he was profoundly unhappy and unable to escape his demons. Offering advice or attempting to help him was futile, as Jessie rightly surmised: 'Only Lawrence might help himself.' Jessie recognised the answer 'lay within himself', but before he could achieve it he had to acknowledge the nature of his malady.

But outwardly, Lawrence was buoyed by his own progress. And no doubt wanting to share his enthusiasm with the one person who he knew would understand his renewed sense of interest in writing – his 'Sternest Critic' according to an article written in 1965[19] – he sent two thirds of the manuscript of 'Paul Morel' to Jessie Chambers, asking her to tell him what she thought of it. Lawrence had written himself into a corner with the telling of Paul Morel's story and hoped that Jessie would provide the key to writing himself out of it again.

The issue was the relationship between the characters of Paul [Lawrence] and Miriam Leivers [Jessie]. Jessie saw the characters as locked together in a frustrating bondage with no way out. Reading it 'oppressed' her with 'a sense of strain'. Lawrence had explored the theme of oppressive motherlove, and through the character of Gertrude [based on Lydia Lawrence] had depicted her opposition to a marriage between Paul and Miriam – but could progress no further. Paul faced a dilemma over his relationship with Miriam, and Lawrence was conflicted as to how he should conclude their story – as well as how he should conclude his own story with Jessie. He had two choices – either he let the two lovers be together, or he let Gertrude Morel triumph. This conflict manifested itself in his manuscript. The internal quarrel he had had over his feelings towards Jessie and the expectations of his mother would come to bear through his writing, and so Jessie suggested Lawrence write the story again, with more authenticity. She felt his treatment of it didn't convey the poignancy and tension of the story, and he had omitted many points of interest that had their foundation in real events, such as Ernest's death. The outcome of these revisions she hoped would be twofold – first that Lawrence would write 'a magnificent story', but secondly (and perhaps more importantly) that by working out the conflict through the medium of the novel, that he might free himself from his obsession with his mother. 'I thought he might be able to work out the theme in the realm of spiritual reality, where alone it could be worked out, and so resolve the conflict in himself',[20] Jessie wrote. She did not reveal this to Lawrence, trusting to his integrity and ability to work it out himself through his writing.

In response, Lawrence asked Jessie for her recollections of their earlier days, which she duly began to write. Where their relationship had failed in real life, Jessie no doubt hoped their fictional counterparts would find salvation instead.

Before Jessie would find out, however, Lawrence would need to battle for a physical salvation of his own.

Chapter 6

Sons and Lovers

Mrs. Morel felt as if her heart would break for him. At this rate she knew he would not live. He had that poignant, carelessness about himself, his own suffering, his own life, which is a form of slow suicide. It almost broke her heart. With all the passion of her strong nature she hated Miriam for having in this subtle way undermined his joy. It did not matter to her that Miriam could not help it. Miriam did it, and she hated her.[1]

As the autumn of 1911 wore on, Lawrence sank further into a mire of self-made misery. Rather than bringing him happiness, his relationship with Louie was dragging him down and he could see no satisfactory end. To mitigate this, he seemed to fill every moment of his spare time with distractions – anything that would help to take his mind off his slide into depression and ill-health. Whether it was visiting the theatre or a concert ('I have been to a Promenade Concert in our Public Hall this week', he commented), spending time with friends ('tonight I've promised to go out for tea and all evening with one of my friends'), even visiting sick friends in hospital ('Gert Cooper is in hospital again – not very serious – so I must go and see her'). He was also regularly visiting Edward Garnett at the Cearne, as well as keeping up a weekly correspondence with him, but even his renewed enthusiasm for working on 'Paul Morel' wasn't enough to stave off an impending feeling of doom. 'The long slow drag of the hours is very trying', he wrote to Louie at the end of October.

He was also finding it difficult to show his true self to Louie. There were things he wanted to say or share with her but felt that he couldn't – he likened it to 'shoving' the words back inside himself. Lawrence could not be who he wanted to be with Louie – and therein lay the crux of the issue, and what would ultimately become the axis on which the relationship ended. He *could* be himself with Jessie but wasn't sufficiently attracted to her sexually to bind himself to her in marriage. Louie knew very little of the real Lawrence – only the carefully curated version Lawrence chose to share with her. This meant that apart from the veiled references he made to his general mood and emotions in his letters and probably in person too, Louie was very much in the dark with regard to the seriousness of the situation, and unaware of how rapidly Lawrence's state of mind was deteriorating.

Things reached a climax for Lawrence in mid-November. His teaching and schoolwork was a burden, but so was the unfinished 'Paul Morel': 'I am really very tired of school – I *cannot* get on with Paul', he complained. Lawrence himself had a sense of foreboding that all was not well, and he was teetering on a precipice: 'I am on the brink of a complaint', he revealed to Louie, although the nature of their relationship meant he couldn't divulge the extent of the 'complaint'. What is more telling throughout Lawrence's correspondence with Louie is what he *doesn't* say. That version of Lawrence – the one that could speak candidly about how he felt – is absent.

Just as it was looking as though Lawrence would have to make a difficult decision as to his future in teaching (and possibly incur Louie's wrath as a result), the final choice was taken completely out of his hands. Following a visit to Edward Garnett's over the weekend of 18–19 November, he had got wet watching Garnett chopping wood, but had stayed in his wet clothes and caught a chill. By the time he returned to his lodgings in Croydon on Sunday evening he had developed double pneumonia.

His sister Ada rushed to his side, arriving on 25 November to nurse him. By 28 November, the situation was grave, and it was only by 2 December that Lawrence seemed to be out of danger, and was keen to see visitors, although he was still bed bound and wouldn't be able to sit up in bed for several more days. And yet, he was still concerned with his writing – he even dictated a letter to Garnett via his landlady (before Ada's arrival) regarding a manuscript and thanking him for his weekend hospitality, during the initial stages of his illness, and later got Ada to send the manuscript of the 'Saga' – which he had finally extracted from Heinemann – to the Cearne for Garnett's opinion.

By 9 December, Lawrence was able to sit up in bed if he was propped up by pillows, and there was talk of him convalescing in Bournemouth. Despite his physical frailty, his mind was still as sharp as ever and he was clearly frustrated with his predicament. Louie found herself on the receiving end of Lawrence's short temper for asking him to be patient. He wanted to read and exercise his mind and didn't need Louie telling him he couldn't. Helpfully, Ada was able to give updates on Lawrence's condition to Edward Garnett, writing rather prophetically on 17 December that the doctor had said Lawrence would be 'very liable to consumption' and that he ought to give up his role as a teacher. Garnett was able to help in practical ways – his financial gift of a loan of seven guineas to help with Lawrence's costs while he was unable to work shows his concern for his young protégé.

Lawrence hoped to be in Bournemouth before Christmas, but his plans were curtailed by his doctor, who insisted he wouldn't be well enough for the journey until well into the new year. Jessie visited him while she was staying with Helen Corke over the Christmas period and remembered him sitting by the fire in his bedroom looking 'grievously thin, but yet somehow so vital'. She saw in him the 'naked flame of life'. It reflects something of the intellectual accord that existed between Lawrence and Jessie that he commented to Garnett along similar lines. He could feel his life 'burning like a free flame floating on oil – wavering and leaping and snapping'. Like the phoenix Lawrence came to use as a metaphor for his own rebirth, he would struggle back to life whatever the cost.

The Christmas period before his time in Bournemouth at least gave Lawrence a chance to reflect on his circumstances. He was becoming disillusioned with Heinemann, to the extent that he was telling Garnett that he would be glad not to have to deal with the firm any longer. Garnett had also read the 'Saga' and was enthusiastic enough to suggest he offer it to Duckworth on Lawrence's behalf – although Lawrence was keen to ensure Garnett did not present him as a beggar. With renewed hope in its merits, Lawrence began rewriting the manuscript with a new title in mind: *The Trespasser*.

He was also considering his future with Louie and seeing Jessie again at Christmas had also prompted a nostalgic, but painful, mental return to the Haggs and all it meant to him. Lawrence would express this in a new story, 'The Soiled Rose' (published in 1914 as *The Shades of Spring*), where he brought the landscape back to life once again before he buried it for good the following year after his final break with Jessie: 'To his last day, he would dream of this place, when he felt the sun on his face, or saw the small handfuls of snow between the winter twigs, or smelt the coming of the spring.'[2]

Lawrence went to Bournemouth to convalesce via his friend Lilian Reynolds at Redhill in early January and stayed a month – during which time he did a thorough revision of his manuscript. He seems to have enjoyed the experience, despite some reservations that he would feel lonely. It also afforded him the time and space he needed to edit his manuscript into the novel it would become, as well as giving him the opportunity to regain his strength and health through a routine of light exercise, socialising, games and about as much food as he could humanly eat: 'We seem to feed so much', he commented to Louie.

Lawrence left Bournemouth on 3 February 1912, 'fatter' but 'very well', bound for the Cearne and Edward Garnett. He was also a changed man. Lawrence's later reflections on the events of 1911 suggest this was a watershed moment for him:

Then, in that year, for me everything collapsed, save the mystery of death, and the haunting of death in life. I was twenty-five, and from the death of my mother, the world began to dissolve around me, beautiful, iridescent, but passing away substanceless. Till I almost dissolved away myself, and was very ill: when I was twenty-six.

Then slowly the world came back: or I myself returned: but to another world.[3]

Lawrence had returned to himself – or at least someone who more closely resembled the 'real' Lawrence – but to inhabit himself fully he needed to cast off his other persona: the version of himself that Louie was in love with. Initially, he used his financial circumstances as a respectable approach to ending the engagement, citing his inability to teach and inevitable struggle to support them both with no income, as the reason. Ada agreed with Lawrence and told Louie as much in a separate letter in which she wrote that Lawrence was 'changed for the worse' and that dragging the engagement out would inevitably 'end in nothing'. Like all loving siblings, she closed the letter with some rather uncomplimentary commentary on her brother, declaring that, 'You really deserve someone better than Bert, Louie. I wouldn't marry a man like him, no, not if he were the only one on the earth.'[4]

Lawrence had engineered a fait accompli, but Louie respected herself enough to ask that they meet in person, which they did – at the Castle Art Gallery in Nottingham on 13 February. Louie recalled being 'simply dumb with misery'. Their meeting in Nottingham was the last time they saw each other.

Lawrence was finally free. Free of his fiancée, free to write, free to travel and free of any responsibility, except to himself. He resigned from his teaching role at Davidson Road on 28 February, telling Arthur McLeod that he'd 'rather be a tramp' than go back to the school. He continued writing at pace, working on 'Paul Morel' with all his pre-illness intensity – sharing the early sections of his revised manuscript with Jessie as he completed each section. The two had become reacquainted following his split from Louie – via a peace offering of a box of chocolates. 'I could hardly believe that we were really together again',[5] Jessie recalled, although there was an underlying tension to the meeting that made itself known when Jessie thought about sitting next to Lawrence:

as plainly as though he spoke aloud, there came into my consciousness the words: 'Don't imagine that because mother's dead you can claim me', and I felt the ground taken from under my feet.[6]

Jessie checked herself without Lawrence uttering a word and the conversation moved on to safer topics such as his plans to visit Germany and how Lawrence wanted to be 'free' rather than become a husband and stay in England. But Jessie could always read Lawrence; instead of freedom she only saw his separateness from everything else in life. 'I was overcome with pity', she wrote of the encounter, 'I slipped my hand into his...'[7]

Yet as a literary pairing, they were still very much connected. Jessie gave Lawrence the notes he had asked her to write before he was struck down with pneumonia, which he incorporated and adapted into 'Paul Morel'– and initially, Jessie was delighted with the early pages: 'Here was all that spontaneous flow, the seemingly effortless translation of life that filled me with admiration...It was his power to transmute the common experiences into significance that I always felt to be Lawrence's greatest gift.'[8]

But Lawrence couldn't allow himself to belong to anyone – least of all Jessie. He was cut off, and despite his obvious gifts, he was unable to connect with others on a normal level. Lawrence didn't just cut himself off from life though. He cut himself off from Jessie too, through the only medium that was keeping them tethered to one another – his writing.

Lawrence wrote himself out of Jessie's life, just as he writes the character of Paul out of Miriam's life in *Sons and Lovers*. And just as Paul struggles to separate himself from his mother – even in death – so too did Lawrence, a fact Jessie was all too aware of:

> ...his mother's ban was more powerful now than in her lifetime. I began to realize that whatever approach Lawrence made to me inevitably involved him in a sense of disloyalty to his mother. Some bond, some understanding, most likely unformulated and all the stronger for that, seemed to exist between them.[9]

Lawrence's bond with his dead mother is immortalised in the closing paragraphs of *Sons and Lovers*, as Paul Morel wills himself to carry on without his mother Gertrude, rather than follow her into darkness: 'And his soul could now leave her, wherever she was. Now she was gone abroad into the night, and he was with her still. They were together.'[10]

And it was within this frame of reference that Jessie had battled for Lawrence, and Miriam had battled for Paul. But betraying Jessie was easier than betraying the memory of his mother. And so, Jessie was once again excluded. As the pages of Lawrence's revised manuscript reached her, it dawned on her that Lawrence had side-stepped the issue of his mother's overbearing influence, and rather than resolve the issue through a union (or at least an understanding) between Paul and Miriam, through which Gertrude Morel's power would be vanquished, he had allowed her to triumph. 'It was his old inability to face his problem squarely',

Jessie remembered bitterly. 'His mother had to be supreme, and for the sake of that supremacy every disloyalty was permissible'.[11]

Lawrence's disloyalty cut deep. Jessie felt strongly he had painted a distorted picture of the bond they shared, as well as giving Miriam a host of unattractive qualities to justify Mrs Morel's dislike of her. The manuscript also ignored the years of devotion she gave Lawrence in nurturing his genius. It was an unfaithful representation in many ways, but Jessie's overriding resentment lay in the martyrisation of his mother at her expense. Lawrence simply could not countenance a world in which his mother didn't emerge victorious. Writing to Helen Corke, Jessie called Miriam 'a slander – a fearful treachery…Don't talk about it, please. If I am to live at all it will be necessary to put David [Lawrence] out of my life – to ignore him entirely, in thought and speech.'[12]

The outcome was exactly that – her utter repudiation of the man she had held so high, for so long. He was the 'philistine of philistines' and his significance shrank. He had 'ceased to matter supremely' to Jessie. The shock of *Sons and Lovers* was the death-knell to their friendship. 'If I had told Lawrence that I had died before, I certainly died again',[13] Jessie wrote.

But Lawrence (being Lawrence) still wanted to know what Jessie thought of his manuscript, even though he was avoiding her. The two arranged to meet at Jessie's sister May's cottage. Jessie made some notes on the manuscript in preparation and took it with her.

He gave her the opportunity during a private walk together to voice her thoughts, asking her whether she had anything to say about the manuscript. But for Jessie, speaking aloud what she felt in her heart was a futile exercise. She simply could not speak to him – her emotions had rendered her mute. Lawrence arrived at May's cottage in an uncongenial mood and there was an atmosphere of tension underneath the gaiety of the gathering – an air of foreboding Jessie knew all too well. So instead, she handed him back the manuscript, simply remarking that she had put her notes in with the manuscript. Jessie knew that to question the novel would lead to further upset, and she almost certainly couldn't face a further onslaught of defensiveness from Lawrence. Words would only exacerbate the situation, she decided. They never discussed the novel again, and only saw each other on two further occasions – one by chance, and one by coincidence. 'I knew that in our wordless way we had come to an end', Jessie commented.

Rather fortuitously for both parties, Lawrence had arranged to visit his German cousins in the Rhineland in May 1912 – a suggestion made earlier in the year by his mother's sister, Ada, who was married to a German academic, Fritz Krenkow. The break would allow Lawrence to focus on his writing – a test to see whether he could indeed make a living from his writing – and by dint of Lawrence's absence, a chance for Jessie to recover from Lawrence's betrayal and move on from a period in her life in which she would later reveal had made her wish she were dead.

In preparation for his upcoming sabbatical, and subsequent reinvention of himself, Lawrence needed to plan his trip to Germany – and he knew exactly who to ask. He had always admired the professor of modern languages at Nottingham University College, Ernest Weekley. Weekley was not only fluent in the language, but his wife, Frieda, was also born into an impoverished aristocratic German family the von Richthofens, and had been brought up in Germany.

A lunch date was arranged in early spring. Lawrence arrived early, spending the first half an hour of his visit alone with Frieda. 'The two of us talked in my room, French windows open, curtains fluttering in the spring wind, my children playing on the lawn…'[14] Frieda related in her memoir, '*Not I, But the Wind…*' It was a different kind of domestic idyll to the Haggs, but then Frieda was a very different woman to Jessie.

Six weeks later, this scene of suburban domesticity was utterly shattered when Frieda left her husband, said goodbye to her children, boarded a train and crossed the channel with Lawrence.

Chapter 7

Frieda

Oh, but she is the woman of a lifetime.[1]

I t is tempting to cast Frieda Weekley as the villain. She was known to have had extra-marital affairs before Lawrence came on the scene and later in their relationship. She made a cuckold of Ernest and left her children motherless for the sake of a six-week dalliance with a man who was six years her junior. Yet to malign Frieda in this way is to misunderstand the complexity of her emotions – the sense of instinctiveness and vitality that was the driving force behind many of Frieda's (sometimes questionable) decisions, and what ultimately drove her into the arms of Lawrence.

Frieda was born Emma Maria Frieda Johanna Freiin von Richthofen in Metz in 1879 – the second daughter of a branch of the famous baronial family, who had fallen on hard times. Her upbringing couldn't have been more disparate from Lawrence's – where Frieda had been presented at court and enjoyed an endless round of balls, banquets and boyfriends, Lawrence had had none of the trappings that came with a famous name or wealth during his working-class existence in Eastwood. Yet the two shared a commonality in the dysfunctional relationships of their parents. Just as the Lawrences grew to openly despise each other, Frieda's parents – career army officer Freidrich and his wife Anna – made no secret of their hatred of each other. Freidrich had frequent angry outbursts and gambled with the family wealth (or what little there was left of it), as well as producing an illegitimate child with his mistress – who subsequently had to be paid off. And Anna, pushed to her limits by her husband's behaviour, existed in a constant state of high anxiety as she struggled to prevent her unruly husband from ruining them all. This was all witnessed by the young Frieda and her sisters, Else and Johanna.

Did it explain Frieda's decision to marry the conventional and reliable middle-class Professor Ernest Weekley? Perhaps. But Frieda was also something of a rebel, and more than a little impulsive. Ernest was fourteen years her senior, and like Lawrence, was academically prodigious, educating himself above and beyond the norm for his class. In Lawrence's words he was a 'middle class, gentlemanly man, in whom the brute can leap up. He is forty six, and has been handsome, is usually ironic, pessimistic and cynical, nice, I like him…He is getting elderly, and a bit tired'.[2]

Ernest had met Frieda while on holiday in Freiburg, Germany in 1898 and by 1899 they were married and Ernest had brought her back to Nottinghamshire, where they settled into some semblance of a normal, respectable, middle-class life. Three children were born – Monty in 1900, Elsa in 1902 and Barby in 1904. Frieda tried to fit in to the life her marriage afforded, just as Lawrence had tried to unsuccessfully fit in to his, but the reality was she was bored, frustrated and desperate for some sort of stimulus to lift her out of the predictability of her life. She wanted to live on her own terms, rather than those dictated by her position as a wife and mother. By her own admission her marriage to Ernest was a failure. A string of love affairs between 1905 and 1910 were the result of her need for sexual satisfaction as well as self-determination, but she would never have left Ernest for any of her former lovers. Not only were they wholly unsuitable as long-term partners (two were far from 'respectable') but also in 1912, adulterous women seeking a divorce from their spouse were not able to gain custody of their children, unless their former husband consented. And Frieda loved her children, or at least loved them more than she cared for her lovers. It was not worth the risk.

So, why was Lawrence different? Of all of Frieda's lovers, Lawrence seemed to ignite some emotion deep inside her that had been lying dormant; 'the consciousness of my own proper self', as Frieda called it. Whether they could simply relate to one another as unconventional people living in a conventional world, or a purely physical reaction that neither of them could control – whatever was initially awakened that day in March 1912, it led Frieda to take drastic action.

Lawrence was similarly spellbound by Frieda, enthusing to Edward Garnett that she was 'the finest woman I've ever met', but also recognising 'how damnably I mix things up'.

Initially, Frieda could not understand where Lawrence's attraction to her lay. She struggled to understand why he wanted her, and how he could love her – after all, she was a 32-year-old married mother of three children. He was a 26-year-old bachelor with no fixed income. But in Frieda, Lawrence saw all the qualities that had been lacking in his former partners. She was sexually liberated, asking Lawrence to spend a night with her in the marital home while Ernest was away – an invitation Lawrence declined out of respect for Ernest. She also spoke as she found and was unafraid to challenge Lawrence – speaking to him as directly as he spoke to her (which would later provoke them both into the fiercest rows), but since he seemed to thrive on opposition, it was an aspect of their relationship that complemented Lawrence's genius rather than contradicted it.

But it was a lucky circumstance rather than a romantic ideal that took them to Germany together just six weeks after their first meeting. Frieda was already planning to go to the continent in May for a celebration of her father's fifty years in the army, and Lawrence was already expected in Waldbröl, near Cologne, to stay with his cousins, the Krenkows. But they were captivated enough by each other for Frieda to share her travelling itinerary with him to ensure they travelled together.

Meanwhile, Frieda was charged (by Lawrence) with telling Weekley what was going on. 'I was frightened', Frieda revealed in her memoir. 'I knew how terrible such a thing would be for my husband, he had always trusted me. But a force stronger than myself made me deal him the blow'.[3] Lawrence believed Frieda had done so and wrote to Garnett to tell him the same – telling him that Weekley loved her in a 'jealous monogamistic fashion' that was unhealthy for them both. Lawrence, in his new ebullient and optimistic frame of mind, had also managed to convince himself that Ernest would eventually come round, writing that, 'He [Ernest] will hate me, but really he likes me at the bottom.'

What Lawrence didn't know is that Frieda had been conservative with the truth. She had told Ernest about *some* of her affairs – those with the psychoanalyst Otto Gross and the German painter and anarchist Ernst Frick – but had neglected to reveal the extent of her feelings for Lawrence. This drip-feeding of information was a test of Ernest's reaction. As Lawrence historian John Worthen suggests, this may have been Frieda's way of examining whether they could have the kind of open sexual relationship that her sister Else and brother-in-law Edgar enjoyed – a relationship that would have appealed to the free-spirited and uninhibited Frieda.

Whatever Frieda's reasons, and not forgetting she would have found delivering her confession to her husband deeply distressing irrespective of her behaviour to the contrary – he was, after all, the father of her three children – she embarked on her journey with Lawrence full of hope that she would find her 'real self', and agony at leaving her children behind.

On Friday, 3 May, Frieda left her two girls with Ernest's parents in Hampstead – Monty stayed with Ernest in Nottinghamshire – and at two o'clock Lawrence met Frieda outside the first-class ladies' lounge at Charing Cross station. Their plan was to take the boat train – a passenger train that would transport travellers directly to their port of embarkation – to Dover, where they would board a steamer to cross the channel. For Lawrence it would certainly have been relief – he confided to Frieda three days before they travelled that he had a portentous feeling about it all. 'I am afraid of something low', he wrote, 'like an eel which bites out of the mud, and hangs on with its teeth. I feel as if I can't breathe while we're in England.'[4]

They reached Metz just after 6 o'clock the following morning. Frieda's parents' house was full of various Richthofen relatives, so they both ended up in the Hotel Deutscher Hof – and Lawrence needed to keep a discrete distance from the festivities – but Frieda was immediately candid with her mother and sister, knowing she would find a sympathetic ear in both. This allowed for Lawrence to be briefly introduced to Frieda's mother, who naturally assumed he was merely her latest lover, and her sister Johanna. But during their stay in Metz, Lawrence was existing on the fringes of Frieda's life and the situation inevitably led to frustration. Despite staying only three miles away, Lawrence could only write to Frieda to express how he was feeling, and the knowledge that eventually their time in Germany together would come to an end loomed over them ominously. It was one thing to carry on clandestinely in a different country, but returning to Nottinghamshire and to their normal lives was something else entirely; something Frieda seemed to have put to the back of her mind. For what else could she do *but* return to Nottingham? For now, Frieda was existing in the moment, but for Lawrence – alone much of the time with his thoughts – the lack of forward planning and the uncertainty of their future together was troubling him. 'I wish I had the management of our affairs', he wrote to Frieda from the hotel.

Lawrence was also up against conflicting advice from Frieda's mother and sisters, who assumed that Frieda would return to Ernest and their married life and keep Lawrence as a lover. After all, that would mean she could stay in her children's lives and remain financially secure. But Lawrence had had enough. 'Now I can't stand it any longer, I can't', he wrote to Frieda from the hotel. He wanted 'no more lies' and had written to Ernest explaining the situation – putting the onus on Frieda to send the letter. 'No, I can't bear it, because it's bad. I love you', he wrote.

The letter written to Ernest that Lawrence alluded to was printed in the national press more than a year later, no doubt to the embarrassment of all parties. Nestled among the sporting news and an announcement that the famous Zulu chieftain, Dinizulu, had died, the *Yorkshire Evening Post* reported Lawrence's 'Excuse for a Betrayal'. The letter was cited in Ernest Weekley's divorce suit against Frieda and was presented as evidence of her betrayal – thus handing all her marriage rights, that of an income and access to her children, to Ernest.

On receiving the 'strange letter' (as the press referred to it) Ernest would have been enraged; or in Lawrence's words, the 'brute' would almost certainly have 'leapt up'. Lawrence naively (or perhaps conceitedly?) suggested that Ernest did not 'suffer alone' in the affair, and that it was 'torture' to Lawrence to have to tell 'the thousand baffling lies' that being in Metz with Frieda entailed. He then proceeded to patronise Ernest with a short lecture on the behaviour of women, specifically his wife, before dealing his final blow: a request for Ernest's forgiveness.

Lawrence put the responsibility for 'the letter' into Frieda's hands – it was up to her to act on it. In the short term at least, Lawrence found some sort of freedom from the situation, but irrespective of the 'stir up' he had caused, he had little option but to leave Metz anyway. While out walking with Frieda one morning, he had been arrested for trespassing (and thus potentially spying) in one of the military fortifications. They had had to provide their names and addresses, and to get themselves out of trouble they disclosed the information that Friedrich von Richthofen was Frieda's father. Frieda had little option but to present Lawrence to him. 'They looked at each other fiercely', according to Frieda. Friedrich was thoroughly unimpressed with Lawrence, the miner's son, and was similarly unimpressed with his daughter's behaviour. The meeting wasn't repeated.

Lawrence was told by the authorities on returning to his hotel that he was suspected of being a spy and was ordered to leave. He left Frieda in Metz and travelled to Trier, eighty miles away. Despite the distance that was now between them, it was clear from Lawrence's letters that some kind of decision had been reached before they parted ways. 'Remember, you are to be my wife…', Lawrence wrote to Frieda on the day he arrived …No doubt there'll be another dish of tragedy in the morning.' Lawrence was beginning to feel more worldly. He had cast off the old vacillating Lawrence when he'd sailed away from England only a week before. Here was a new Lawrence; one that was decisive and knew what he wanted. He had predicted as much in an earlier letter to Louie Burrows: 'I go straight, like a bullet, towards my aim. I cannot loiter by the way…I cut straight through like a knife to what I want. I cannot, cannot slowly enjoy watching the rose open…I love my rose, and no other: and when I can have her I shall want no other.'[5]

And what Lawrence wanted was Frieda.

The dramatic maelstrom the two lovers had created had forced Lawrence to take on the role of protector – he had to be the stronger partner to steer Frieda through the emotional turmoil of being away from her children and leaving her husband. Frieda only saw the romanticism of the situation, stating that, 'He seemed to have lifted me body and soul out of all my past life' – but there were obvious practical concerns too. And so among Lawrence's pledges of love and utter devotion to Frieda, there was also a dispassionate appraisal of the reality of what they were doing. Lawrence wrote to Frieda from the Krenkows' residence in Waldbröl: 'Tell me exactly what you are going to do. *Is* the divorce coming off?…*Are* we going to have enough money to get along with? Have you settled anything definite with Ernest? One must be detached, impersonal, cold and logical, when one is arranging *affairs*. We do not want another fleet of horrors attacking us when we are on a rather flimsy raft – lodging in a borrowed flat on borrowed money.'[6]

But most importantly, and at the heart of it all, was an epiphany – that Lawrence *could* love someone other than his mother. 'I know I only love you', he wrote on a postcard to Frieda.

Yet love would only get them so far. There was heartache on all sides as the respective families – the Weekleys, the Richthofens, and (eventually when they finally found out) Lawrence's family and friends back in Nottinghamshire – tried to see a way through that wouldn't end in public disgrace. 'It is so sad to think how many innocent people must be wounded to the heart by such an event',[7] Ernest Weekley wrote to Frieda's mother.

Frieda's family were sympathetic of her affair but furious that she had pledged herself to Lawrence for the sake of her financial security, her children and her respectability. Her father informed her that he would never see her again if she stayed with Lawrence, and Ernest Weekley seemed to swing from one emotional extreme to the other – telling Frieda's father that he hoped she would be happy in the future, and Frieda that he bore Lawrence 'no ill-will', to threatening to kill himself and their children. Ernest's primary concern was to 'save something out of such a shipwreck',[8] which meant that Frieda needed to quietly agree to a divorce. Ernest only had two goals – to make Frieda free so she could marry Lawrence and provide for the future of their three children. Her Nottinghamshire friends even tried to remonstrate with her, but it was futile. In a heart-wrenching letter to Frieda, Lily Kipping, the wife of Ernest's closest friend, stated emotionally just what was at stake:

Whatever you have done, said or thought, come back, back here to me if you like and then tell me everything and let me keep you, but don't spoil your own life and the lives of all the others – the little girls without a mother, no mother's love, and Monty, he must have a mother to protect him. Frieda dear, our friendship is a true one, but do, do listen to an older woman, a woman who really knows that there is only one true happiness in life. Hold by your responsibilities. His life is not to be ruined like this. You took it into your care and the children you brought into the world can't be cast off like this.[9]

Ultimately, as history proved, Frieda ignored all the well-meaning advice and stayed the course. Lawrence would later comment humorously, 'I like the way you stick to your guns. It's rather splendid. We won't fight, because you'd win, from sheer lack of sense of danger.'[10] But fight they did – as history would also prove – passionately, and at times, violently.

Lawrence stayed with the Krenkows in Waldbröl until 24 May, during which time he managed to convince himself that one of his relatives, Hannah, had fallen in love with him ('Why is it women *will* fall in love with me', he lamented to Garnett), before moving on to Munich. Frieda was already there, having escaped the tension at her parents' house with her sister Else. During his time in Waldbröl, Lawrence continued working on 'Paul Morel' and writing a travel series for the *Westminster Gazette*, which was published in stages over the summer of 1912. The village in which the Krenkows lived was so remote that there was precious little else for Lawrence to do except write and mull over his predicament.

In Munich, Lawrence and Frieda were reunited and their life together began. Else's lover, Professor Alfred Weber, lent the couple a flat to live in in the village of Icking, and it was here that they finally found the emotional and physical space to live as a proper couple. This was as close to marriage as they would get for now, but it was enough. Lawrence even referred to the eight days before they moved into the flat, which they'd spent in the Alpine village of Beuerberg, as their 'honeymoon'.

Lawrence dashed off several letters and missives to his Eastwood friends during these first heady days. Jessie Chambers recalled receiving the news via a sealed letter inscribed with the words *pour vous seulement* [for you only] accompanied by a general newsy letter for the rest of the family. 'It contained a hysterical announcement', she wrote, 'of the new attachment he had formed, and enjoined the strictest secrecy upon me: "Don't tell M [May]., don't tell N.C., don't tell *anybody*. Only A. [Ada] knows..." I felt it was probably the last request Lawrence would ever make of me, and I kept his secret.'[11]

Liberation from Lawrence came at a cost. Although Jessie felt relieved that she was free (and she replied as much to Lawrence), the end of their friendship was a deep blow that was 'comparable to a kind of death', and it left her feeling suicidal. Jessie's final act to purge herself of Lawrence was to return his final correspondence to him. In the spring of 1913 Lawrence sent Jessie a copy of his first poetry collection, followed by the proof-sheets of 'Paul Morel', telling her that he wanted her to see it before it went to print, and rather audaciously inviting Jessie to visit him and Frieda. Jessie had no intention of reading 'Paul Morel' again, and neither did she particularly fancy spending time with Lawrence and his soon-to-be wife. So, she directed the proofs to Ada unread, and returned Lawrence's ill-judged letter to him. 'I was not sorry for my action. It was somehow necessary. Indeed, I never did regret it...' Jessie recalled. 'I had gone with him as far as I could go. Nothing further was possible.'[12] Lawrence and Jessie never saw or spoke to each other again.

It would take Jessie several years to recover, but she did. In 1915 she married a schoolmaster named John (Jack) Wood whom she had met on a holiday in France – and the couple settled in Nottinghamshire. Jessie died fourteen years after Lawrence in 1944.

Aside from Jessie, Lawrence also wrote to his old socialist friend Sallie Hopkin, telling her how much he loved Frieda and requesting reassurance that the Hopkins would support them should they ever need the help of their friends. This was important to Lawrence, for the 'honeymoon' was now over and the reality of day-to-day life was beginning to kick in. They may have enjoyed 'lovely things' according to Lawrence – notably the flowers, wading through glacial waters, glittering snowy mountain tops – but they also needed to be able to live, and to do that Lawrence needed to work. 'Paul Morel' was finally sent off to Heinemann, which Lawrence hoped would provide some income, and he began working on some new short stories. *The Trespasser* had finally been published by Duckworth, and lauded as 'the supreme glorification of the intensity of life'[13] in a publicity advert that appeared in the *Westminster Gazette*, which would have pleased Lawrence. This was backed up by some excellent press reviews: *The Bystander* called it a 'remarkable piece of writing…Indeed, he invests his story with some touch of greatness',[14] and the *Saturday Review* enthused that 'There are pieces of writing which could not be surpassed'.[15] Yet it did little to mitigate Lawrence and Frieda's misery over their predicament, exacerbated by the letters being sent backwards and forwards between the warring factions. They were living in bliss but under a storm cloud. This inevitably led Lawrence and Frieda to quarrel – something that would become an intermittent soundtrack to their relationship.

In early July, Ernest Weekley was still deliberating. He wanted Frieda to return to England and be with him and their children, but when she told him she would never come back, Weekley retaliated by threatening that she would never see her children again. 'She [Frieda] lies on the floor in misery', Lawrence wrote, '-and then is fearfully angry with me because I won't say "stay for my sake".' Lawrence, rather unfairly, told Frieda that she had to decide what she wanted most – to be with him with his 'rotten chances' or go back to domestic security and her children. Frieda's anguish over being separated from her children was an ongoing source of tension between the couple. From Lawrence's perspective, Frieda had chosen to abandon her children and was thus disavowed of any right to complain about it. It went against the idea that they had broken with their 'old selves' and were starting anew. Frieda's children were a silent, but constant presence between them. They represented the antithesis to how Lawrence wanted to live.

The situation caused Frieda considerable anguish as she grappled with the twin emotions common to betrayal: regret and guilt. Yet these instinctive reactions were anathema to Lawrence, and Frieda suspected his efforts to detach her from her role as a mother stemmed from his own troubled relationship with Lydia Lawrence. His tolerance for the grief Frieda felt at losing her children was notable by its absence. Instead, he used it as an emotional stick to beat her with; at first consoling her by telling her things would inevitably work themselves out, but then quickly turning furious and shouting that her children didn't love her. He made Frieda feel her guilt acutely.

But somehow, among the frantic letters, handwringing, arguing and penny-pinching ('we had very little money, about fifteen shillings a week', Frieda wrote), Lawrence and Frieda found themselves, and found each other. They revelled in the newness of their relationship and the world they were creating together. Lawrence had given himself to Frieda – 'I am yours', he told her – and she gave herself, body and soul, to him; 'I had found what I needed.'

They drew strength from each other – a strength that would be tested over and again throughout their life together. The first test of their new life came on 1 July 1912.

> *Dear Mr Lawrence*
>
> *I have read Paul Morel with a good deal of interest and, frankly, with a good deal of disappointment, especially after what you wrote to me with regard to your feeling about the book and the view you took that it was your best work.*
>
> *I feel that the book is unsatisfactory from several points of view; not only because it lacks unity, without which the readers interest cannot be held, but more so because its want of reticence makes it unfit…it is a real disappointment to me to have to decline this book. The manuscript goes back to you in a separate parcel, registered.*[16]

The letter was from William Heinemann, but luckily Garnett thought differently, having read the novel himself, and with some suggested alterations, he recommended it to Duckworth. Heinemann's decision not to publish would mean Lawrence and Frieda would have to stretch their meagre finances even further, but his initial disappointment was easily overcome with Garnett's assurance that the novel would be on Duckworth's list.

Their time at the Icking flat came to an end at the beginning of August. Lawrence packed the revised version of 'Paul Morel' into a knapsack, along with some clothing, a few personal possessions and a little spirit lamp for outdoor cooking, and the couple embarked on what would turn out to be a great adventure. They were heading for Italy, where they hoped they would be able to live a more frugal existence. They sent the bulk of their combined belongings ahead of them to Lago di Garda, and on a misty morning they set off for 'unknown parts'.

Their wanderings over the Alps were part blissful, part full of mishaps – some of these were innocent, some were not. On the second night they got 'hopelessly lost' and were caught out by the weather. They had little option but to shelter in a hay loft that, fortuitously, was one of Frieda's long-held desires. Frieda conceded later that it was 'uncomfortable', and they got soaked, but their spirits weren't dampened, and they traipsed on the following morning for a further five miles before taking a room – possibly the 'hunters cottage' Lawrence alludes to in his letters – in the small watch-making town of Glashütte. Via a combination of omnibuses, walking and train journeys, the couple eventually made it to Mayrhofen where they took a room in a farmhouse for two weeks. Here they were joined by David 'Bunny' Garnett, Edward's 20-year-old son, and his friend, the 21-year-old Harold Hobson. From here, Lawrence wrote to his long-time friend Sallie Hopkin, describing openly how his relationship with Frieda was blossoming into something real and wonderful: a 'wonderful naked intimacy' that he knew 'at last is love', although he also spoke about the 'ghastliness' of the affair, and his feelings of regret that they had hurt so many people.

The hay loft was to play a further part in Lawrence's and Frieda's adventures – this time as the scene of Frieda's first betrayal. The group of four dispatched their suitcases to Bozen (Now Bolzano) and set out across the Pfitscherjoch pass. The terrain was challenging and their carefree attitude towards the journey so far was certainly tested at this point. They eventually reached Sterzing, after an 'exciting scramble' on 30 August, exhausted and with tempers slightly frayed. Bunny and Hobson departed from Sterzing early to catch a train back north, with Lawrence and Frieda staying on at Sterzing a few days longer before they started the next leg of their journey up the Jaufen pass. More uphill trudging ensued – this time for eight hours – on the 'highroad from Germany to Italy',[17] as Lawrence called it, in difficult conditions and with none of the enthusiasm they had had at the start of their journey. It was at this point that Frieda decided it would be a good time to confess to Lawrence that she had been unfaithful to him with Bunny's friend Harold – allegedly in the hay loft they had slept in on the Pfitscherjoch pass, while Lawrence and Bunny were out hunting for Alpine plants. This moment was retold in a thinly disguised comment made by Bunny, who remembered, 'leaving Harold and Frieda to amuse each other as best they knew how...'[18] Frieda was not untouched by his good looks and masculine charm. Frieda may have committed her soul to Lawrence, but she had no intention of giving up her independence or her autonomy to choose who she gave her body to. As Lawrence himself had pointed out to Weekley only three months earlier, 'Mrs Weekley must live largely and abundantly. It is her nature.'[19] If their relationship was to thrive, Lawrence had to accept that Frieda *would* live abundantly in all areas of her life – including sexually. Frieda was also testing her own, and Lawrence's, boundaries. Their journey to Italy gave them the chance to confront, head on, exactly who each other was and what their limits were. It was a metaphorical journey of discovery, as well as a physical one.

As always, Lawrence explored his feelings in his fiction. His comic novel *Mr Noon*, which Lawrence drafted but abandoned, was published posthumously by Martin Secker as a long-short story in 1934 as part of a larger volume of stories. In the story, the latter part of which has been widely accepted as based on Lawrence and Frieda's early relationship, the young schoolmaster Gilbert Noon (Lawrence) is forced to meet the challenge of his lover Johanna's (Frieda) indiscretion with Stanley (Harold Hobson). Johanna explains to Gilbert that 'he had me in the hay-hut – he told me he wanted me so badly', but Gilbert forgives her. Yet his over-the-top reaction is charged with an air of condescension:

> *He dropped her knapsack and threw his arms around her. 'Never mind, my love,' he said. 'Never mind. Never mind. We do things we don't know we're doing.' And he kissed her and clung to her passionately in a sudden passion of self-annihilation. His soul opened, and he gave himself up. He rose above the new thrust on wings of death.*[20]

Johanna then decides that 'He seemed to have put her more in the wrong, and assumed a further innocent glory himself'.[21] Despite Gilbert's initial forgiveness he begins to feel irritated: 'for the first time he felt a pang of hate and contempt for Stanley', yet, 'in the end the irritable waters would boil up over this same business'.[22] Whether Lawrence's reaction was close to this, only Lawrence and Frieda knew, but to live as vitally as he wanted to, Lawrence knew he had to experience a range of emotions – good and bad – and be comfortable confronting the truth. This was the moment at which Lawrence faced what life with Frieda meant. She was the woman he so frequently characterised in his fictional works, from the independent and strong-willed Clara in *Sons and Lovers* (1913) to the fearless and defiant Ursula in *The Rainbow* (1915) – a new kind of woman who celebrated the freedom to make her own decisions and enjoy life in its fullest sense. But he was also fearful of women and what they represented, something Frieda touched on in her own recollections:

> *In his heart of hearts I think he always dreaded women, felt that they were in the end more powerful than men. Woman is so absolute and undeniable. Man moves, his spirit flies here and there, but you can't go beyond a woman. From*

her man is born and to her he returns for his ultimate need of body and soul. She is like earth and death to which all return.[23]

For now, Lawrence kept his inner thoughts on the matter to himself. Their eight hours of meandering had convinced both that they had crossed the pass from Germany into Italy and so they set off again the following morning believing they would soon reach Meran, just fifteen miles from their destination of Bozen. Unfortunately, the path into the valley they chose to follow for the best part of a day merely returned them both to Sterzing. This was the final straw and despite their lack of money, they decided to get on the train to Bozen where they spent one night – in a room over a pig sty according to Lawrence – before heading further south to Trento. Their stretched finances (and tramp-like attire – both were garbed in torn and stained clothing) would only allow for a cheap hotel and Frieda was dismayed by the 'marks on the walls and doubtful sheets', and worst of all the toilets, which were thoroughly grim.

It was all a bit too much for Frieda, whose 'abundance' didn't extend to the cleanliness of the local toilets, and she was quickly in tears – lamenting not only the horrible WCs but probably her life choices too. They decided there and then to abandon Trento and take the train to Riva on Lago di Garda (Lake Garda), which at that time was an Austrian garrison town. They found a room in a house that belonged to two old, sympathetic ladies, who 'instead of fearing the worse for their silver', were kind enough to provide fresh fruit for the two travellers while they cooked their meals on the spirit lamp they had used in the mountains. With, presumably, much relief, their trunks arrived, and they were able to dress presentably again. They stayed in Riva for two weeks, before they found a flat in the Villa Igea in Gargnano: a beautiful fairyland according to Frieda. And things were looking up financially too – Edward Garnett managed to secure Lawrence the welcome sum of £50 from Duckworth, which may have been royalties for *The Trespasser*. They only knew about ten Italian words, according to one of Lawrence's letters, but they had managed to find a place they could call their own – somewhere they could, at least for a time, find enough peace and tranquillity for Lawrence to write and Frieda to establish herself as a 'housekeeper' for the first time in her life.

Initially, it did not go as well as Frieda hoped. She was far from a natural domestic – having been brought up in a wealthy household she was used to a retinue of servants and staff to see to all her daily needs, and these circumstances would have changed little on her marriage to Weekley. In 1911, the Weekleys lived at 'Cowley', a nine-roomed residence on a private road in Nottingham. They employed two live-in servants – a nursery governess and a domestic cook – and would certainly have had further 'help' in the form of a housemaid or cleaner, someone to take care of the laundry, and perhaps even a gardener, all of whom would have lived locally. It was now up to Frieda and Lawrence to fulfil these roles between them, with Frieda taking on the bulk of the responsibility while Lawrence wrote.

Suffice to say, Frieda quickly realised that even 'fairyland' came with a large degree of domesticity. Frieda admitted in her memoir that Lawrence often had to rescue her attempts at cooking and a disaster involving the laundry, in which the sheets were so large and wet from washing that their 'wetness was overwhelming', leading Frieda to inadvertently flood the kitchen.

Lawrence was tolerant to a point but on occasion his patience wore extremely thin – whether out of genuine frustration at what he saw as Frieda's laziness (or, more likely, ineptitude) or because of some deeper-rooted anger at the failings of the class system that Frieda, the baron's daughter, embodied – it is difficult to tell. In one particularly ugly scene, recalled by an acquaintance of the couple, Cecily Lambert, Lawrence humiliated Frieda quite appallingly for her lack of competence in the house. On this occasion he had been riled by a mishap Frieda had had with a borrowed sewing machine:

> ...the result was a tornado so shocking that even we were terrified, fearing the outcome. He slated Frieda unmercifully, saying she was lazy and useless and sat around while we did all the work. He then ordered her to clean our kitchen floor which was large with the old-fashioned, well-worn bricks, none too easy to get scoured, in fact real hard labour. To our amazement she burst into tears and proceeded to work on it, fetching a pail of water and sloshing around with a floor cloth in a bending position (although he had told her to kneel), bitterly resentful at having to do such a menial task quite beneath the daughter of a baron, at the same time hurling every insult she could conjure up at D. H., calling him an uncouth lout, etc. He appeared to love an opportunity to humiliate her – whether from jealousy or extreme exasperation one could never tell. I was only surprised that she listened to his abuse or obeyed his orders.[24]

To outsiders, Lawrence and Frieda's relationship was at times unfathomable. Frieda commented in a letter to Edward Garnett in the autumn of 1912 that she was never *quite* sure whether she loved or hated Lawrence. The feeling was certainly mutual and when it came to their separate roles – Lawrence as writer, and Frieda as reluctant housekeeper – they found much to criticise in each other's success (or indeed, lack thereof). Her comment came while she was in the depths of helping Lawrence to reshape 'Paul Morel'. Lawrence had entered another period of frenetic creativity and during the autumn of 1912 he transformed 'Paul Morel' into *Sons and Lovers*, despite his many arguments with Frieda over its characterisation.

Understandably, Frieda got fed up with the novel and Lawrence's endless deep dive into what his characters were feeling or thinking, and turned against the central Oedipal thread, the 'house of Atreus' feeling' as Frieda called it, referencing the classical Greek family tragedy. In humorous retaliation, she wrote a skit she called 'Paul Morel, or His Mother's Darling', which she then showed to Lawrence, who didn't find it in the least bit amusing: 'He read it and said, coldly: "This kind of thing isn't called a skit."'[25]

But they battled on – together, against the world; apart, against their own inner turmoil; and with each other (often publicly, much to everyone's distaste). No one understood Lawrence and Frieda, except Lawrence and Frieda themselves. But the dynamic somehow worked. 'Everyone seemed to condemn us and be against us', Frieda wrote, 'and I couldn't for the life of me understand how the whole world couldn't see how right and wonderful it was to live as we did; I just couldn't.'[26] Lawrence may have had little control over his real-life relationships, but he *could* control those of his characters, and he seemed to draw creative energy from conflict and drama; it was a necessary requirement for the genius-at-work. As he famously quipped to Cynthia Asquith in 1913: 'I like to write when I feel spiteful: it's like having a good sneeze.' And with Frieda, 'spiteful' was what he got in spades.

So, despite the quarrels, the sheer emotional determination it took to defy convention in the way that they did, and the uncertainty of their future ('Heaven knows how we are going to untangle these knots',[27] Lawrence wrote to Frieda's sister Else), Lawrence somehow managed to turn 'Paul Morel' into *Sons and Lovers*. Arguably, it was *because* of these uniquely challenging circumstances that *Sons and Lovers* was crafted. Circumstances that were manifest because of Lawrence's love for Frieda, and Frieda's love for him.

Chapter 8

Untying the Knot; Tying a New One

'You know,' says D. seriously, as we go, 'when I'm middle aged, I shall probably be married and settled, and take my family to church every Sunday...'[1]

L awrence dispatched the manuscript of 'Paul Morel' to Duckworth on 18 November 1912, writing to Edward Garnett that it was made 'out of sweat, and blood'. His likening of the process to something visceral – not unlike the physicality of a baby being born – wasn't far from the truth in terms of the effort involved in birthing *Sons and Lovers*. It was a labour of love, and Lawrence was quick to defend it against any lingering doubt that Garnett had as to its greatness. 'I've written a great book',[2] Lawrence declares triumphantly, and in case Garnett isn't sure – 'it's a great novel',[3] he repeats just three lines later; an act of reassurance to himself as well as to his friend and mentor.

Frieda and Lawrence were living in paradise, and with little of their earlier financial concerns to worry about for at least a few months, they could re-immerse themselves in that dreamy, quixotic world they had discovered at the beginning of their adventures. At least, that was what they wanted to do. But the letters from England regarding Frieda's marriage kept up a regular pace, thus curtailing any chance they had of immersing themselves fully in their romantic idyll. The mail always seemed to bring fresh tragedy – but one letter struck Frieda the biggest blow so far. It was from Ernest telling her that if she didn't come home she would never see the children again. One can only imagine Frieda's anguish – she was like 'a cat without her kittens', as Frieda herself put it. Yet it wasn't enough for her to leave Lawrence; she was in his orbit and his pull was stronger.

Lawrence's ongoing annoyance over the question of the children had a note of jealousy attached to it – an emotion he explored in the poem 'She Looks Back', where he accuses Frieda of partly faking her joy at being with him when really she is pining for her children:

> But the shadow of lying was in your eyes,
> The mother in you, fierce as a murderess, glaring, to England,
> Yearning towards England, towards your young children,
> Insisting upon your motherhood, devastating.[4]

Perhaps Lawrence had already reconciled himself to the inevitable: that Frieda would be prevented from seeing her children, therefore making Frieda's 'insistence' on motherhood futile. The law was on Weekley's side and Lawrence probably acknowledged this quicker than Frieda did. The strength of her motherlove (or the 'curse' of it in Lawrence's mind) wouldn't allow her to consider a life that didn't include her children, even though Lawrence was correct in his summation. Yet his words jar. To deny Frieda the liberty to mourn the loss of her children, and accuse her of murdering their love because of this, seems particularly cruel if considered in this context.

As it turns out, Lawrence wasn't the only one with murdering in mind.

'Weekley threatens us alternately with murder and with suicide (the latter his own)', Lawrence wrote to Bunny Garnett in December 1912. 'I always expect a streak of greased lightning to fly out when we open an envelope from him. The Richthofen's and W [Weekley] have made a grand onslaught this week. I believe it is their Waterloo. God knows what sort of a Napoleon I feel, nor where my St Helena is.'[5]

Frieda's choices were clear – she either accepted a flat of her own in London, paid for by Weekley, where she could see her children, but without any contact with Lawrence; or she stayed with Lawrence and had no further contact with her children. Lawrence was firm – he would not stand aside and order Frieda back to her children. It wasn't his choice to make. So, Frieda found herself locked in a stalemate with her husband and lover. To cope with the perpetual drama and with her emotional resources depleted, Frieda rather feebly hoped that she would be able to stay with Lawrence, but somehow see her children in the spring of the following year and more regularly after that. When it came to her children, Frieda's hope always sprung eternal – for what other option was there?

The Christmas of 1912 was to be a particularly troublesome time for everyone. Just two days before Christmas, Lawrence revealed to Sallie Hopkin that Ernest was considering a divorce – which must have cheered the couple somewhat, although it didn't change the situation with the children – but Frieda reached her lowest point. The knowledge that she was spending the festive season away from her children – with no cards or presents, or the trappings of Christmas to share with them, and a sense of gloom rather than gaiety pervading the atmosphere – led her to fantasise about drowning herself in the lake.

Lawrence was also finding Weekley's indecision maddening. Fortunately, England's divorce laws in 1912 were such that if Weekley or Frieda were seen to have 'colluded' on the divorce to obtain it, i.e. by cooperating in an arrangement where one party stages an act of adultery with the knowledge of the other – thus presenting a false case – then it wouldn't be granted. This meant that Weekley took the decision to stop corresponding with Frieda so as not to prejudice any future case he was planning to take against her, so by the end of December his vitriolic letters were seemingly to come to an end.

During this difficult time, Lawrence started work on some new full-length material. The first took the life of Scottish poet Robert Burns as its inspiration, although Lawrence re-set its location, confessing that 'I'm not Scotch. So I shall just transplant him to home – or on the hills of Derbyshire' – although by January 1913, Lawrence was already wondering if he'd ever get it done and his interest in it appears to wain after this. Since only a fragment of this manuscript remains, we can only assume he abandoned it completely. He also started writing something called 'Elsa Culverwell', which he abandoned twenty pages in, before starting on a novel called 'The Insurrection of Miss Houghton', which was also eventually abandoned – although some of the material was rewritten and rejigged for *The Lost Girl* (1920). Lawrence predicted Garnett would hate it, so perhaps it was just as well that Lawrence didn't see it through to publication. And if other accounts of this time in Lawrence's life are anything to go by, the material was too sexual ('thrilling' in Lawrence-speak) to be considered publishable anyway. It was Lawrence's modus operandi to start with a sketchy idea and begin writing to see where it took him – often with no idea where he'd end up. 'He did not always himself understand to what results it was tending', Herbert Asquith wrote after Lawrence's death:

> he had great reverence: if a work seemed unsatisfactory, sooner than trimming its fringes or entering on long petty labours of minute corrections, he would wait for the mood to come on him again and re-write the whole manuscript. The result of this method, though it sometimes produced defects of form, was a freshness whose bloom may sometimes be brushed away by too much finish.[6]

This perhaps goes some way to explain his rather stop-start method, the abandonment of his works in varying stages of completion, and the merging of one work into another.

Alongside this group of stop-start novels (mostly stopping according to the sources), Lawrence also worked on sketches of Italian life, which would be worked up into his first travel book, *Twilight in Italy and Other Essays* (1916), and had his first poetry collection published by Duckworth, *Love Poems and others* (1913). The poems were haunted by the ghosts of girlfriends' past, so it was unsurprising that Frieda wasn't keen on the book, but the poems were noted for their 'musical, modern, free lines'.[7] It also marked another break from the Lawrence of old – the unhappy Croydon schoolteacher he had left behind in England.

But this period during Lawrence and Frieda's residence in Italy also gave rise to one of Lawrence's best plays, *The Daughter-In-Law* (1913), which was published and staged posthumously, as well as the embryonic beginnings of what would become *The Rainbow* (1915) and later, *Women in Love* (1920). Lawrence originally called this work 'The Sisters', and it was begun in March 1913 around the same time that a 'mangy old gentleman' appeared on their doorstep. The gentleman was from the British Consul and after establishing Lawrence and Frieda's identities, they were both handed some official-looking paperwork. Ernest Weekley had finally served the long-awaited divorce papers, in which Lawrence as co-respondent was accused of having 'habitually committed adultery'. One of Weekley's sisters had already travelled to Italy in the January of 1913 to gather the 'evidence' Weekley needed to secure his divorce from Frieda.[8] It is not known whether Lawrence and Frieda were aware of her presence, but it is also possible that she had made herself known to them and they had cooperated with her evidence-gathering task.

Word reached Lawrence in March that Jessie Chambers had written an autobiographical novel – a sort of counter narration to *Sons and Lovers*. Encouraged by Edward Garnett and Ford Madox Hueffer, Jessie had originally called the manuscript 'The Rathe Primrose' when she began writing it in 1911, but by 1913 she was referring to it as 'Eunice Temple' – the initials E. T. would eventually be used on her published memoir after Lawrence's death. Frieda was particularly keen to see the manuscript and was quick to reference it in a letter to Ada Lawrence, telling her (even though Frieda hadn't read it herself) that Garnett had said it was 'good, but not quite good enough'. Frieda also refers to Jessie's decision to return Lawrence's final note; the simple but symbolic act that eventually allowed Jessie to move on from her relationship with Lawrence. Frieda tells Ada: 'L.'s letter, I suppose wasn't high falluting enough, but I did think it was nasty of her...'[9] One person who *had* seen Jessie's manuscript and could therefore comment on it with some authority was Helen Corke. Helen had read the early chapters and described its style as 'that of an etching, simple, telling and direct', and she looked forward to reading it once Jessie had completed it. By May 1913, Lawrence and Frieda had also seen a copy of the initial chapters; Frieda commenting that it was 'a faded photograph of *Sons and Lovers*...she does make one ache!', and Lawrence remarking that he barely recognised Jessie in the writing. 'But it isn't bad', he conceded, 'and it made me so miserable I had hardly the energy to walk out of the house for two days.'[10]

Jessie's novel would go no further than this. With the literary and spiritual values she had once shared with Lawrence lying in tatters, she turned her back entirely on her own creative aims. She burnt the manuscript, together with the letters that had been exchanged between them, in a final act of catharsis.

Lawrence and Frieda had other distractions though. They were supposed to be taking a break from the Villa Igea to travel to Florence, but Frieda's desire to be as close to her children as she could physically get without incurring Weekley's wrath meant that by early April they were heading back to England. Lawrence also wished to be present at his sister Ada's wedding to fiancé Eddie Clarke in Eastwood – although as the estranged wife of another man, Frieda wouldn't be able to accompany him. The couple took a circuitous route back to England, journeying first to San Gaudenzio ('a lovely place', according to Lawrence) where they spent ten days, before travelling on to Verona to see Else, and then Irschenhausen, just south of Munich. Lawrence's heart was still in Italy though. He felt a kind of kinship with the Italian way of life with its 'non-moral' ways that Lawrence felt freed his soul from the binds of English society, and the 'tightness' of Germany that he felt choked him. He admired the way the Italians lived by their senses, believing that the senses constituted the very essence of who he was. 'But the senses are superbly arrogant', Lawrence wrote in *Twilight in Italy*:

> *The senses are the absolute, the god-like. For I can never have another man's senses. These are me, my senses absolutely me. And all that is can only come to me through my senses. So that all is me and is administered unto me. The rest, that is not me, is nothing, it is something which is nothing. So the Italian, through centuries, has avoided our Northern purposive industry, because it has seemed to him a form of nothingness.*[11]

Italy had none of the uptight, class consciousness that Lawrence had been exposed to in England and Germany. Instead, it was care-free, having 'no thought for the morrow', and a naturalness that was at odds with England's artificiality.

It was with some trepidation that Lawrence and Frieda left Germany to embark for England on 17 June 1913. Lawrence was particularly troubled by a plan Frieda had devised to see her children. She would intercept her eldest child, Monty (now 13), on his way out of school and get him to arrange for her to see the two girls, Elsa and Barby, without Weekley's knowledge. She hoped the children would then petition their father for further contact with their mother. Not only was it risky but it was also over-optimistic. 'It is a plan I don't like',[12] Lawrence confided to Garnett.

With *Sons and Lovers* published on 29 May, Lawrence returned to England as a fully fledged author. The day it was released he wrote to Helen Corke for the first time in a year, telling her that he felt he had lived 'several lives' since he had begun 'Paul Morel', and those lives were all 'queerer than novels'.

It was understandable. Not only had the novel been completely rewritten, and large sections of it removed and replaced with different material, but Lawrence had also completely rewritten his own life. Life had stopped imitating art – and in this case, the truth was altogether 'queerer' than the fiction. He *was* a different person. He knew himself; and just as Paul had been on a journey of self-development, so had Lawrence. The deliberately ambiguous ending of *Sons and Lovers*, in which Paul pledges not to 'give in', suggests a sense of promise and success; something Lawrence hoped to emulate in real life. Paul Morel's story ended there. Lawrence's didn't – but he knew which of his 'several lives' he wished to leave behind, and which he wished to take with him into the future.

On arrival in England, Lawrence and Frieda headed straight for the Garnetts at the Cearne. It was the only place they could stay together as a couple. Lawrence felt cut off from his past life, as though he had been 'reincarnated', but it had also left him isolated. But staying with the Garnetts wasn't as easy as they hoped it would be. First, Edward wasn't there initially and so they were welcomed by his wife, Constance, and David 'Bunny' Garnett. Bunny was in the middle of revising for his Associateship of the Royal College of Science exam and Constance was thoroughly unsettled by Frieda and Lawrence's constant arguments about the Weekley children. Bunny was categorical in whose fault it was, as he later described in his recollections of their stay:

> ...*there was a streak of cruelty in Lawrence; he was jealous of the children and angry with Frieda, because she could not forget them. Now that she had come back to England, she was longing to see them, and the spiteful, ill-conditioned, ungenerous side of Lawrence's character was constantly breaking out in different ways... Of course, he rationalised his jealousy and his spite, attributed the whole trouble to faults in Frieda's character and never admitted the existence of imperfections in his own.*[13]

Little wonder that just before they arrived in England, a similar incident had resulted in Frieda smashing a plate over Lawrence's head. But Lawrence reassured Garnett that they were 'trying to be good' for Bunny's sake, although he wasn't sure whether they were succeeding in that department. But apart from being a natural reaction to an incredibly stressful situation, quarrelling with Frieda was a necessary part of Lawrence's need to understand the human condition and the relationships between men and women – all of which Lawrence felt strongly about, and which naturally fed into his writing. Conflict rather than harmony characterised Lawrence's relationships in the flesh and on the page.

Lawrence's exploration of the male-female dynamic coincided with a transitional phase in his writing – and ultimately signalled a slow departure from Edward Garnett's influence on his future works. Lawrence had already anticipated Garnett's reaction to his new work, 'The Sisters', as he was writing it, commenting frequently in his letters to Garnett that, 'I think you will hate it', and, 'you may dislike it'. The knowledge that his writing was entering a new phase was confirmed to Lawrence when he received his bound copy of *Sons and Lovers*, with which he declared to Garnett that he wouldn't be writing in that style anymore because it marked the end of his 'youthful period'. But it would take the rest of 1913 for Lawrence to make his departure complete, for he wouldn't submit 'The Sisters' to Duckworth until early 1914.

In the interim, there were more pressing personal matters to deal with. Now back in England, Frieda's priority – as it always had been – was to see her children, and so the couple travelled to London from the Cearne on 26 June in the hope that Frieda would be able to see Monty as he was leaving his school, Colet Court, in West Kensington. Four days later she was successful in her illicit endeavour, but the outcome was disastrous. Frieda managed to talk to Monty, and gave him some money and a letter, but both were discovered by Weekley's sister Maude, who reported the incident back to Weekley himself, who then obtained a court order preventing Frieda from 'interfering' with her children. Frieda relates how her children had danced around her 'in complete delight' asking, 'Mama, you are back, when are you coming home?' when she initially managed to engineer the meeting with Monty. But by the time she saw them again, they had been told that they were not allowed to speak to her, and only 'little white faces' looked back at her, as though she were an 'evil ghost'. Coincidentally, it was exactly the reaction Ernest Weekley hoped his children would have, for he had written to Frieda via her mother telling her that she would henceforth be 'dead to the children' and little more than a '*verfaulte Leiche*' – a decomposed corpse.

But Frieda was soon to gain an ally. In July, Lawrence and Frieda met another bohemian couple who were defying convention: journalist and critic John Middleton Murry and his girlfriend, the talented short story writer Katherine Mansfield. Twenty-four-year-old Murry was Oxford educated but from the lower middle-classes, having grown up with an Inland Revenue clerk for a father in pre-high-rise Peckham; and the 25-year-old Katherine was born in New Zealand but had been schooled in London before emigrating permanently to the city in 1908. Katherine had been married (disastrously) and was attempting to obtain a divorce from the husband she had left on their wedding night. Murry and Mansfield's joint venture, the literary magazine *Rhythm* (Murry was the editor, Mansfield provided the funds to keep it going), was on the cusp of being rebranded as *The Blue Review* and its literary and artistic focus – and its potential as an outlet for his work – had already been recognised by Lawrence

The D. H. Lawrence Birthplace Museum.

View of the kitchen in the D. H. Lawrence Birthplace Museum. A typical 'miner's kitchen' such as this provided inspiration for Lawrence when writing *Sons and Lovers*. "She glanced round the kitchen. It was small and curious to her, with its glittering kissing-bunch, its evergreens behind the pictures, its wooden chairs and little deal table."

View of the parlour in the D. H. Lawrence Birthplace Museum. Lydia Lawrence loved to play the piano, and Lawrence went on to recreate similar scenes in *The White Peacock* (1911). "Mother sat before the little brown piano, with her plump, rather stiff fingers moving across the keys, a faint smile on her lips."

The Breach, Eastwood. Lawrence's childhood home and setting for 'The Bottoms' in *Sons and Lovers* (1913). "Moreover, she [Mrs Morel] had an end house in one of the top blocks, and thus had only one neighbour; on the other side an extra strip of garden. And, having an end house, she enjoyed a kind of aristocracy among the other women of the 'between' houses, because her rent was five shillings and sixpence instead of five shillings a week."

D. H. Lawrence in 1906.

Annesley Old Church graveyard.

The ruins of Annesley Old Church are described in Chapter 11 of *The White Peacock*: "As I drew near an owl floated softly out of the black tower. Grass overgrew the threshold. I punched open the door, grinding back a heap of plaster and entered the place…"

Annesley Old Church is also linked to Byron's 'Hills of Annesley.'

Ford Madox Ford (Hueffer), 1905.

Home of Louie Burrows, Church Cottage, Cossall. Lawrence describes the cottage in *The Rainbow* (1915). "It was the cottage next the church, with dark yew trees, very black old trees, along the side of the house and the grassy front garden; a red, squarish cottage with a low slate roof, and low windows." © Oxymoron/CC BY-SA 2.0.

'An Idyll' (1891) by Maurice William Greiffenhagen. The painting fascinated Lawrence and he recreated many versions during his younger years.

D. H. Lawrence in 1912.

Katherine Mansfield.

John Middleton Murry in 1917.

D. H. Lawrence & Frieda von Richthofen in 1914.

Lady Ottoline Morrell by Adolf de Meyer, circa 1912.

Portrait of Rosalind Baynes nee Thornycroft, 1913.

Samuel Solomonovich Koteliansky, seated in the centre, also known as 'Kot' to Lawrence and Frieda – London, 1928.

Rosalind Thorneycroft, Frieda, D.H. Lawrence and Bertie Farjeon in the woods behind Spring Cottage, Bucklebury, West Berkshire, in 1919.

Rosalind in Italy with her three children. It was during her time in Italy that Lawrence and Rosalind became intimate.

A portrait of D. H. Lawrence, painted by Millicent Beverage in 1921.

The front cover of *Sea and Sardinia* (1921) by D. H. Lawrence with paintings by Jan Juta. Published by Thomas Seltzer (New York). Some of Lawrence's finest writing can be found in the descriptions of the places he visited. (*Image from Wikimedia Commons*)

Mabel Luhan in 1934.

Mabel Dodge Luhan House, the 'Big House' in Taos, New Mexico.

Aldous Huxley, 1927.

Giuseppe 'Pino' Orioli in 1935, Florence. Pino was the first publisher to privately publish *Lady Chatterley's Lover* for Lawrence in 1928.

Photograph of D. H. Lawrence, enclosed in a letter to Bernard Falk (1882–1960), dated 24 February 1929.

The D. H. Lawrence Memorial, near Taos, New Mexico.

Inside the D. H. Lawrence memorial.

Frieda Lawrence in 1950.

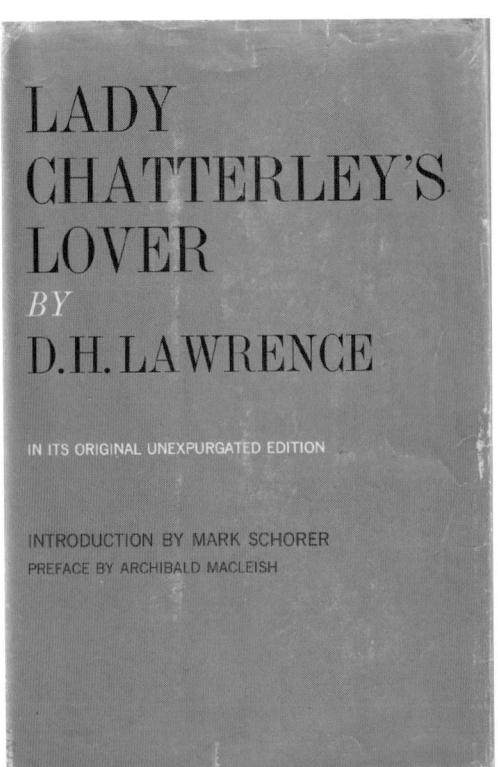

Lady Chatterley's Lover (1959) by D. H. Lawrence. Published by Grove Press Inc. (New York). The unexpurgated edition was published in the United States a year before the British version by Penguin. (*Image from Wikimedia Commons*)

Memorial flagstone in Poets' Corner, Westminster Abbey. © 14GTR.

in the winter of 1912, although he also referred to it as a 'daft paper' on one occasion – it's 'daftness' mitigated only by the fact it was edited by folk who 'seemed rather nice'.

The two couples immediately hit it off, finding more than enough common ground on which to build a friendship. Frieda remembered how arresting the couple were as she caught them quite unexpectedly 'making faces' at each other and 'putting their tongues out' on their bus journey with Lawrence and Frieda to have lunch in Soho. Murry attributed this to the fact that Lawrence and Frieda had formed the idea that the couple were wealthy and important people: the kind of people 'who finance daft magazines'. Irrespective of first impressions on both sides, Murry concluded that the two couples were made for one another.

Frieda was particularly taken with Katherine, admiring her exquisite looks and style, brown hair and delicate skin. But more importantly, she was sympathetic to Frieda's plight and was, in Frieda's words, the perfect friend; she helped her try to contact her children, visiting Colet Court on several occasions to pass notes to Monty from Frieda.

The friendship that Lawrence and Frieda struck up with Murry and Katherine in the summer of 1913 meant more than just the enjoyment of each other's company. Lawrence and Frieda had been social pariahs since their elopement in the spring of 1912, and besides the Garnetts, the couple had lived a lonely existence. It is unsurprising then that Lawrence, particularly, found solace in his relationship with Murry; a feeling that manifested itself in Lawrence's intensity and desire to understand the young critic. 'In an astonishingly short time he knew all about me',[14] Murry wrote.

Buoyed by the confidence of having made new friends, Frieda and Lawrence departed from the Cearne to rooms in Kingsgate, near Margate in Kent. But Lawrence was quickly unhappy with the arrangement. Whether it was because Frieda had visited Margate previously with Ernest and their children and was ruminating on all she had left behind – which no doubt annoyed Lawrence – or that he simply felt he no longer belonged in England, having cut many of his ties in Nottinghamshire; it is difficult to determine. As was customary for Lawrence, he found an outlet for his frustrations in his writing, and he explored these sentiments in his 1914 short story 'The Shadow in the Rose Garden'. It is possible Lawrence was rewriting it in Kingsgate under its previous title 'The Vicar's Garden', and its themes of bittersweet wistfulness and the sentimentality of past-love may reflect Frieda's 'rose-tinted' remembrance of her previous visit to the area. The story also revolves around the unsuitability of the honeymooning couple who form the two principal characters: the crossing of class boundaries reflecting Lawrence's own experience of first his mother and father's marriage, and second his relationship with the aristocratic Frieda.

Yet despite the 'jolly little flat' they had found for themselves, Lawrence seemed to feel uncomfortable in his surroundings. But he was also fed up with moving around – his and Frieda's wanderings without any real purpose or firm plans to lay down any roots were clearly troubling him. He had no plans to stay in Nottinghamshire – except a brief visit for Ada's wedding – or see his old school chums in Croydon – and even if he had wanted to, there was every chance Frieda would have been unwelcomed. His agenda was very much 'out with the old, in with the new' during this time as he continued to forge a path that suited him and no one else.

Via the civil servant and editor Edward Marsh, whom Lawrence had met through Marsh's poetry anthology, *Georgian Poetry*, Frieda and Lawrence were also introduced to Herbert 'Beb' Asquith and his wife, Cynthia. Beb was the second son of the prime minister (Herbert Henry Asquith) and himself a writer and poet, and Cynthia a novelist, ghost story writer and renowned socialite. Frieda was thrilled to be among such prestigious company, particularly Cynthia, who seemed 'like Botticelli's *Venus*' to Frieda, and Beb was equally as enthralled with Lawrence.

This sense of deeply human perception resonated in the reviews that *Sons and Lovers* was beginning to receive in the press. 'No other English novelist of our time', wrote the *Standard*, 'has so great a power to translate passion into words. Mr Lawrence shows that he is a master.'[15] This was echoed by the *Saturday Review*, who stated that 'we know of no English novelist – today – who has his power to put into words the rise and fall of passion.'[16] *Sons and Lovers* was 'glowing reality'. It had 'glorious flashes of imagination' and an 'insight into the hearts of men'. This was the opinion of the critics. But getting the public to buy the novel was something else entirely. 'I don't know whether it has sold so well', Lawrence lamented to artist Ernest Collings towards the end of July. 'The damned prigs in the libraries and bookshops daren't handle me because they pretend they are delicate skinned and I am hot. May they fry in Hell.'[17]

The problem was some of the reviews had highlighted the 'passion' Lawrence depicted as a point for criticism. 'Mr D. H. Lawrence is not reticent', reported the *Illustrated London News*. 'It may be, perhaps, that he might have been more reticent with advantage to his book'.[18] The *Nation*'s reviewer, Ethel Colburn Mayne, was particularly scathing of the 'incessant scenes of sexual passion' and Lawrence's 'morbid brooding on the flesh'. Lawrence clearly thought this noteworthy for he mentions it in a letter to Arthur McLeod – marking the beginning of Lawrence's longstanding association with sexual and erotic content; a connection that gained traction as his writing career progressed.

Yet, the reviews were overwhelmingly positive. *The Clarion* waxed lyrical, hailing Lawrence as a, *great artist in words, a man who can arrest and hold the attention of even a hardened reviewer, a penman who produces something very little short of a literary masterpiece, an author with four books to his credit, and but for the thoughtfulness of Messrs. Duckworth and Co. I should have known nothing about him or his work, and so missed a glorious feast, not to mention the thrill of a big discovery.*[19]

This must have cheered Lawrence somewhat as he focused on his short stories that summer, first at the Cearne, and then at Kingsgate. But the issue of Frieda's access to her children, and her divorce were still unresolved. Matters had, in fact, worsened, with Frieda telling Ernest that his 'decayed corpse' still lay in her bones. It was an odd reference and something of the original German was probably lost in translation (the retort was made via Else, Frieda's sister), but just as Lawrence explored the physicality of men and women in his writing, Frieda too used visceral descriptions to depict the strength of her emotions. 'To tear myself loose from the children is horrible', she wrote to Else, 'it is as when living pieces of flesh are torn from one…'[20]

Yet despite this, Frieda still seemed to believe that he would calm down – which seems astonishing given the vehemence of his letters. The situation was not helped by Katherine Mansfield's attempts to speak to Monty on Frieda's behalf. Monty sent a message back via another pupil that 'he was not to talk to people who came to the school to see him'. Frieda's main concern was that the Weekleys had prejudiced her children against her irrevocably and had instilled a 'horror of her' into Monty.

Frieda resolved to leave England. If she couldn't see her children, then there was little to be gained from staying any longer. On 31 July she left to see her parents, who were staying in Bavaria with Else, leaving Lawrence to head back to the Cearne alone. Lawrence stayed with Edward Garnett for two days, although it seems the visit was somewhat marred for him by the presence of Constance Garnett ('I don't like Mrs G', he commented), who no doubt changed the dynamic in the house whenever the three of them were together, before heading up to Eastwood for Ada's wedding to William Clarke on 4 August.

Lawrence left Nottinghamshire on 7 August to join Frieda in Irschenhausen where he resolved he would stay, at least until they could work out a more permanent living arrangement. Lawrence was glad to have left England, regarding his experience over the previous two months as 'dull and woolley', as opposed to the vitality – 'so living; so quick' – he sensed abroad. The change clearly made a difference to Lawrence – he wrote the first hundred pages of a revised version of 'The Sisters' while he was staying in Germany, as well as revising his play *The Widowing of Mrs Holroyd* (1914). But he knew it wasn't where he wanted to write in the long term, and he commented as such to Edward Garnett in early September. And so, despite Lawrence's objections to their constant wanderings, within four weeks he was on the move again, hiking over the Swiss Alps to Basel with a rucksack, while Frieda went alone to Baden-Baden to spend time with her parents. Their plan was to meet in Basel and then get the train to Lerici, on the northwest Italian coast, where Else's husband, Edgar Jaffe, was holidaying with his mistress. The location did not disappoint, and the couple quickly found themselves a 'perfect' little four-roomed cottage on the beach in Fiascherino – a 'delicious' idyll that Lawrence described prosaically to Garnett:

> *You run out of the gate into the sea, which washes among the rocks…at the mouth of the bay. The garden is all vines and fig trees, and great woods on the hills all round…. Yellow crocuses are out, wild. The Mediterranean washes softly and nicely, with just a bit of white against the rocks.*[21]

Frieda was equally as enthralled, describing lazy days lying in a hammock watching the fishermen, and their swimming excursions that Lawrence described humorously as 'trying to drown myself'. The days were long, and they spent most of their time outdoors, taking walks, eating on the beach, and marvelling at the beauty of their surroundings and the wonder of living. Frieda had found liberation of a sort: she found that she enjoyed having no money and 'didn't want to play a role in the world', which was unhelpful given Lawrence's precarious financial situation, and her own lack of money. But what they did not find was acceptance among their neighbours. The couple decided that they would be honest about their relationship to the other English and American villa owners in the area. But the middle-classes of Lerici weren't ready for an unmarried couple – one of whom had run away from her husband. Frieda recalls in her memoir how one 'friend' of the couple had declared how fond she was of them both but was adamant that they were wrong and that their life together was a mistake. Rather than feel judged by such a condemnation, Frieda – who was still basking in the warm romantic glow of a new relationship – chose to feel sympathy for the woman's narrowmindedness.

That autumn and winter of 1913, Lawrence and Frieda were, for the most part, happy. They sang, painted together, and Lawrence finally found the freedom of expression he needed to continue work on 'The Sisters', which he was confident he could finish in a month. The distance Lawrence had created between himself, and the rigid expectations of English society allowed him to explore the idea of the modern woman; shaping Ursula Brangwen, the main protagonist in 'The Sisters', as a product of three generations worth of cultural influence. But this was at odds with Garnett's more traditional approach to novel writing, where 'form' was given more weight than 'life'.

Lawrence wanted to depict how his characters felt, the concept of who they were, rather than what they could see happening around them – a complete departure from the traditionally plot-driven novel where action, or factual realism, trumps multi-layered characterisation. Lawrence was searching for the *truth* in his work, which in 1913 was ground-breaking stuff. Virginia Woolf's *Mrs Dalloway* (1925) was more than ten years away, and James Joyce's *Ulysses* wouldn't be properly published until 1922; just two examples from the early twentieth century that explored a more sensitive, artistic and profound way to represent character. Woolf argued in 1924, in her famous essay 'Mr Bennett and Mrs Brown', that the shift in human relationships that had occurred at the beginning of the twentieth century had heralded a new approach to writing. This was because the changing dynamic in human connection simply couldn't be sufficiently represented by the literary conventions of the Edwardians, such as a reliance on describing what exists outside of a character's psyche and external fact. Woolf likens this to the novelist 'looking very powerfully, searchingly and sympathetically out of the window',[22] while ignoring the character in the corner: 'never at her, never at life, never at human nature'. 'For us', she asserts on behalf of the modern writer, 'those conventions are ruin, those tools are death.'[23] Fortunately, Lawrence did not have to look far for the inspiration he needed to lose himself in the female psyche; he had Frieda, and she was just as dedicated as Lawrence in ensuring truth in all he was writing.

As a result of his own desire to do justice to this new approach, and no doubt incorporating input from Frieda also, 'The Sisters' grew extremely long, morphing into a multi-generational novel covering the emotional lives of just one family, the Brangwens – a dynasty of farmers and craftsmen living on the borders of Nottinghamshire and Derbyshire. The first part began with Tom Brangwen and his experiences in the 1840s (representing the old ways) and ending with his granddaughter Ursula in 1905 (representing modernity). This was followed by a second part that took the story of Ursula even further into the twentieth century, and included her sister Gudrun, whose relationship with Gerald Crich provides a foil to that of Ursula's relationship with her husband Rupert Birkin.

By January 1914, Lawrence was ready to send the first half of 'The Sisters' to Garnett, under a new title, 'The Wedding Ring'. But first, Frieda's real-life marriage came to an end. On 18 October 1913 the hearing took place in the High Court, Probate, Divorce and Admiralty Division to grant Ernest Weekley his decree nisi, although it would take a further six months for it to be made absolute. Nevertheless, it was an important milestone in what had been a tumultuous period, and as they were abroad, the couple were also spared the indignity of having to face the inevitable press reports on the case. 'A CO-RESPONDENT'S STANGE LETTER/EXCUSE FOR A BETRAYAL' ran the headline in the *Yorkshire Evening Post* that very same day – an allusion to the infamous letter written by Lawrence and sent to Weekley from Metz, which proved Frieda's affair. The 'thunderstorms of tragedy', as Lawrence called them, convinced him that he was destined for the 'mad-house', and that Frieda would be 'buried under a nameless sod'. 'We are the most unfortunate, agonised, fate-harassed mortals…'[24] he wrote to Cynthia Asquith.

But the new year seemed to bring renewed hope for Lawrence. In early January 1914, he was waiting optimistically for Garnett's response to 'The Wedding Ring'. Lawrence thought it was good – good enough for him to suggest in a letter to Garnett that the version he had sent him was its 'final form' and that any faults could be quickly dealt with, and the novel rushed to print. It is possible Lawrence's confidence had been buoyed by approaches from several publishers – most likely Pinker and Curtis Brown – who believed *Sons and Lovers* had not received the sales that it deserved and offering an advance of £200 for rights to publish his next novel. So, it was within this context that Lawrence posted 'The Sisters' to Garnett.

Lawrence knew he was taking a risk with his new material, especially under Garnett's critical gaze, so he was unsurprised when his mentor's response eventually arrived on 29 January. Garnett responded negatively but Lawrence was ready to defend his approach. He didn't want to create 'vivid scenes' as he had done in *Sons and Lovers*. Rather, he asserted his needs as a writer and creator to 'write differently'. But he was still influenced enough by Garnett's opinions to pledge that he would leave the book altogether if the second half also disappointed him and abandon his new method. Lawrence recognised that he needed to transition to grow – not just as a writer but as a person. His pledge, really, was an empty one. It is difficult to conceive of a Lawrence who would readily submit to the conformities of established writing methods to the detriment of his own need to be authentically himself: 'I must write to live', he wrote – not just for practical and financial reasons, but to really feel *alive*.

Garnett persevered in his attempts to remonstrate with Lawrence over the form of 'The Wedding Ring' well into the spring of 1914, but Lawrence became increasingly defensive about the direction he wished to take his writing in. His conflict of feelings towards Garnett – his friend and mentor, but also an associate of Duckworth – was evident in his letters. From Garnett's perspective, he was torn between supporting Lawrence the friend, but preventing Lawrence the writer from committing career suicide.

Lawrence wrote with frustration to Garnett, imploring him to 'have patience' and understand what he wanted to do with his writing, reminding him, 'I am not a child.' Lawrence was also caught between the need for his novels to be a commercial success and generate enough money for him and Frieda to live on and maintaining his friendship with Garnett, whom he 'couldn't separate from Duckworth and Co'. Lawrence knew that Garnett wouldn't be able to sell his novels commercially if he didn't believe in them. It was stalemate – either Lawrence put aside his quest for truth and fall in with Garnett (and Duckworth's) expectations of him, or he find a different publisher, and potentially, a new mentor.

Sons and Lovers complicated matters further for Lawrence. Here was a critically acclaimed novel, on the strength of which Lawrence was on the cusp of breaking through – so much so, in fact, that the agent J. B. Pinker had approached him with a lucrative three-novel contract worth £300 per book with the publisher Methuen. Lawrence was clearly interested, and in the spring of 1914 he had two copies of 'The Wedding Ring' typed while he was still writing it, indicating that he was intending to submit it to other publishers, rather than just Duckworth. He believed in it – he just needed to find a publisher who believed in it too. Lawrence trusted in his genius and was certain it wouldn't let him down – and it would be acknowledged eventually, but not before several decades had elapsed. Nevertheless, it must have been an extremely tempting proposition from Pinker et al, despite Frieda's assertion that she 'enjoyed being poor'.

Lawrence had outgrown Garnett, and Garnett had little choice but to let him go. He wasn't just another 'discoverer' of Lawrence's genius – he had helped him to nurture it until Lawrence had enough self-belief to follow his own path with conviction. Or as the editor of the *Spectator*, Rolfe Arnold Scott-James, put it, 'till the genius ran away and mocked him by becoming a best seller, or stayed by his side and languished'.[25] This fits entirely with Lawrence's own declaration in a letter to Garnett in 1921:

> *No, my dear Garnett, you are an old critic and I shall always like you, but you are a tiresome old pontiff also and I shan't listen to a word you say, but shall go my own way to the dogs and bitches, just as heretofore. So there.*[26]

It says something about the strength of their affection for each other that the two men were still conversing way beyond their difference of opinion in 1914. Edward had, after all, offered support to Lawrence at one of the most testing times of his life thus far, and was one of only a handful of people who accepted Lawrence *and* Frieda together, and welcomed them into his home – the importance of which was never lost on Lawrence. Edward did believe in Lawrence as his friend, and as a new voice that needed to be heard, but not within the confines of his advisory role with Duckworth, and so on a professional level, the two men parted ways.

The summer of 1914 was notable for two reasons: money and marriage. On 24 June the couple arrived back in London, having travelled separately so that Frieda could visit her ailing father in Baden-Baden, for what would be the last time. Lawrence wasted no time in trying to untie the knot that was binding him to Duckworth so that he could submit 'The Wedding Ring' (now called *The Rainbow*) to Methuen instead. Lawrence's trump card was the knowledge that Duckworth – as a less commercially minded and therefore less well-off publisher – would never be able to match the £300 offered by Methuen – and Lawrence was proved right.

However, to offset the fact that he hadn't delivered the promised manuscript to Duckworth – and to compensate for Garnett's time and input into 'The Sisters', Lawrence promised a collection of short stories instead, which was published in November as *The Prussian Officer and Other Stories* (1914). What Duckworth thought of Lawrence's withdrawal of *The Rainbow* isn't recorded, but given Garnett's categorical rejection of it in the form Lawrence wished it to be published, it can be surmised that he probably felt he'd had a lucky escape.

With Frieda's divorce made absolute at the end of April, the couple were finally able to marry, and so on 13 July the couple made their way from Gordon Campbell's house in Selwood Terrace, South Kensington, where they were staying, to the nearby registry office. They made a quick stop on the way so that Lawrence could buy Frieda a ring, and she dispensed of the ring Weekley had given her by gifting it to Katherine. According to Frieda, Katherine was buried with it on her death in 1923 in Fontainebleau. Thus, after one of the most tumultuous periods of both their avant-garde lives, they finally tied the knot – the photographs, probably taken by Gordon Campbell, afterwards showing Lawrence sporting a moustache and in a straw boater and cravat, and Frieda looking a little matronly, but carrying it off with her customary aplomb. None of Lawrence's family were present, so the couple were accompanied by Katherine Mansfield (looking fragile and demure) and John Middleton Murry, looking rather dapper with a book stuffed under his arm. Most importantly, Lawrence and Frieda were now respectable – even though their wedding photo features Gordon Campbell's washing in the background.

For the already once-married Frieda, the act itself changed nothing in their relationship. It was a simple and undignified ceremony, which suited her belief that it made no difference to them as a couple. Yet Lawrence had always believed in the idea of marriage – despite the example he grew up with – and to have found a woman who respected both his need for a binding union and the needs of the individual within it was a rare and beautiful thing.

As a married couple the Lawrences found they now *both* had a seat at the table, and with Lawrence's star on the ascent, their time in London presented an opportunity for them to accumulate more friends of a similar ilk to themselves and the Murrys. During this time, they made the acquaintance of artist Mark Gertler, the poets Rupert Brooke, Amy Lowell and Richard Aldington, who was also the editor of *The Egoist*, and Aldington's wife, the American poet and novelist H. D. (Hilda Doolittle), among other members of London's literati.

Among this milieu of intellectualism and modernist individualism, which centred around Hampstead, politics and ideas were passionately discussed, including events on the continent. 'Is it War?'[27] the newspaper headlines asked on 31 July as the precarious diplomatic situation reached a crescendo and Serbia and Austria began to mobilise troops. On the same day, and in the baking heat of one of the hottest summers on record, Lawrence left Frieda in London and set off on a week's walking tour of the Lake District with a group of friends. When Lawrence returned to London, the country was at war. 'We are so miserable about the war' was all Lawrence could comment at the time. And Frieda's nationality was a problem they couldn't escape from. It was only later in January 1915 that Lawrence was able to fully articulate how he felt about the war, choosing to juxtapose the simple joys of his walking holiday, the splendid scenery and 'visionary beauty' with the 'immense pain' they saw all around them – the pain of separation and a country readying itself for conflict.

Lawrence's life before war was declared on 4 August looked promising. He had two publishing contracts for his full-length fiction (Methuen) and his short-story collection (Duckworth), a non-fiction work on Hardy to deliver, and was regularly placing his short-stories in various magazines and journals. But the war cruelly changed everything for everyone. Lawrence would at least escape with his life come 1918, unlike many of his contemporaries, but the dreary, joyless atmosphere of a world at war would curtail any demand for writing like Lawrence's. It belonged to another world – a pre-war world. As did many of Lawrence's friendships, as tensions surfaced, and sides were taken.

But the greatest test would be closer to home, as the newly united couple were now forced to confront one of their major differences – their nationalities.

Chapter 9

The Lawrences at War

So when war broke out his whole instinct was against it: against war. He had not the faintest desire to overcome any foreigners or to help in their death. He had no conception of Imperial England, and Rule Britannia was just a joke to him.[1]

In the immediate aftermath of the announcement, Lawrence and Frieda's primary concerns were money and their living arrangements – with good reason. Within a week of war being declared, Methuen sent back Lawrence's manuscript of 'The Wedding Ring', asking him to resubmit in six months' time when they hoped the economic situation would have stabilised.

This was a problem. Lawrence and Frieda had spent much of Lawrence's advance over the summer because they knew that the forthcoming publication of 'The Wedding Ring' would provide another sum of money that they could draw from, but the hiatus in publication would now leave them short. But more depressingly, there was little hope of them being able to return to their beloved Fiascherino.

In the interim, they stayed in Kensington while they worked out what they would do. From there, Lawrence wrote to his recently acquired agent, J. B. Pinker, asking, 'What is going to become of us?' and wondering how he would support himself and Frieda. The couple couldn't return to Italy, so they began to look for a 'tiny cottage' instead.

The 'tiny cottage' they found was at the end of the Metropolitan line in Chesham, Buckinghamshire, where after Lawrence had whitewashed and cleaned the interior, they hoped to live the simple life. Lawrence was keen to reassure his friends that it wasn't too bad – his letters following their move stress that it was 'very pretty and nice', and 'tiny, but jolly', but one suspects he was trying to convince himself as much as the outside world that they were coping with their financial crisis. As Lawrence put it, they were sitting 'very tight' on their last sixpence. 'It is nice', he reiterates with regard to the cottage at the end of one letter, having already used the same adjective several times in the preceding paragraph.

While Lawrence busied himself with practical tasks, he was mentally contemplating the war, 'grinding it over' in his soul. He was clearly conflicted, alternating between 'hating it thoroughly' and 'yearning over it'. Frieda was indignant at the xenophobic sentiment that was beginning to permeate their lives. Stories of atrocity in the press, and propaganda posters – some of which Frieda would have seen on her journey into London on the Metropolitan line – all fuelled the public appetite for anti-German feeling. There was nothing heroic or glorious about it, thought Frieda – only waste and stupidity. 'Nationality was just an accident and here was grief',[2] she wrote in her memoir.

But many thought differently, and the Lawrences were only too aware that Frieda (and Lawrence, by association) were now 'the enemy'. Suspicion was all around, despite their rural location. Even the simple act of gathering blackberries in the nearby hedges prompted a policeman to pop up from behind a bush wanting to know who they were. And on one of their trips back to London, they were returning home over Hampstead Heath when they saw a Zeppelin, prompting Frieda to contemplate that it might be piloted by the men she had known as boys in her youth. She worried that if the onlookers knew she was German they would tear her to pieces. As the war progressed, suspicions naturally increased, and the Lawrences would face frequent intrusions into their lives as they strove to maintain their neutrality and natural aversion to what they perceived to be a pointless destruction of civilisation.

The Lawrences were unified against the notion of war, but that didn't necessarily strengthen the bond between them. The war posed not only a threat to the stability of the country but also to the stability of their relationship. It was yet another test for them to endure, and it would at times bring them almost to breaking point. Frieda was still grieving for the children she had lost to Weekley, and she would come to grieve her father too when he died in 1916 without her having seen him again. She was also trying to cope with the sense of alienation of being a German woman living among 'the enemy', and the atmosphere of suspicion that status implied. Lawrence himself didn't help matters by making barbed comments – sometimes to her, but more often to their friends – about the atrocities perpetrated by the German military. He told Lady Ottoline Morell in 1915 that he would 'like to kill a million Germans' as retribution for the sinking of the passenger ship, the *Lusitania*, by a German submarine in May of that year. He could also be spiteful. He commented to E. M. Forster in June 1915 that Frieda was in London looking for a flat, 'unless a bomb has dropped on her – killed by her own countrymen – it is the kind of fate she is cut out for'.[3] Lawrence's antipathy towards everyone around him when he was in the grip of one of his black moods was well known, and the war only amplified a trait that was accepted by Frieda as being an integral part of Lawrence's character – irrespective of how disagreeable it was. Frieda felt Lawrence had turned against her, but Lawrence felt alienated too – from his fellow countrymen, the jingoistic patriotism that pervaded everything, and from civilisation and the age in which he lived. The war destroyed Lawrence's core belief in the oneness and wholeness of humanity. It was the climatic crisis of his life, the result of which drove him eventually into total rebellion and exile.[4]

But Lawrence's physical exile was still to come, because for the foreseeable future he was trapped in England, and any hopes of returning to Italy were now dashed. He poured his unhappiness into his writing instead, hoping to find the solution there. He began work on his book about Thomas Hardy in September, commenting to his agent that it would be 'queer stuff' and about almost 'anything but Thomas Hardy', which must have been slightly alarming for Pinker. So instead of writing a manuscript that stuck to the brief, e.g. a format of 15,000 words covering Hardy's life and works, Lawrence used it as an opportunity to express his feelings about the 'just and righteous' war against Germany, and it morphed into a 50,000-word examination of everything he was thinking and feeling. 'We go to war to show that we can throw our lives away', railed Lawrence in what became known as 'A Study of Thomas Hardy:

> *Indeed, they have become of so little value to us. We cannot live, we cannot be…*
> *Tell me no more we care about human life and suffering. We are, every one of*
> *us, revelling at this moment in the squandering of human life as if it were*
> *something we needed. And it is shameful. And all because that, to live, we are*
> *afraid to [risk] ourselves. We can only die.*[5]

Lawrence would never pick up a gun, but he could pick up his pen. He remarked to Garnett regarding *The Prussian Officer* that it was 'the real fighting line, not where soldiers pull triggers'. Lawrence worked on 'the Study' until late November, by which point he was ready to pick up 'The Wedding Ring' again, probably with a view to sending it back to Methuen now the sixth-month submission hiatus was at an end. But instead, his recent exploration of what it meant to be human in 'the Study' took Lawrence down a new path with his novel – the path to self-fulfilment and liberation. Lawrence split the novel into two, creating two volumes: *The Rainbow*, as it would become, and *Women in Love*. The new work would challenge notions of the male-female relationship like never before and reject society's acceptance of the old-world order in favour of individual growth and progression.

It was risky. Lawrence warned Pinker that he had to be prepared to fight for *The Rainbow* with Methuen. He would take out sentences and phrases but refused to take out multiple paragraphs or pages. Lawrence wasn't just risking his reputation on *The Rainbow* but any kind of financial security that could be derived from the novel; the ongoing war wasn't just occupying Lawrence's thoughts, but it was starving him of income. In October 1914 Lawrence was forced to apply to the Royal Literary Fund for a grant – the 'Cause of Distress' in his financial situation given simply as 'The War'. Yet Lawrence continued to make friends in high places – during this time he made the acquaintance of Lady Ottoline Morrell, the society hostess and patron of the arts whose country estate, Garsington, became a meeting place for artists and intellectuals opposed to the war. Through Ottoline, Lawrence became acquainted with philosopher and mathematician Bertrand Russell, and the writer E. M. Forster, who would later defend him posthumously at the *Lady Chatterley* trial. In true Lawrence form, not all these connections would last the course, but one that did was his intimate friendship with Samuel Solomonovich Koteliansky, or 'Kot' as he was known to Lawrence and their friends. Lawrence had met Kot that summer during his walking tour of the lakes in Westmoreland (now Cumbria) and the Russian translator became the person Lawrence corresponded with most frequently during his lifetime – the two men no doubt finding much in common having both elevated themselves out of humble backgrounds and into the intellectual world on their own merit.

It was through Kot that the concept of 'Rananim' was born over the festive season of 1914–15 – Lawrence et al's fantasy of a self-sustaining community far from Europe in which they could establish their own set of ideals, objectives and rules away from the oppressive expectations of western society. 'I want to sail away from this world of war and squalor', Lawrence wrote to Willie Hopkin in January 1915, 'and found a little colony where there shall be no money but a sort of communism as far as necessities of life go, and some real decency.'[6] The name 'Rananim' was an adaptation of the Hebrew word for 'Rejoice', which itself was taken from a song sung by Kot that Christmas.

The idea, noble though it was, never came to fruition – the closest Lawrence would ever get was his time living in Mexico during the 1920s. And although the idea has been oft-mooted as evidence of Lawrence's long-term utopian goal, the reality wasn't quite so high-minded; the notion was concocted over several festive gatherings between the Murrys, Mark Gertler, Kot, and the novelist Gilbert Cannan and his wife Mary – probably as a merry way to pass the time on a chilly winter's evening. Nevertheless, Lawrence did return to the vision time and again in his letters. It provided a form of escapism from the horrors of the war, and the strain of his financial situation. 'What about Rananim?' he wrote to Kot in early 1915, and nearly two years later he is still asking 'Where is our Rananim?', fearing that they had let the moment to establish it pass them by. It was a subject he gave much consideration to, if only to indulge the idealist and visionary in him, and it is unsurprising that he adopted the phoenix – a symbol long-associated with Lawrence – as part of Rananim's iconography.

The new year of 1915 brought a move to Greatham in West Sussex, which not only alleviated the lack of space the Lawrences had in their tiny Buckinghamshire cottage but also probably alleviated many of the arguments Lawrence and Frieda had had over the lack of space in the tiny cottage. More importantly, Lawrence finished *The Rainbow* on 2 March 1915 – although Lawrence was never truly 'finished' with any of his novels when he declared them finished, for he would revise every one extensively before it was committed to the press. He wrote that he was 'frightfully excited' that it was done, and even produced a celebratory sketch that he sent to the owner of their Greatham cottage, Viola Meynell. *The Rainbow* was the culmination of everything Lawrence had come to understand about human consciousness and the microcosm of mankind that exists in each of us.

Inevitably, the shorter works Lawrence produced during the First World War were tainted by the war itself. When he wasn't revising *The Rainbow*, he was rewriting his 'Hardy' manuscript to reflect his developing philosophy on the disintegration of society. Lawrence eventually shaped his thoughts into a series of six essays entitled 'The Crown', three of which appeared in a fortnightly paper/pamphlet Lawrence launched with Murry later that year called *The Signature*. The paper was a reaction to events abroad; Lawrence and Murry's answer to 'doing something'. It was aimed at people 'who care about the real living truth of things', and its subscribers were mostly recruited from Lawrence's literary friends and associates and their wider circles. The 'helpless little brown magazine', as Lawrence later described it, was printed three times and then quietly dropped. In true Lawrence fashion, he downplayed the endeavour ten years later, when all six essays were printed in Lawrence's *Reflections on the Death of a Porcupine* (1925): 'To me the venture meant nothing real: a little escapade. I can't believe in "doing things" like that. In a great issue like the war, there was nothing to be "done," in Murry's sense.... So that, personally, little magazines mean nothing to me.'[7] The text was somewhat esoteric, and Lawrence would have been hard pushed to convince the average man or woman on the street to join his cause because of the obscurity of his argument and themes, but it captured the spirit of revolution in him, and gave him a medium through which he could express his discontent. 'It says what I still believe', he said of it later, 'But it's no use for a five minutes' lunch'.[8]

'England, My England', a short story by Lawrence, and the title given to a larger volume of ten stories published in 1922, gave an insight into how Lawrence perceived the war to be affecting life. Using the motif of sentimentality for the past, followed by a failed marriage, and the nihilism of the central character in battle, Lawrence explored the death of Englishness and the aesthete in the darkest of terms:

Better the agony of dissolution ahead than the nausea of the effort backwards...
Utterly, utterly to forget, in the great forgetting of death...to lapse out on the
great darkness...Let the black sea of death itself solve the problem of futurity.
Let the will of man break and give up.[9]

This sense of utter despair was redolent of Lawrence's attitude towards war
and civilisation at the time.

The autumn of 1915 brought further disappointments and failures. The most
significant by far was the reception *The Rainbow* received when it was published
in early October 1915. Methuen had attempted to rein in their wayward genius
by censoring some parts of the manuscript at the proof stage but had failed
miserably. The resulting outcry was thus expected – but Methuen was wholly
unprepared for what followed. The reviews started innocuously enough – *The
Globe* pointed out that it was 'most emphatically not a book for everyone', and
that it ought to have a notice printed inside it to state that it was 'in no way
suitable for the youthful and inexperienced'.[10] But the fickle tide of opinion
rapidly turned, and the floodgates opened to a barrage of hostility.

'There is no form of viciousness, of suggestiveness, that is not reflected in
these pages', wrote *The Sphere*'s reviewer.

I can only suppose that Mr. Methuen and his two partners for some reason
failed to read this book in manuscript and published it upon the strength of the
previously well-deserved reputation of the author. Let them turn to the chapter
entitled 'Shame,' and unless they hold the view that Lesbianism is a fit subject
for family fiction I imagine that they will regret this venture. The whole book
is an orgie of sexiness.[11]

Much of the concern voiced at the time was around protecting the public – a
responsibility that *The Sphere* believed should have been brought to bear by
Methuen – and two reviews categorically stated that the book should be
suppressed. At a moment of national crisis, and heavy losses on the Western
Front, *The Rainbow* was incongruous; a glaring reminder of a time that was now
lost in the muddy, rat-infested trenches of Belgium and France. The misery of the
human relationships conveyed in *The Rainbow* was of little consequence when
compared to the misery being played out on the continent. Consequently, the
book was not only unpopular with the critics but also its sexual content made it
an unpopular choice with public libraries and booksellers. Inevitably, the shouts
of outrage grew louder until in early November 1915 all undistributed copies
of *The Rainbow* were confiscated from Methuen by the police, on the orders of
the Director of Public Prosecutions. By now, the Lawrences were residing at 1

Byron Villas, Vale-of-Health in Hampstead – a red-brick terraced house that had been partitioned into apartments. On hearing the news, Lawrence wrote wearily from their ground-floor flat to his agent, Pinker, to merely state that he was beyond being emotionally moved by the turn of events and that he 'cursed them to eternal damnation'.

Under the Obscene Publications Act of 1857, the case was brought before the Bow Street Magistrates on 13 November. Among reports of the loss of a British submarine in the Sea of Marmora and the suicide of a soldier who was home on leave and couldn't face going back to the front, the press picked up the story:

> *At Bow-street Police-court on Saturday, the well-known publishers, Messrs. Methuen and Co., of Essex-street, Strand, London, were summoned to show cause why 1,011 copies of a book called "The Rainbow," by D. H. Lawrence, should not be destroyed...the defendants, publishers of old standing and recognised repute, offered no objection to an order being made in the terms of the summons.*[12]

Methuen's refusal to defend the novel was a devastating blow for Lawrence. Frieda likened it to the murder of Lawrence's soul. The court heard how the absence of obscene words was a misdirection, because it was 'in fact, a mass of obscenity of thought, idea, and action throughout, wrapped up in language which he [Lawrence] supposed would be regarded in some quarters as an artistic and intellectual effort'.[13]

Those 'quarters' were hardly leaping to Lawrence's defence either, despite his hope that he could 'move a body of people' and get the decision reversed. Ottoline Morrell's husband Philip, the MP for Burnley, raised the matter in the House of Commons on 14 December but his intervention came to nothing. And while the Murrys would argue against censorship, they weren't prepared to defend *The Rainbow* – a novel they both disliked anyway and which Katherine 'quite definitely hated' in parts according to Murry. Thus, Lawrence's cries for support went unanswered. Methuen merely stated that they regretted publishing it. All 1,011 copies were seized and destroyed.

Lawrence later denied that he was upset by the events of 1915, but it is difficult to believe that such a profound betrayal – by his publishers, by his circle of friends and by his country – didn't leave him deeply disappointed. But while he never expressed candidly his feelings at the time, beyond the general annoyance he conveyed through his letters, he did express his bitterness through his actions. England had turned its back on Lawrence, and now he would turn his back on England.

Lawrence and Frieda had mooted the idea of moving to Florida before the suppression of *The Rainbow*, and the latest blow to Lawrence's credibility gave the whole idea a sense of urgency. 'If I don't go away I shall die', Lawrence wrote to one of his correspondents on 6 November, and to Pinker he declared it was 'the end of my writing for England'. Lawrence hoped North America would offer them a more liberally minded market – after all, his books all had US editions, and were therefore already in circulation – as well the security of living in a country that wasn't at war with its nearest neighbours. He petitioned friends to lend them the money to cover their passage across the Atlantic as well as the £10 each that they needed to be allowed to land in New York. Lawrence's plan was crystallised after a break at Lady Ottoline's manor house, Garsington. The time he spent at the seventeenth-century house, and the sense of nostalgia it provoked, only served to remind him of what was at stake as Britain marched towards modernity. 'I feel as if the whole thing were coming to an end', he wrote to civil servant and scholar Eddie Marsh from Garsington:

> the whole of England, of the Christian era: as if ours was the age only of Decline and Fall. It almost makes one die. I cannot bear it – this England, this past. I am staying with Lady Ottoline till tomorrow. Here one feels the real England – this old house, this countryside – so poignantly. I wonder if ever I shall have strength to drag my feet over the next length of journey. It isn't my novel that hurts me – it's this hopelessness of the world.[14]

But Lawrence was attempting to hold on to a version of the past that no longer existed – if it ever really did. Given his lapse into sentimentality, North America seems an odd choice given that it was flexing its progressive muscles and boasted a booming economy at the early twentieth century. But Lawrence was nothing if not contradictory. So while *The Rainbow* was being condemned for being too 'revolutionary' in its treatment of relationships, Lawrence himself was hankering after 'the beauty and pathos of old things'.[15] But above all else, what he really wanted was a sense of community – the very foundations of what British civilisation was built on – and it was this that he saw disintegrating.

Lawrence and Frieda were ready (and somewhat desperate) to travel but there was a last-minute stumbling block. To leave the country, Lawrence needed to attest, i.e. swear, an oath of allegiance as a military recruit and be ready to enrol for military service if the time came for him to be called up. But this would mean committing himself to a cause in which he didn't believe, and to a war he felt was deeply wrong. A passport was no longer enough, and with heavy losses in France, and Kitchener informing all able-bodied males that 'Your Country Needs You', conscription was looking ever more likely.

So, for the sake of getting out of England, and thus escaping Europe, he duly joined the queue at Battersea Town Hall on 11 December. Unfortunately, the queue was two hours long, which gave Lawrence plenty of time to reflect on what was important to him and talk himself out of it. Integrity would always trump hypocrisy for Lawrence, and he couldn't bring himself to perform a deception and betray his core values for the sake of leaving the country. Lawrence told Lady Ottoline that the experience had been false, degrading and an 'utter travesty of action', and that leaving the queue was as good as 'a triumph'.

Florida was no longer an option, but neither did Lawrence wish to stay in Hampstead. Whether the proximity to London – the place that had brought him both publishing joy and utter despair – was too much, or whether he needed to simply remove himself from the hot-housed intellectualism of Hampstead isn't clear, but as was often the case for Lawrence, he was rescued by another member of the writing community. The novelist and writer J. D. Beresford offered the Lawrences the use of his holiday home in Porthcothan on the north Cornish coast, and after a short trip over the festive period to his sister Ada's house in Ripley, Derbyshire, the Lawrences travelled to Cornwall on 30 December 1915, with a promise from the Murrys that they would join them later.

They had hardly any money and, at that moment, no prospect of earning any more. What could possibly go wrong?

Chapter 10

Living on the Edge

And they talked for a while of the bleak, lonely northern coast of Cornwall, the black huge cliffs, with the gulls flying away below, and the sea boiling, and the wind blowing in huge volleys: and the black Cornish nights, with nothing but the violent weather outside.[1]

Lawrence and Frieda arrived in Cornwall with £100 – the money that would have bought them their passage across the Atlantic. Instead, they could only look on from the upstairs window of their Cornish cottage, as the waves of the Atlantic crashed beneath them. They were living on the edge of the British Isles, but also on the edge of existence. 'There remains only to fall off into oblivion', Lawrence wrote. Their decision to separate themselves physically and mentally from the world into rural seclusion meant beginning again – as they had done so many times already.

Lawrence had just one book and a volume of poetry from which he could derive an income – his collection of essays on Italy that would be published in June 1916 with the title *Twilight in Italy*, and the collection of poems, *Amores*, in September 1916. Frieda's recollection of that time is imbued with her usual gaiety at being somewhere different. Written almost twenty years after events took place, the dual obfuscators – time and sentimentality – are no doubt to blame for her cheerful account of the fun they had buying furniture and arranging their meagre belongings.

Despite their poverty, and the pressure Lawrence would have felt to support them both, Lawrence felt a deep connection to Cornwall. Its 'black rocks like solid darkness' and 'great seas like twilight' made it difficult for him to thoroughly dislike England. 'I am incurably English', he announced. 'I seem as if I can't leave it. But I feel like sulking in one of its remotest caves. I can't go away.'[2] Yet despite wishing he could sulk in a cave, alone and unhindered by the emotions of others, he still needed to be around others. Within days of moving to Cornwall, the Lawrences were joined by the composer Philip Heseltine (also known as Peter Warlock), who then invited his lover, Minnie Lucie 'Puma' Channing, to the cottage, and before January 1916 was over, they also had Bulgarian novelist Dikran Kouyoumdjian (originally named Michael Arlen) to stay for several days. Lawrence also kept up a constant stream of correspondence. But this was also a time in which several important relationships in Lawrence's life came to an end. In March, Lawrence's friendship with the mathematician Bertrand Russell came to an end, just over a year after meeting him for the first time. While the two men had found much to admire in each other, they fundamentally disagreed on several key points – the most critical of these being their differing opinions on war. They had already quarrelled violently via letter in the autumn of 1915 – a situation that seemed to make both miserable at the time – but in the spring of 1916 the matter came to a head, their relationship broke down irretrievably and they had no further correspondence.

The other casualty during this time was Lady Ottoline Morrell, who had been caught in the crossfire between Russell and Lawrence (it was Ottoline who had introduced the two men in the first place). The Morrells had been staunch supporters of Lawrence, despite Ottoline's ambivalent attitude to *The Rainbow*, and her acts of kindness towards Lawrence are well documented in his letters. She sent him a jumper to help him ward off the worse of the Cornish winter in early 1916 and a piece of embroidery to hang on the wall of the cottage. She also offered money, which Lawrence turned down, and he relied heavily on Ottoline for the succession of books that she had sent from London to keep him occupied, and his appreciation of these acts was genuine: he dedicated *Amores* to Ottoline, 'In tribute to her noble and independent sympathy and her generous understanding.'[3] Ottoline was invited to Cornwall to stay with the Lawrences several times during 1916, but the visit never came off. On at least one of these occasions Ottoline was genuinely unwell, but she was also reluctant to step into Frieda's domain, particularly after one especially vitriolic letter from Frieda in May 1916, which Frieda subsequently described in a letter to Cynthia Asquith:

> *I had a great "rumpus" with dear Lady Ottoline, finally; I told her what I thought of her.*
> *All her "spirituality" is false, her democracy is an autocrat turned sour, inside those wonderful shawls there is cheapness and vulgarity.*[4]

Frieda felt she had uncovered the *real* Ottoline – i.e. the Ottoline Frieda belived to be a gossiping socialite who liked nothing better than discussing other people's lives in the drawing rooms of Bloomsbury – which she had thus far managed to conceal under an aristocratic upbringing and ladylike manners. Lawrence was aware of the quarrel, and he was also aware that Ottoline had been discussing his marriage to Frieda with other people in their circle. Whatever the truth of the matter, the split between the two women was irreconcilable, despite Lawrence's efforts to repair the damage.

Lawrence also managed to upset Philip Heseltine by interfering in his romantic affairs – who in turn was also engaged in an argument with Ottoline, who was accusing him of getting her into trouble with Lawrence. Heseltine was unrepentant when it came to Ottoline, and he also concluded that it was impossible to have a normal relationship with Lawrence: 'All he likes in one is the potential convert to his own reactionary creed. I believe firmly that he is a fine thinker and a consummate artist, but personal relation with him is almost impossible.'⁵ Lawrence was aware he had been cut loose by his London friends. 'Nearly everybody has dropped off from me – even Ottoline is *very cool*', he wrote to E. M. Forster. 'It is better to be alone in the world, planté [stand] by oneself.'⁶

Most importantly though, Frieda and Lawrence's relationship with the Murrys remained strong – for the time being at least – and they wanted their true friends around them. So much so, that they persuaded the Murrys to come back to England from where they were settled in the south of France. Lawrence wanted to 'unite forces' and 'become an active power' with the Murrys, and together they could create 'our Rananim'. The Lawrences even found two neighbouring properties for them all to reside in, just outside of Zennor, at Higher Tregerthen Farm, among the wild gorse and 'great grey granite boulders' and 'wide stretching sea'.

The Murrys moved into the cottage next door to the Lawrences in April 1916; their arrival prompted a new burst of creativity in Lawrence, and he began reacquainting himself with the material he had left out of *The Rainbow*, which was now back in his possession after a hiatus of three years. In July, Lawrence attempted to type it himself, probably to save money, but soon gave up. Not only did he find it boring but it also got on his nerves – which then made him irritable and miserable.

Lawrence had shaped the older material into a new novel, *Women in Love* – forming a sequel to *The Rainbow*. The story continues following the lives of Gudrun and Ursula Brangwen but moves the action gradually away from the England Lawrence had grown to despise, to the modern society of Europe. It is certainly bleaker – not just because it was written in a time of war and disillusionment, but because it reflects Lawrence's bitterness and disappointment. The banning of *The Rainbow*; his feelings about England; issues in many of his closest relationships; his intermittent quarrels with Frieda and their struggle to live an existence that felt normal to them but was anything but that to the wider word – all became situations and experiences that fuelled Lawrence's artistic treatment of *Women In Love*. As such, he melds the complex psychological forces of his characters with all the cultural and relationship issues he himself was experiencing. As Tedlock reiterates in his study of Lawrence's fiction, 'problems that are for him both causes and expressions of those forces.'⁷

One source of tension that almost certainly found an expression in the novel was the stifling proximity of the Murrys and the Lawrences to each other. What had seemed like the perfect set-up rapidly turned into a hostile environment – predominantly for the Murrys, who found Frieda and Lawrence's constant fighting emotionally exhausting. Their rows frequently turned violent, with smashed plates (over Lawrence's head on one occasion) and physical blows exchanged. Katherine had been unsettled from the start, declaring to Murry, 'I shall *never* like this place,' and Frieda disliked sharing Lawrence with the Murrys. Katherine almost certainly wanted a life with Murry that didn't involve having the Lawrences only a few feet away. The Murrys began to feel that the communal life wasn't something that either of them were suited to – and they had concerns over Lawrence's mental state too. Katherine wrote to Ottoline that 'he [Lawrence] has gone a little bit out of his mind', and Murry was convinced that in Lawrence's actions he could detect mental illness or hysteria. There was no doubt some exaggeration in these descriptions for Ottoline's benefit, but Lawrence did frequently complain of feeling 'seedy', i.e. unwell, during this period, and Lawrence's physical and mental health were so closely entwined that it is not difficult to imagine that his tendency to brood was manifesting itself physically too.

Both Murry and Lawrence were also living under the threat of conscription. Murry had already had a near miss when a policeman turned up on their doorstep with a warrant to arrest him for not joining up. He was able to produce his rejection certificate, and the policeman left empty-handed, but it was the closest Lawrence had got thus far to being forced to confront what was an inevitability for most able-bodied men in 1916.

By the middle of June, the Murrys had moved out and Lawrence's dream of communal living was over. Inevitably, he questioned the authenticity of the relationship he had previously enjoyed with the Murrys, feeling that he had deceived himself over the strength of their intimacy. It was another blow – the result of which was that he decided to stop having 'intimate friends'. Yet by the autumn he was hopeful that a reconciliation with Murry could take place if they shed their old selves and embraced 'a new young me, and a new you'.

Lawrence's own brush with conscription came later that month. He revealed in a letter that he had to go and 'join the colours' in Penzance, from where he was conveyed to Bodmin with thirty other conscripts and kept in a barracks overnight. Lawrence was shocked by the experience in which he was lined up on a station platform and marched 'like a criminal' through the streets to a barracks. He was put through a medical examination and received a full exemption. Going to war would almost certainly have killed Lawrence, physically and emotionally: 'I should die in a week if they made me a soldier', he confessed.

But in some respects, the exemption only added to their woes. An air of suspicion was already following the Lawrences around. They were consistently bothered by the local police, who sent a constable to their cottage regularly to check Lawrence's papers. Even simple tasks such as carrying home a loaf of bread in a rucksack came under the suspicion of the local coastguard, who thought they were concealing a spy camera.

The 'creeping foulness' seemed to follow them around. One evening in 1917 they had dinner with the composer and friend of Philip Heseltine, Cecil Gray, at his residence Count House. A light was left on in a bedroom and could be seen from the sea, which led the coastguards to believe they were signalling to German submarines. The confusion was cleared up, but Frieda took some small pleasure that the coastguards had fallen into a ditch and got covered in mud while listening under the windows.

Worse was to come in the autumn of 1917. Early one morning they opened the door to four officials who ordered them to leave Cornwall. They had just three days to pack up their belongings and say their goodbyes, with no real explanation as to why. Their house was then searched, but nothing could be done, 'so we left Cornwall, like two criminals', recorded Frieda. According to her, it changed Lawrence forever.

Despite the sour ending, Cornwall had at least gifted Lawrence the time and space to complete *Women in Love* – and while he had been rejected by Cornwall itself, he could at least retreat into the world of his novel, a place where he could live apart from what he thought was a 'foul world'. But even Lawrence himself was unsure of his fictional world, and he wasn't sure if he hated the novel. By the end of October he had given himself over to the process instead – he was ready for his fictional world to be given life through publication. The final pages were sent to Pinker with a note: 'It is a terrible and horrible and wonderful novel. You will hate it and nobody will publish it. But there, these things are beyond us.'[8]

Lawrence was initially correct in at least one of his predictions. In early 1917 Pinker offered *Women in Love* to Methuen (he was obliged to) but they refused it – as did the 'faithful' Duckworth. Lawrence feigned indifference to this turn of events, as the spurned artist is oft to do, but he still wanted Pinker to send him progress updates, asking him relentlessly how far he had got with it and what the publishers were saying. He was also still trying to make good his escape from England, as though his absence would somehow negate the impact of further rejection. He enlisted the help of several of his London friends for the necessary forms to renew his and Frieda's passports and was assured by civil-servant friend Eddie Marsh that he would be allowed to travel if he could show evidence of necessity, but that Frieda's nationality would be the main sticking point. Lawrence planned to list three reasons: his continuing ill health, his failure to make money in England, and the necessity to publish *The Rainbow* and *Women in Love*; and place his short stories and articles so that he had an income. Lawrence wanted to be in the place that he thought would give him the best chance of being accepted and succeeding as a writer. And that place was America.

The rejection of *Women in Love* by the publishing houses was to be expected, but it was probably a surprise to Lawrence that among his circle of friends there was only a handful who were prepared to speak in favourable terms about the novel. The issue wasn't helped by the fact that several of them recognised aspects of their own personalities in Lawrence's 'fictional' characters – notably Ottoline Morrell, who found Lawrence's use of her as inspiration for the character of Hermione utterly unforgiveable. When she received the manuscript and read the novel, she went 'pale with horror...nothing could have been more vile and obviously spiteful and contemptuous than the portrait of me that I found there':

> *I was called every name from an 'old hag,' obsessed by sex-mania, to a corrupt Sapphist. He described me as his own discarded Mistress, who, in my sitting-room, which was minutely described, had tried to bash him over the head with a paper weight...In another scene I had attempted to make indecent advances to the Heroine, who was a glorified Frieda. My dresses were dirty; I was rude and insolent to my guests...*[9]

The Morrells threatened to bring action for libel if the manuscript was published as it stood, but it never came to that – ostensibly because the novel was unpublishable as it was, and the three years it would take Lawrence to get it published gave him the opportunity to revise and reshape it. But the damage was done. Ottoline's overriding feeling was one of betrayal rather than anger. 'The hurt that he had done me made a very great mark in my life', she said of their fractured relationship. She never saw Lawrence again.

While Lawrence waited for the opportune moment to make good his escape to America, his thoughts turned to American literature, and he began a series of essays on the subject – initially as a money-earner. But just as his work on Thomas Hardy had been about 'anything but Thomas Hardy', his new project took a similarly esoteric turn. Using the literature of Poe, Hawthorne and Melville among others, he argued that love is the most important force for humanity and reveaed more about his own psychological and moral beliefs than those of the authors he was examining. Six years later, it was published as *Studies in Classic American Literature* (1923). It was reissued ten years later – three years after Lawrence's death – and was still raising perplexed eyebrows among the critics even then.

'D. H. Lawrence uses these persons [the authors] and their writings as pegs on which to hang his own self and philosophy', commented one. 'There is in the book far more of Lawrence than of any American writer – and perhaps the book is all the more interesting and valuable on this account.'[10] The critic also remarked on 'Lawrence's staccato sentences, hurrying out from an over-charged mind and almost falling over one another'.[11] It was all very un-scholarly, particularly with phrases such as 'Flop goes spiritual love', and 'The perfectibility of Man! Ah heaven, what a dreary theme!'[12]

But as was typical of Lawrence, he turned a work of non-fiction into a mode of self-expression – his author's voice coming to the fore and drowning out any objective assessment of the literature he was critiquing. As ever for Lawrence, what may have begun life as a dispassionate examination of the canon of American authors of the eighteenth and nineteenth century became an opportunity for him to communicate his own insights. And in a moment of glaring self-awareness he observes, 'Never trust the artist. Trust the tale'.[13]

The work also coincided with Lawrence's new acquaintance with two young American journalists, Robert Mountsier and Esther Andrews. The pair had visited the Lawrences over the Christmas and New Year of 1916–17 and Andrews lodged with the Lawrences on her own in late spring 1917. With the insight that only an American native could provide, Mountsier helped Lawrence develop his essays, and Andrews's visits probably encouraged Lawrence to further his plans for residency in the States. He was by now certain of his decision, and although he recognised all that was 'worse...falser' about America, he also recognised a fast-moving, progressive society that was closer to freedom than England, which was on a slow path to certain death.

But Lawrence's plans were delayed yet again in April 1917, when the USA declared war on Germany. 'Bravo, Uncle Sam!' the *Sunday Mirror* ran as their headline. 'And now let us raise our glasses to the United States of Britain and America and all their gallant Allies',[14] the reporter enthused. But Lawrence had little to toast or celebrate. Apart from working on the American literature essays, and revising *Women in Love* and rewriting his philosophy, he only had one book published in 1917, by Chatto and Windus – a small volume of poetry titled *Look! We Have Come Through!*, which centred on his fledgling relationship with Frieda during 1912–13. It was an intensely personal collection of poems that Lawrence had always been reluctant to publish, but his outlook on love and his concept of two people being together but maintaining their autonomy was also emerging, and the poems were revised accordingly.

The optimistic title of the volume was a rare flash of hope in a time of abject misery for so many. By the autumn of 1917 the British public were reminded daily of the dreadful toll the war was taking on their menfolk. Passchendaele had ensured 90,000 Allied casualties in the first two months of battle and suspicion of anti-war sentiment had reached fever pitch. This air of suspicion was made tangible in the Lawrences's eviction from Cornwall, and under the Defence of the Realm Act the couple were forbidden to reside in the county or any coastal region or port.

With their meagre belongings packed up, the Lawrences left Cornwall on 15 October 1917 bound for London; homeless and with their dreams of rural living shattered.

Chapter 11

Exile

I will not live any more in this time…I know what it is.
I reject it. As far as I possibly can, I will stand outside this time.
I will live my life and, if possible, be happy. Though the whole world slides in
horror down into the bottomless pit…[1]

The Lawrences's removal from Cornwall did little to remove the stain of suspicion. Instead it followed them to London, where they were ordered to register at the nearest police station and put under surveillance. Fortunately several of their acquaintances and friends rallied around them to provide a roof over their heads. Initially, Dollie Radford provided space for them at her terraced house in Hampstead, but Lawrence was thoroughly displeased to be back in the city. 'I hate London', he wrote to Catherine Carswell, and as far as Lawrence was concerned the feeling was justified. Everywhere he went he was confronted by reminders of the war he so vehemently opposed. 'London is really very bad: gone mad, in fact. It thinks and breathes and lives air-raids, nothing else', he remarked in a letter. He signed off with a comment that echoed what was going on abroad: 'It is like being slowly suffocated in mud.'

Fortunately for Lawrence, and unlike many other men his age, he would never experience that sensation during the war years – beyond what his imagination could muster. But London did affect both Lawrence and Frieda physically, albeit in a minor way to begin with. Frieda caught a cold and took to her bed within days of their arrival in the metropolis, and Lawrence then came down with something similar that went onto his chest. But undoubtedly, being reconnected with some semblance of a friendship network and being immersed in wider society was good for them both. Two weeks after their arrival, Lawrence was no longer in a hurry to go back to Cornwall, at least not immediately. He felt 'vitally active' in London and being around others was giving him a 'strange new response'.

In some respects, their situation forced them into mixing with other people – new acquaintances and old friends alike. Being homeless meant they were relying on the generosity of those around them to provide support, and often found themselves co-habiting with the other guests and friends of their host. This was certainly true when they moved into H. D.'s (Hilda Doolittle) tiny flat in Mecklenburgh Square in the heart of Bloomsbury. It was already providing lodgings for Arabella Yorke – her husband, Richard Aldington's, mistress – and at times a translator called John Cournos. Space was at a premium, so the Lawrences had no choice but to rub along with whomever happened to be staying in the same abode. Aldington also visited Mecklenburgh Square when he was on leave from the army, whether to see his wife or lover (or both) isn't known, but at least he had the convenience of knowing they were in the same place. This no doubt caused a degree of awkwardness for all parties, including Lawrence and Frieda.

Following a month in Mecklenburgh Square, their composer friend Cecil Gray convinced his mother to lend them her flat in Earls Court Square, although Lawrence confessed he 'loathed' the 'bourgeois little flat'. They stayed for as long as Lawrence could tolerate his surroundings (which included a retired Admiral in the flat downstairs), which was approximately two weeks before they moved on again – this time back to H.D.'s flat, before travelling out of London to Hermitage in Berkshire where Dollie Radford had a cottage she could lend if her daughter and her did not need it. The Lawrences also travelled back to the Midlands to stay with Lawrence's sister Ada Clarke – Lawrence finding that he felt 'better and happier in the country'.

Lawrence also conceived another fictional world. If he couldn't put down roots in real life then he would do so in his imagination. The 'Island' Lawrence conceived was in the Andes, and it became 'so concrete and real' to him that it 'occupied his heart'.

Unsurprisingly, their chaotic existence moving around from house to house and room to room meant that Lawrence got very little work done. He tried to learn Greek. Frieda made an evening dress. Lawrence learnt songs. They both got ill. And so the cycle continued into early 1918.

Look! We Have Come Through! was published at the end of November 1917, and by the early months of 1918, it was clear it was following a similar trajectory as Lawrence's other published works. The critics were confused – the critic writing for *The Sketch* couldn't even get past the book's jacket, commenting that the 'incomprehensible Futurist cover-design which looks like a mixture of two broken combs and the fragments of a knife-cleaner, ought to warn you to expect something desperately eccentric'.[2] Lawrence, though, seemed to be happy with the finished volume, although he conceded it was a little gaudy.

As for what was inside the garish jacket, the *Times Literary Supplement* were their usual disparaging selves, writing that 'we need hardly say that he has much of the art of writing and avoids banality. By no means, however, does he avoid verbiage,' which was 'varied by orgies of extreme eroticism'. The review concludes with a final, damning statement: 'An excited morbid babble about one's own emotions which the Muse of poetry surely can only turn from with a pained distaste'.[3] Lawrence was now used to such barbs, writing resignedly to American poet Amy Lowell that, 'as usual the critics fall on me…I don't really care what critics say, so long as I myself could personally be left in peace'.[4]

But Lawrence was very far from being left in peace. Instead he was consistently hounded at the end of 1917 by the authorities, who would periodically arrive wherever the Lawrences were residing; on one occasion even accosting Cyril Gray and demanding information from him on the couple. 'We are followed everywhere', Lawrence lamented to Cynthia Asquith, '…it is *very* maddening.' The pressure of being under surveillance seemed to ease when the Lawrences departed London for Dollie Radford's cottage in Hermitage. Instead they now faced a different sort of pressure – finding enough money to survive what Lawrence called the 'fag end of poverty'. They took to trawling the woods around the cottage for wood chips left behind by the local woodsmen, and Lawrence complained to Pinker that if the situation continued he wouldn't even have money for a loaf of bread and margarine. Lawrence was not unduly bothered – although he recognised that perhaps if he was, he would ensure he was a better provider. What bothered Lawrence more was the boredom of being penniless, and the impact that had on his creativity. 'I shall have to turn beggar', he wrote to Lady Asquith. Or find a patron, although he clearly wasn't keen on the idea of having to engage with said patron: '…if you know anybody that would be likely to patronise me – at a distance – I am very happy to be patronised – at a distance – why not…It is time I found my Pharoah – but the connection would have to be distant.'[5] Frieda was concerned less about the lack of money and more that its absence would contribute to Lawrence's 'seediness'. She wrote to Koteliansky in February 1918, 'There's no money, no house, nothing…It is quite a struggle now to exist – getting food and everything.'[6]

The cottage had brought them geographical distance, but now Lawrence craved mental and emotional isolation. The experience of being spied upon had left him both angry and paranoid, and thoughts of someone creeping up behind him haunted him. Lawrence's dire financial circumstances eventually drove him out of his hermit-like existence and forced him back into some semblance of society. In the spring of 1918 Lawrence was considering Ada's suggestion that he move back to the Midlands so that she could assist him financially. Lawrence couldn't afford to refuse, but he knew the sort of place he wanted: a house that was isolated so he wouldn't be 'jammed in amongst people' anymore. A move back to the Midlands would be on his terms, and so Mountain Cottage, on the edge of a steep valley in the 'navel of England', near Middleton, Wirksworth, was a natural choice.

Lawrence and Frieda arrived back where they started their relationship just six years earlier on 2 May 1918, feeling 'queer and lost and exiled'. Yet surprisingly – and probably to Lawrence's surprise too – he was soon received back into the bosom of his family and Eastwood friends and found that it was good for him. On 28 May he saw his father again for the first time in years, along with Emily King (Lawrence's elder sister) and her daughter Margaret (Peggy), and Ada's son Jack. His nieces and nephew visited frequently that summer, often staying for several weeks, and Lawrence was a doting uncle. He conceded it was 'a bit irritating, to be en famillie again' but that being with people was 'soporific'; 'it saves one', he commented. The presence of the children no doubt drew Lawrence out of his introspection. Unencumbered by the opinions, judgements and expectations that Lawrence frequently butted heads with, they acted as levellers. They also provided a distraction from his natural propensity for introspection. 'I was very glad of their presence', he remarked.

Remarkably, his attitude towards his native town of Eastwood – a place he had denounced but ten years earlier – also mellowed. He told Mark Gertler he felt 'quite amicably' towards it. Yet he was never quite settled enough in the Midlands to reach the same levels of creativity he had had before to 1915. He did, at least, complete his American essays in draft form at the end of the summer of 1918, but he also had to contend with the shocking realisation that he *might* still be called up – even at this late stage of the war, irrespective of his poor health. A physical examination in September left Lawrence feeling utterly disgusted. He was given a Grade III classification, which meant he was 'Fit for non-military service.' In other words, he could be called upon to perform a clerical or sedentary role as part of the war effort. Lawrence was furious about the entire episode – from being 'pawed by the swine' to fears that he would have to re-enter the workplace (ideally for Lawrence, at the Ministry of Education) so that he could avoid being 'kicked about like an old can'.

It was probably not a coincidence that the Lawrences absented themselves from Mountain Cottage during October and November. 'I shall just remove myself and be a deserter', he told Lady Asquith. 'I'm out on a new track – let humanity go its way – I go mine.'[7] Instead they moved about – dividing their time between friends in London and Dollie Radford's cottage in Berkshire. The couple were in Hermitage when the Armistice was declared on 11 November – and it has been suggested that the 'Nightmare' chapter of *Kangaroo* (1923) describes how the couple might have spent that evening, singing German songs and with Frieda crying – although transplanted to St Ives in Cornwall, rather than Berkshire.[8] 'Lawrence knew it signalled a fresh opportunity to leave England. But there was no sense of rejoicing. 'How strange peace is. Is it peace?' Lawrence commented just after the Armistice. Lawrence and Frieda's feelings about the Armistice were at odds with the general cheeriness of the nation. Rather than the happy outcome celebrated by everyone else, they recognised the temporality of the previous four years of bloodshed. Instead of peace, all that war had done was provoke further hate and evil, thus leading to another war in the future.

Yet Lawrence was sure of two things following the Great War: that it certainly didn't mean 'peace' as everyone hoped – writing somewhat portentously in a letter that, 'even if this war ends in our lifetime, war in the same sort will go on'; and that for him personally, it was better for him to die than to do something that he felt violated his soul. Death may not have been 'desirable' for Lawrence for many reasons when it did eventually come for him in 1930. But in some respects it was his salvation. 'It is so sure, death, that one is always strong in it', he wrote during one bout of illness in 1916. 'It is only the faith in what is beyond, that saves us.'

Chapter 12
The Savage Pilgrimage

It has been a savage enough pilgrimage...We keep faith.
I always feel death only strengthens that –
the faith between those who have it.[1]

L awrence's faith in the beyond was put to the test in dramatic fashion in early 1919. As the jubilant mood that immediately followed the Armistice waned, a new enemy lurked in the shadows, and this time it was invisible. The country was amid the Great Influenza epidemic of 1918–1920 – and just as the Great War had devastated Europe's population of young adults, so too did the 'Great' epidemic. Unlike most influenza outbreaks that disproportionately preyed on the young and old, the 'Spanish Flu' – as it unjustly came to be called – had an unusually high mortality rate in young people. On 13 February 1919, the *Derby Daily Telegraph* published the following advice, under the rather disheartening headline 'Weak People Catch Colds': 'When a person is strong, hearty, able to enjoy a brisk, cold day, chills and infections are set at defiance. But when the system is below par, run down, bloodless and nervous, the germs influenza are quick to seize their opportunity. Go to bed at the first feverish sign of influenza, eat little or nothing, and call the doctor'.[2]

Lawrence was right to be concerned. Even within his own circle, the epidemic was wreaking havoc. Don Carswell, husband of Lawrence's friend Catherine, went down with it in late 1918 – as did Lawrence's sister Ada, who was 'rather sick and wretched'. Kot was ill with flu over the festive season of 1918 and Lawrence was forced to confront mortality again with the death of one of his childhood friends from Eastwood, Frances 'Frankie' Cooper. Frankie was consumptive, so her death wasn't unexpected, but with Katherine Mansfield's recent diagnosis of the same chronic condition – as well as his own medical history of ongoing infections – the influenza epidemic was a very real and grave danger to him.

He began 1919 well enough. But the recurring sense of feeling trapped – in poverty, in England, and probably inside his own head too – plagued him just as it had in the latter half of 1918. He felt 'paralysed' and 'caged' – trapped by their lack of money, and the after effects of the war – although he conceded it was better than being 'tied tight to a job', or 'to a sickness'. Lawrence was currently tied to neither, and so he began to think about leaving England again, and he was more determined than ever. 'I must get out of England, of Europe', was his refrain throughout early 1919. He wrote to Cornish farmer and friend William Henry Hocking to tell him that he and Frieda would probably be going abroad and had decided to give up the smaller of the two Tregerthen Cottages they had stayed in from March 1916 to October 1917 and that he could sell the furniture.

It was a practical step, taken with intention. They *could* go back to Cornwall now the war was over, if they wished, but they chose not to. Around the same time, Lawrence also completed a non-fiction commission for Oxford University Press – an educational textbook titled *Movements in European History*. It was a potboiler – Lawrence himself made no attempt to claim otherwise, although in the end he was 'rather pleased with it' – but he hoped the money it would bring in would provide some relief to their circumstances. It was eventually published in 1921 under the pseudonym 'Lawrence H. Davison' due to the controversy surrounding Lawrence's fictional works.

The bad weather in Derbyshire at the beginning of the year (Lawrence described it as 'vicious') meant the couple had limited opportunities to leave the house. Instead Lawrence spent his time contemplating their plans to go abroad and writing letters to all his friends and associates telling them how much he wanted – no, *needed* – to leave England. The weather suited his mood – all was 'gloomy', the air was 'poisonous' and although there was snow on the ground, it was under a 'dark sky'. Even the windows were covered with what Lawrence called 'ice flowers', obscuring their view 'as if in a frozen under-sea'. Lawrence was once again plagued by a cold and took to his bed.

A visit from Lawrence's eldest sister Emily and his niece in early February brought some relief from the solemn atmosphere of Mountain Cottage as well as a short hiatus in Lawrence's disagreeable attitude – in his letters at least. Writing to Katherine Mansfield on 9 February, Lawrence returns to form, describing vividly the world outside his window:

I climbed with my niece to the bare top of the hills… The upland is naked, white like silver, and moving far into the distance, strange and muscular, with gleams like skin. Only the wind surprises one, invisibly cold; the sun lies bright on a field, like the movement of a sleeper. It is strange how insignificant, in all this, life seems. Two men, tiny as dots, move from a farm on a snow-slope, carrying hay to the beast. Every moment, they seem to melt like insignificant spots of dust.[3]

The creative release Lawrence gained from being immersed in nature again is profound. He drew his energy from such experiences. The scene that follows – of domestic bliss inside the little cottage – and the warmth of human nature he conveys is the perfect juxtaposition – sitting as it does in the wide, cold landscape of the hills.

The sense of contentment Lawrence seemed to achieve that day wasn't set to last, despite a rhetorical appeal: 'While we live, let us live.' A week later, Lawrence collapsed at his sister Ada's house in Ripley. He had caught influenza – but this time it came with 'complications' due to the poor health of Lawrence's lungs. He came close to death again, and his recovery was slow – he couldn't even sit up in bed and write a letter until 26 February, and he didn't venture out of bed to sit in a chair until 2 March. By 6 March he was contemplating an attempt to 'creep downstairs' so that he could rejoin his family and by 10 March he was managing to negotiate the stairs for tea, although he described himself as 'wretched…like a drowned ghost creeping downstairs'. The 'putrid disease', as Lawrence described it, had him trapped again. There was no question of going back to Mountain Cottage until he was sufficiently recovered – a state of health he wouldn't achieve until 17 March, a full month after his collapse. Even then he still needed injections for his lungs and Ada to nurse him ('she is the responsible nurse', he told Kot – clearly he didn't trust in his wife's skills), so she travelled back to Middleton with Lawrence and Frieda.

Inevitably the illness didn't just bring Lawrence down in body, but in mind also. Life was 'unbearably foul', and the world seemed 'so nasty' that Lawrence was reluctant to rejoin it. Predictably, this mood affected his attitude towards Frieda, whose famous lack of sympathy for illness did her no favours in Lawrence's mind, so much so that he told Kot he could leave her without 'a pang of guilt'.

Just as Ursula in *Women in Love* feels 'repulsed' by illness, asking Birkin, 'But doesn't it make you feel ashamed? I think it makes one so ashamed, to be ill – illness is so terribly humiliating, don't you think?'[4] Frieda similarly saw illness as evidence of physical and mental weakness. It was just as well Ada was there to act as a buffer between the warring couple. But the reality was, there was no truth to Lawrence's assertion that he would leave Frieda – it was just one example of many in which Lawrence or Frieda declared their intention to break with the other. These empty threats were a constant feature of their life together, and while they invariably drove each other to extremes of emotion, the foundations of their relationship were strong enough to weather these moments of frustration. Yet it did mark the beginning of another challenging phase in their relationship.

Frieda knew better than to rise to Lawrence's frustrations during his convalescence. She may not have expressed her worries outwardly, but her concern for his health was so great that she barely slept during his illness. She wrote to Kot, 'It's been pitiful to see him try so hard to *live* if he *hadn't*, it would have been all over. I feel so bitter, so bitter against the world, if they had only given him *some* response, he would be happy! I feel two-hundred years old – haven't slept at all.'⁵ Frieda rightly surmised that Lawrence's anger was misdirected – what he *really* railed against wasn't her but the rest of the world. But he was alive. He had cheated death again.

Lawrence was left feeling weak and depressed, but above all he was irritable: with the snow and the 'blank stupidity' of life, but most of all with his own ill-health. He was still convalescing into April – although he did at least manage to pick up his pen again to revise *Movements in European History* in early April, and by the end of the month he was in good spirits, rejoicing in a letter to Kot that he was now a 'free man' because he had completed the manuscript. That freedom opened the gates once again to a flurry of creativity, and Lawrence managed to write three new short stories in the space of six weeks: 'Fannie and Annie', 'Monkey Nuts' and 'Hadrian' (published as 'You Touched Me'). At Pinker's suggestion, Lawrence wrote these with the American market in mind. He also placed several stories in the *English Review* and the *Athenaeum*, and the *Strand* took 'Tickets Please'.

By the end of April, Lawrence was well enough to return to the cottage in Hermitage (and hopefully warmer climes) and he was able to resume his work on *Aaron's Rod* – a novel he had begun while living in London in the autumn of 1917, which tells the story of frustrated amateur flautist Aaron Sisson. In July, Lawrence heard the welcome news that 'The Fox' – a short story written in 1918 – had sold for £30 to *Hutchinson's Story Magazine*, as did *Touch and Go* – a play written by Lawrence in 1918, which was destined to be published in a series called *Plays For a People's Theatre* by C. W Daniel. The £30 he would receive for 'The Fox' was a healthy sum, but Lawrence wouldn't be able to benefit from the money until publication, and in the end it wasn't printed until November 1920. Nevertheless, Lawrence's output, and his overall success at placing his works, was increasing little by little during this time. By September English publisher Martin Secker was even expressing an interest in publishing *Women in Love*, although Lawrence was adamant that its first print should be in America because he would 'never forgive England *The Rainbow*'.

He was almost back on track – but it wasn't all down to his agent, J. B. Pinker. Lawrence was increasingly making his own contacts and sending his work out himself. After all, not having to pay a 10 per cent agent fee was an extremely tempting proposition for Lawrence in the cash-strapped years during the war and immediately following it – particularly as he felt Pinker hadn't fought his corner strenuously enough over the previous five years. Pinker had also unaccountably failed to send *Women in Love* to Lawrence's principal American publisher Benjamin Huebsch. This was only discovered later when Lawrence tried to place the novel himself and was offered a £50 advance for it by Thomas Seltzer – much to Huebsch's annoyance.

What Pinker had provided was a modicum of financial support, which cannot be overlooked. Even so, Lawrence had already considered breaking with Pinker in late 1918, and he now gave the idea serious consideration – but he had to be careful how he managed the situation. While Lawrence was recovering from influenza he also received an invite from John Middleton Murry, now editing the *Athenaeum*, to contribute to the journal. The essay 'Whistling of Birds' was printed under a pseudonym, 'Grantorto' – the only one of several pieces submitted by Lawrence to Murry that was accepted. The rest were rejected with a 'very editorial' note from Murry, the outcome of which was Lawrence's total break with his former friend.

Despite the slight improvement in Lawrence's fortunes (both financially and creatively) in England, he was still impatient to leave. His feet felt 'unfastened'; he could sense that he and Frieda would be departing soon, 'somewhere, somehow'. He was confident enough in this assertion to begin thinking about how he would support himself and Frieda, should he make it to his desired location, America. He hoped his American publisher Huebsch would arrange some lecturing for him. But privately, he had his reservations – and these were amplified by a letter he received from American poet Amy Lowell in which she warned Lawrence not to expect America to be an 'El Dorado'. 'I am afraid you will find America a very different place from what you imagine; and what will be disgusting to you, as it is to me, is that they cannot see the difference between envisaging life whole and complete, physical as well as spiritual, and pure obscenities like those perpetrated by James Joyce.'[6] Crucially though, she also warned him that he would be unwelcome in her little corner of the country, New England, for she had found *Sons and Lovers* in the 'locked up' section of the Boston Athenaeum. 'Now if a superb volume like that is not considered proper to put into the hands of the public, what can you think of the attitude over here?'[7] she wrote.

'I don't want El Dorado: only life and freedom', Lawrence replied. Six weeks later, Lawrence's doubts resurfaced. In a letter to Catherine Carswell he revealed that he didn't know where he and Frieda would eventually end up. Frieda had made clear her intention to return to Germany to see 'her people' – particularly her elderly mother – and she was finally able to make the journey on 15 October 1919, almost a year after the Armistice. Yet Lawrence felt no desire to accompany her, and he had also rethought his plan to travel to America. He also needed to be away from Frieda, for reasons that he never expressed explicitly, but undoubtedly her desire to lay down roots (like an 'unhappy hen' fluttering from 'roost to roost', according to Lawrence) was at odds with his constant indecision regarding where they should go when they left England. Lawrence liked 'not to have a home' but Frieda preferred to be rooted – even if that meant a temporary return to a country that was war-battered and broken: 'A sad, different Germany', Frieda observed.

Lawrence finally hit on a suitable destination – ironically, the one that made most sense – his beloved Italy. 'I want to go to Italy', he announced in his letters. And this time, he did.

On 14 November 1919, Lawrence finally bid farewell to England, sailing for the continent from Dover. 'Lawrence felt the wrench of the departure, but he was glad, very glad, to be going',[8] Catherine Carswell commented in her narrative of Lawrence, *The Savage Pilgrimage*. He didn't know it then, but he would only return to the 'corpse-grey cliffs'[9] three more times, in 1923, 1925 and 1926 – and even then for no more than twelve weeks in total. Viewed from the ship, England was a 'long, ash-grey coffin slowly submerging'[10] until it disappeared completely. The vision Lawrence recreated in *The Lost Girl* was probably close to how he felt about leaving the country of his birth. England had betrayed him, so now he turned his back on it – imagining it as dead meant Lawrence could disassociate himself from it. 'England' and 'Englishness' were no longer alive in him, and so he symbolically buried his association with it. Koteliansky, who had seen Lawrence off from London that day, recorded later that Lawrence was 'not like his best'.[11]

Lawrence was bound for the island of Capri, where he planned to spend the winter with fellow writer Compton Mackenzie. He made several pit-stops en route – stopping in Turin to stay with diplomat Sir Walter Becker and his wife, and then on to Florence via Lerici. In Florence he met up with novelist and essayist Norman Douglas and met for the first time the American writer Maurice Magnus. Douglas introduced him to other English and American 'personae non gratae' living on the continent – although Douglas was careful exactly whom he allowed Lawrence to meet, writing to his friend Reginald Turner that, 'I am going to prevent his [Lawrence] meeting certain other people, because he is a damned observant fellow and might be so amused at certain aspects of Florentine life as to use it for "copy" in some book: which would be annoying.'[12] From what we already know of Lawrence, they were right to be suspicious.

Lawrence waited in Florence for Frieda to arrive from Baden-Baden before heading south, enjoying the 'blessed insouciance' of the Italians. It was during his time in Florence that Lawrence wrote 'David' – an essay on Florence that takes the statue of 'David' as its central theme: 'Michaelangelo's David is the presiding genus of Florence. Not a shadow of a doubt about it. Once and for all, Florence. So young: sixteen, they say. So big: and stark naked. Revealed. Too big, too naked, too exposed. Livid under today's sky.'[13] This he sent to Murry, although its unconventional style and classical references make it difficult reading – the rain and 'perpetual sound of water' echoed throughout in the short, staccato sentences Lawrence used. But a more literary depiction of Florence did find its way into *Aaron's Rod*. The rain makes another appearance, but Lawrence captured the sense of it being a 'new world' through the eyes of his eponymous character:

> *Aaron went along close to the tall thick houses, following his nose. And suddenly he caught sight of the long slim neck of the Palazzo Vecchio up above, in the air. And in another minute he was passing between massive buildings, out into the Piazza della Signoria. There he stood still and looked round him in real surprise, and real joy. The flat empty square with it's stone paving was all wet. The great buildings rose dark. The dark, sheer front of the Palazzo Vecchio went up like a cliff, to the battlements, and the slim tower soared dark and hawk-like, crested, high above. And at the foot of the cliff stood the great naked David, white and stripped in the wet, white against the dark, warm-dark cliff of the building... And he felt that here he was in one of the world's living centres, here, in the Piazza della Signoria. The sense of having arrived – of having reached a perfect centre of the human world: this he had.*[14]

Lawrence was reunited with Frieda on 3 December and on 10 December they travelled to Rome, where according to Catherine Carswell's account of the events, they met with two misfortunes. First, they were refused entry to a pensione on account of Frieda's nationality. Fortunately, Carswell's friend agreed to provide them with temporary lodgings but while they were there, their money was stolen. This was a double blow to him because he had already had his wallet stolen in Florence, an incident that left Lawrence feeling as though 'his heart had dropped from his breast through the soles of his feet', and then a rising fury 'that flushed him to the roots of his hair'.[15] From Rome, they went to Picinisco ('*so* primitive, *so* cold', according to Lawrence) and then Naples via Atino and Cassino, to catch the boat to Capri. The last leg of their journey from Picinisco to Atina was a five-mile walk, followed by a ten-mile ride on a post omnibus from Atina to Cassino, and then a train journey to Naples. After more than twelve hours of non-stop travel, the couple were within sight of Capri but frustratingly the sea-level was too high for them to get from the boat to the shore. 'There was nothing for it but to go back and seek the semi-shelter of Sorrento, there to roll horribly all night with a shipload of moaning Italians',[16] writes Carswell.

Once in Capri, Lawrence and Frieda took an apartment of two beautiful rooms and a shared kitchen at the top of an old palazzo. The landscape was idyllic, and Capri was 'pleasant and bohemian', but Lawrence was rather less enamoured with the cosmopolitan society that populated the island. 'The English-speaking crowd are the uttermost uttermost limit for spiteful scandal', Lawrence wrote to Catherine Carswell. 'London is a prayer meeting in comparison.'[17] Frieda also complained, writing in her memoir: 'I didn't like Capri; it was so small an island, it hardly seemed capable to contain all the gossip that flourished there.'[18]

In contrast to the previous year, in which Lawrence and Frieda had spent Christmas Day at Ada's house in Ripley lamenting that the fact that the new year would bring 'the same dreariness as before', and a feeling of paralysis, Frieda and Lawrence spent Christmas Day 1919 in a 'little apartment of our own', watching the ships sailing into the bay of Naples, and out again to Africa, wondering what the future held. Lawrence still felt as though he was merely en route to somewhere else, and Capri was just a 'stepping-stone' rather than an 'abiding place'.

Before the year was out though, he took decisive action regarding his professional relationship with Pinker. On 27 December, Lawrence wrote to him expressing his view that there was little point in them being bound to one another as author and agent, and that he wished to break their agreement. The man credited as being one of the first modern literary agents only lived a further two years, dying in a New York hotel in February 1922. By then, a bitterness had set in – brought about by various legal complications regarding the rights to Lawrence's works. A lack of confidence on both sides led to a certain amount of viciousness from Lawrence and on hearing of Pinker's death and the subsequent take-over of his literary agency by his sons he wrote, 'One's enemies fall slowly but surely into oblivion. The sons are said to be semi-idiot.'[19] The words were condescending, not to mention rude – but oddly they would turn out to be prophetic with regard to Pinker's sons. Eric and Ralph Pinker, who took over from their father in New York and London, undid much of their father's hard work. Both ended up in prison on charges related to diverting authors' royalties into their own pockets.

Lawrence stayed in Capri for as long as his tolerance would allow – which amounted to a little over two months. Life within the inner circle of Capri's expatriate society, of which his friend Compton Mackenzie was at the centre, provided creative fodder for Lawrence for a short time, as well as some amusing anecdotes in his letters home. He could observe their goings-on mostly unnoticed – after all, he and Frieda were the 'Poor Relations at the other end of the table' – as well as hearing various bits of tittle-tattle from their friend Mary Cannan, who was also on the island and staying with an 'arch-scandalmonger', according to Lawrence. But even he would tire of the constant gossip, eventually deciding that he was 'very sick of Capri'. Yet the irony that he himself had a huge capacity for spite and gossip in his letters – many of which he sent at this time contained unflattering accounts of other people's behaviour and way of life – was lost on Lawrence. And his most injurious letter was yet to come, for it was in early 1920 – just before his departure from Capri – that Lawrence turned on two of his oldest acquaintances, Katherine Mansfield and John Middleton Murry.

'Lawrence sent me a letter today', Katherine wrote to Murry in early February, 'he spat in my face and threw filth at me'.[20] Lawrence's letter was in response to her own letter describing the impact of her illness on her emotional state, but also her practical arrangements since she couldn't engage an Italian maid because of her disease. Katherine then relates exactly what Lawrence had written: 'I loathe you, you revolt me stewing in your consumption…The Italians were quite right to have nothing to do with you.'[21] The words are shocking, even from an objective standpoint, but Lawrence biographer John Worthen offers the most sensible and impartial reason Lawrence so suddenly, and viciously, turned against Katherine – and was so calculating in his choice of words. Worthen suggests that the combination of postal strikes in Italy and Lawrence's ongoing frustration with getting his work into print (a matter of days before, Lawrence had discovered that Pinker had never sent *Women in Love* to America) exacerbated his venomous outpouring. Murry had also just returned the articles Lawrence had provided for the *Athenaeum*, which no doubt irritated Lawrence, especially as he'd pledged to himself not to send work to Murry again but had evidently rescinded that idea. His reaction was to call Murry a 'dirty little worm', but worse than that, the articles had been returned from Katherine's address in Italy, where Murry had been staying in December and January – the same address from where she'd written to Lawrence complaining about her isolated circumstances and disease, with no mention of the articles. Her letter had been delayed in reaching Lawrence, and she'd had no knowledge of the articles when she wrote it – but given the address on the letter, Lawrence jumped to the conclusion that she had been part of the decision to refuse them, and was deliberately obscuring the fact, while 'still asking for his sympathy'. It was a low blow to use Katherine's illness to attack her – particularly as he was frequently ill himself (although still undiagnosed as consumptive at this point) – and a dreadful way to end a relationship that although bumpy at times had genuine fondness on both sides. 'The episode gives us a momentary revelation, for once preserved, of what he could be like when really vengeful', writes Worthen. 'He not only believed in saying what he felt; he could be calculatedly vicious, too.'[22]

Murry subsequently wrote to Lawrence telling him that he hoped they would never meet again, because if they did meet again, Murry would 'thrash' him. Yet astonishingly, both Murry and Mansfield eventually forgave Lawrence – an act of charity that was, arguably, undeserved – but Lawrence never forgave either of them. Katherine's weakness, poured out to Lawrence in the letter that formed the crux of the episode, was his own. Her self-indulgent introspection was a trait she shared with Lawrence, and his violent reaction was the result of being confronted with an aspect of his own character that he was clearly uncomfortable with.

Shortly after this depressing episode, the Lawrences left Capri. All Lawrence had written during their stay was the first draft of *Psychoanalysis and the Unconscious* and made another start on the manuscript of 'The Insurrection of Miss Houghton', which had been languishing in Germany since 1916, and begun three years before that. What was more pressing was their need to move from Capri and find a more permanent dwelling further south. They ended up in Taormina in Sicily, where Lawrence discovered a 'lovely house and garden'. The 'Fontana Vecchia,' (Old Fountain) was set away from the main town in its own landscape of fields and gardens. Lawrence called its location the 'brink of Europe'. They planned to stay a year so that Lawrence could earn the money they needed to travel onwards again. The savage pilgrimage had only just begun.

Chapter 13

Affairs of Love and Literature

A kiss, and a vivid spasm of farewell, a moment's orgasm of rupture.
Then along the damp road alone, till the next turning.
And there, a new partner, a new parting, a new unfusing into the twain,
A new gasp of further isolation,
A new intoxication of loneliness, among decaying, frost-cold leaves.[1]

Lawrence's new landscape in Sicily seemed to bring a renewed enthusiasm for writing. Not only did he work feverishly on the 'forgotten' manuscript he'd had sent from Germany – now renamed *The Lost Girl*, which seems apt given how long it was missing for – he also began work on *Mr Noon*, a sardonic tale about a young Nottinghamshire schoolmaster, Gilbert Noon, who loses his job due to a romantic encounter and subsequent unplanned pregnancy. The young bounder, whose story is loosely based on that of Lawrence's childhood friend George Neville, then decides to leave England for Munich to escape the narrow expectations of provincial middle-class society. Lawrence also returned to *Aaron's Rod* in the summer of 1920, although it remained unfinished for another year.

The three novels formed a witty commentary on English society, although they had Lawrence's customary disillusionment with middle-class marriage and love at their core. He returned to the theme of love in the autumn of 1920 in a sequence of poems that were later published in a volume titled *Birds, Beasts and Flowers* (1923). The poems have been regarded as some of Lawrence's best. In them he presents the reader with his reflections on the natural world – both internally and externally, human and non-human – and the 'otherness' that is inherent in so many of Lawrence's works. He challenges the reader to reflect on the idea of process rather than appearance, deliberately creating tension through his exploration of creation and decay, as well as the unconscious and the consciousness, pain and pleasure, and the self and the other.

Lawrence also had another influence at this time – Rosalind Baynes. Lawrence first became acquainted with Rosalind in the spring of 1919 via the poet and writer Eleanor Farjeon. At that time Rosalind had recently separated from her husband, the doctor Godwin Baynes, and was planning to escape to Italy with her children. Whilst 'house sitting' herself she lent Frieda and Lawrence the use of her own house in Pangbourne, Berkshire and a friendship was struck up. Lawrence continued his correspondence with Rosalind, providing practical advice regarding life in Italy, and she took up his recommendation on where to stay when they arrived. Rosalind and her children eventually settled in the Villa La Canovaia just outside Florence, but they had been forced to evacuate it when the windows were blown in following an explosion in the nearby powder factory. They moved to another local villa, leaving La Canovaia empty barring the gardener and his family.

In early autumn 1920, Lawrence found himself in Florence. Sicily had proved far too hot in late spring and into summer and after an aborted trip to Malta – Lawrence likened it to being in a 'biscuit oven for a month' – Frieda decided to go to Baden-Baden to see her mother, and Lawrence to Florence via Milan, Lago di Como and Venice. The accommodation in Florence didn't suit Lawrence ('too intimate – old ladies', he commented) and so on 3 September Rosalind lent him the window-less villa she had vacated so that he could camp somewhere, which Lawrence found to be 'great fun', even though he was, ostensibly, alone.

But Lawrence wasn't completely alone. It was during this time that Lawrence had a very brief affair with Rosalind. The only account in existence is Rosalind's for Lawrence makes no reference to it in any of his letters – not even those to Rosalind herself. According to Rosalind, the two of them took a walk together sometime around Thursday 9 September, and the subject of conversation turned to sex and their mutual fastidiousness. To Rosalind's surprise, Lawrence asked if they might 'have a sex time together', to which she was happy to agree, telling Lawrence, 'Yes, indeed I want it.'[2] They embraced and kissed in agreement, but did not rush into their intimacy, preferring instead to wait until they were both sure of their decision. Lawrence spent the following Sunday with Rosalind, helping her to make dinner and playing with her children, before taking a walk together at sunset. Rosalind's memoir describes the moment just before their union:

'*How good it is here. It is something quite special and lovely, the time, the place, the beloved.*'
  My heart jumps with joy. We sit there until it is quite dark, our hands held together in union. And so to bed.[3]

The poems that were the result of this experience combine what Lawrence saw, felt and tasted that day *before* he slept with Rosalind. The sexual undertone comes from our knowledge of what came to pass immediately afterwards. Indeed, knowing the events that inspired these poems gives them their meaning. As Rosalind explains,

We walked out after the heat was over, up behind Fiesole town through the trees and the passing Sunday strollers. Italian girls in fluffy voile dresses along the country roads. We saw the black grapes – 'black to make you stare.' [Lawrence writes in *Grapes*, 'Look how black, how blue-black, how gloved in/ Ethiopian darkness] *We saw the grand turkey cock…* [in *Turkey-Cock* he writes, 'Your sort of gorgeousness/ Dark and lustrous]… *We come down the long rather squalid village street. Sorb-apples we buy –* 'Suck them and then spit out the skin!' ['I love to suck you out from your skins', Lawrence writes] – *and home with things to cook for our supper on the terrace, three hundred feet above Firenze.*

This was as close as Lawrence got to admitting the affair on paper. Yet the poems also speak of decay; the ending of the relationship is just as sure as the 'grape turning raisin', leaving nothing but 'intoxication of loneliness'. The affair was over as quickly as it had started – a few days after Lawrence slept with Rosalind for the first time he wrote to a friend that he didn't want to wait for Frieda to join him in Florence and that he was considering a return to Capri. It later transpired that Lawrence felt the affair had been 'a miserable failure',[4] although this account was from the pen of Mabel Sterne, whose remembrance of details was decidedly shaky.

Unsurprisingly, Frieda hated *Birds, Beasts and Flowers*, and although Rosalind's admission came well after Frieda's death, and Lawrence never confirmed the truth of the matter to Frieda in his own lifetime, she almost certainly guessed it herself. If she had, she was unlikely to have minded for very long – after an initial outburst of anger, her own loose interpretation of marital values would have protected her from any ongoing emotional distress the situation was likely to cause. If anything, it affected Lawrence more profoundly, and his reflections on his brief affair with Rosalind took shape on paper in the relationship between Aaron Sisson and the Marchesa he makes love to in *Aaron's Rod*. Aaron is left similarly dissatisfied with the affair: 'He wanted to be gone. He wanted to get out of her arms and her clinging and her tangle of hair and her curiosity and her strange and hateful power,' Lawrence wrote in *Aaron's Rod*. The experience leaves Aaron 'withered' and 'scorched' and he is thankful he can 'go to bed, alone, in his own cold bed, alone, thank God'.[5] Thus it is relief that courses through Aaron/ Lawrence's veins, rather than passion or any desire to repeat the experience.

Lawrence left Florence for Venice on 28 September, leaving behind any thoughts of Rosalind, save writing her a note to thank her for the panforte she gave him to eat on the train. He had several days of 'mouching about' waiting for Frieda to arrive – which he was well and truly sick of by the time she did on 7 October. The couple returned to Taormina in Sicily on 18 October, and shortly afterwards, copies of *The Lost Girl* arrived from Secker (looking 'brown and demure' according to Lawrence), and a set of proofs of the English edition of *Women in Love*. The following two months followed a familiar pattern for Lawrence – a sense of nervous excitement that his work was going to be imminently published, followed swiftly by the crashing disappointment of a less than enthusiastic reception. And this was despite various alterations that he had been asked to make to the novels to make them more palatable to audiences on both sides of the Atlantic.

But Lawrence's biggest concern was how *Women in Love* would be received: 'it is the book I have most at heart', he wrote to Secker in late November. It was enough to make him question whether review copies should be sent out, and whether it would be better just to publish it regardless. The geographical distance he had put between himself and England wasn't enough to mitigate his feelings towards the publishing fraternity and its 'poisonous' critics back home. He turned to painting as a diversion – copying a painting from the Uffizi in Florence, *La Tebaide*, and attributing it to Lorenzetti.

While Lawrence awaited the coming storm (quite literally – the weather had been atrocious since their return to Sicily), he turned his thoughts to *Mr Noon* again. He was struggling to end *Aaron's Rod* and so he poured his frustrations into *Mr Noon* instead. The result was an obvious attack on both the 'imbecile reader' and the 'darling' critics whom Lawrence begs, 'don't *look* at the nasty book anymore: don't you then: there, there, don't cry, my pretty.'[6]

Yet reviews of *The Lost Girl*, when they did come, were decidedly mixed. It wasn't the outright dismissal that Lawrence had been expecting and the book *was* selling – albeit slowly. Seltzer wrote to Lawrence in early 1921 to let him know that the American edition had sold 1,000 copies in only two days – principally in New York City – with some orders going unfilled. In the same letter he commended Lawrence for *Women in Love*, telling him that 'It is not only your best novel but one of the best ever written' – words that Lawrence needed to hear, despite Seltzer's obvious bias. The English edition had also made a promising start. Martin Secker wrote to Lawrence in December with news that the book was doing well, and that sales were approximately 2,000, of which 'library orders count for about half'. This was despite Virginia Woolf's disparaging write-up in the *Times Literary Supplement*, and the *London Daily News's* assertion that it was 'abominably written'.[7] Other reviewers were a little less censorious. *The Sketch* called it 'masterly'[8] and *The Scotsman* felt that the character and environment of the novel were 'vividly suggested',[9] although the reviewer felt the central characters were less convincing than 'the background' of the novel. The *Weekly Dispatch* were positively enthralled by the 'fascinating'[10] novel, and unlike *The Scotsman*, they found the characters to be 'extraordinarily interesting', and the narrative 'brilliant'.

Some of the most balanced reviews were remarkably perceptive in their analysis of Lawrence's modus operandi – and what he wanted to achieve. 'Mr Lawrence is very much of his time, hot, controversial, uneasy, with the sudden fury of the bird that beats against the bars of his cage',[11] wrote the *Aberdeen Daily Journal*:

> *In one sense he is like Blake, in that sex to him is mystical and divine; he explains this again and again in his novels and plays, and, behold, a low-pitched world misunderstands and sneers. Both Blake and he have message, but neither one nor the other speaks in terms which the majority of readers find it easy to translate. Mr Lawrence's chief characteristic is sincerity. He says what he thinks, and he thinks a very great deal.*[12]

The writer of the piece concluded that, 'Mr Lawrence's penetrative passion carries him away. He sees too much, analyses too fully, and discovers what is not there. Introspection leaves him hectic, and, overbalanced by excessive sensation, he lets his intensity of feeling run away with him…'[13] In essence, they felt that he had gone *too* far in his desire to portray the reality of human emotions and the complexity of human relationships. He had probed too deeply into human psychology – and as a result was alienating his readership. Alec Waugh, older sibling of the more famous Evelyn, writing for the *Pall Mall Gazette* (and probably with more inside knowledge than most owing to his literary pedigree) called Lawrence a 'martyr of modern letters…a most uncomfortable writer',[14] while recognising that *The Lost Girl* marked a change in tone:

> *It is quiet, serene, placid. The characters are gentler, sweeter, more unselfish. The author is more tolerant. There is rich mellowness about the first few chapters. We feel hopeful… 'The Lost Girl' will no doubt be highly praised. It is quite moral; it is quite comfortable. Many will be relieved. But to those who really care for D. H. Lawrence's work, will prove little, little beyond the fact that it is the work of a tired man, worn out by conflict, by adversity, by antagonism. It is exhaustion, not serenity, that has tempered this story and made it gentle.*

Yet again, Lawrence had polarised his audience, and it was against this backdrop that in early 1921 he abandoned the 'peppery' and experimental *Mr Noon*.

The New Year brought new sights and a brief change of scene. Tired of the 'shabby and frowsty foreigners' and ex-pats in Taormina, Lawrence and Frieda decided a short sojourn to the more unspoilt (but as it turned out, less civilised) Sardinia would help them decide whether they liked it enough to move there more permanently. They both enjoyed the island but decided to stay put in Fontana Vecchia for another year. There was another motive for their lightning visit to Sardinia. Lawrence wanted material for another book, and the island provided him with plenty to work with. The fruits of this trip became *Sea and Sardinia* (1921) – an ironic portrait of his search for a community unblemished by the march of time, and Sardinia, which as Lawrence subsequently wrote 'is like nowhere', was the ideal location. It was also a portrait of his relationship with Frieda, which was now approaching the ten-year mark, and a wry account of some of the more mundane aspects of their marriage and daily life. Ironically, it is the study of that banality that makes it so relatable. It is simple and uncomplicated, and in many respects showcases Lawrence at his best. For instance, take the morning of their departure from Sicily:

> *The dreary black morning, the candle-light, the house looking night-dismal. Ah, well, one does all these things for one's pleasure. So light the charcoal fire and put the kettle on. The queen bee* [Frieda] *shivering round half dressed, fluttering her unhappy candle.*
> *'It's fun,' she says, shuddering.*
> *'Great,' say I, grim as death.*[15]

This was writing that could easily be 'translated' by its readers. It had all the Lawrentian vigour but none of the psychological depth of his other fictional works. Instead it focuses on the landscape, the people and their way of life, with the same vivid lyricism that he puts to such effective use in his novels. But perhaps it is most memorable for presenting to us a Lawrence who is likeable, despite the bad-tempered outbursts of his fictional equivalent. It was written quickly and by the beginning of March 1921, Lawrence had a complete manuscript. By the end of that year it appeared in extract form in American magazine *The Dial*, before being published by Seltzer in late 1921. The English edition followed in 1923.

America was still very much Lawrence's preferred destination, and there was much discussion regarding the lease on a ruinous farm in Connecticut, but in early March Frieda's mother fell ill with heart issues and the idea of travelling across the Atlantic was put on hold (again). Frieda rushed to Germany while Lawrence arranged to keep Fontana Vecchia for another year. He then travelled north, stopping at Capri, where he met the American couple Earl and Achsah Brewster. The friendship he made with the intellectual duo lasted the rest of his life. After a two-day stop in Florence, Lawrence reached Germany on 26 April, finding it 'very quiet and empty-feeling.' Frieda wanted to stay for the whole summer, but Lawrence wasn't so sure, merely commenting in a letter, 'We shall see.'

Lawrence was unsettled again. 'I don't know what I'm going to do next', he lamented in a letter to Robert Mountsier. What he *did* manage to do next was finish *Aaron's Rod*, telling Kot that he'd suddenly had a 'fit of work – sitting away in the woods'. In May, *Psychoanalysis and the Unconscious* (1921) was published in America – a literary rejoinder to a psychoanalytic criticism of *Sons and Lovers*, and along with his later essay *Fantasia and the Unconscious* (1922) the two works explored Lawrence's thoughts on education, marriage, social and political action, as well as providing a counterproposal to Freudian psychoanalytic theory. The two pieces were also a demonstration of how much Lawrence had changed in the previous ten years. He was no longer the self-professed 'priest of love' from 1912, championing the joining of souls and the love between man and woman. Instead he actively discouraged what he perceived to be the 'disease of love': 'the whole man and woman game has become just a hell, and men with any backbone would rather kill themselves than go on with it…' His solution to this was to advocate individuality. 'You've got to know yourself as far as possible', Lawrence wrote. 'But not just for the sake of knowing. You've got to know yourself so that you can at last *be* yourself.'[16] From Germany, Frieda and Lawrence travelled into Austria to see Frieda's sister Johanna, before returning to Taormina via Florence, where he wrote several of the poems that would be published in *Birds, Beasts and Flowers*.

Women in Love was finally published in England in June of that year. The reviews were as expected. 'A gross insult to all womanhood',[17] was the opinion of the *Sunday Illustrated*, who were so aghast as to offer nothing further. The *Pall Mall Gazette* went into a little more depth, adding that, 'The characters are abnormal and uniformly unpleasant; their interminable talk is tedious; and, for all his undoubted power, Mr Lawrence is able at times to be uncommonly dull.'[18] But it was his former friend John Middleton Murry's lengthy review in the *Nation* that was the most bitter. In 'The Nostalgia of D. H. Lawrence' Murry argued that Lawrence's 'genius', and the originality that made him thus, were now 'dissolved in the acid of a burning and vehement passion'.[19] As such, *Women in Love* was, 'five hundred pages of passionate vehemence, wave after wave of turgid, exasperated writing impelled towards some distant and invisible end…'[20] Murry's final, damning sentence read, '…by the knowledge that we have we can only pronounce it subhuman and bestial, a thing that our forefathers had rejected when they began to rise from the slime'.[21] As far as Murry was concerned, Lawrence had passed his prime 'long before reaching it'.

It was of course impossible for Murry to be objective, given the prior breakdown in his relationship with Lawrence. But it was deliberately provocative. Just over a month later Lawrence discovered via Secker that former acquaintance Philip Heseltine had threatened to bring libel action against him for his depictions of

Halliday and Pussum in the novel. Although Lawrence thought it all 'perfect nonsense' and Heseltine a 'filthy rat', he was obliged to change his descriptions of the characters so that Halliday was swarthy with black hair and Pussum was blue-eyed and fair haired – 'as if there weren't dozens of little Pussums about Chelsea, and dozens of Hallidays anywhere', he commented irritably to Secker. To compound his exasperation, he also learnt that Secker had paid £50 and reimbursed Heseltine's legal costs (Lawrence referred to it later as 'hush-money'). But more worrying was Heseltine's assertion to his lawyers that the book should be prosecuted for glorifying homosexuality. It was an empty threat – Heseltine couldn't afford to continue with further legal action, but the seed had been planted, and Heseltine wasn't alone in his opinion. The conservative weekly magazine *John Bull* dedicated half a page to the 'loathsome study of sex depravity', under the title 'The Book the Police Should Ban'. The opinion of the reviewer was expressed in the clearest possible terms: 'I know dirt when I smell it and here it is in heaps – festering, putrid heaps which smell to high Heaven...It is ugly, repellent, vile.'[22]

The message was clear: neither Lawrence or his novels were welcome in England. Inevitably, Lawrence's thoughts again turned to America – the only place where he seemed to feel any kind of acceptance, despite the fact he had never set foot in the country. But he was also flirting with the idea of travelling east – his new friends, the Brewsters, had invited Frieda and Lawrence to join them in Ceylon (now Sri Lanka) where Earl Brewster was studying Buddhism. But what eventually settled the matter was an unexpected letter from American patron of the arts Mabel Dodge Sterne, inviting the Lawrences to an art colony in Taos, New Mexico. Knowing the importance of the senses to Lawrence, she rather cleverly included perfumed leaves and medicinal liquorice in the envelope – hoping he would be guided there by scent and taste. She also rather generously offered a furnished adobe house near the Native American Pueblo.

Lawrence was sold, and a plan for their next adventure slowly began to take shape. 'Taos is a little Indian town, on a mountain, 2000 metres above the sea, and 35 Kilometres from the railway', Lawrence wrote excitedly to Frieda's mother in November 1921. 'There's a tribe of Indians, free, who have been there since the Flood. They live in great pyramidal houses, and worship the sun. They say Taos is the solar centre of our universe. I think it would be interesting.'[23] All that remained was to work out how to get there.

As the end of the year approached, the thought of living in a colony of 'American artists' began to seem less appealing to Lawrence. His doubts started to surface in almost every letter he wrote describing the 'little colony of American artists', which he thought 'may be horrible' to live among. Their time in Taormina had gifted the couple 'months of quiet, peaceful living' and the thought of re-immersing themselves in an environment made up of 'arty', 'literary' types suddenly seemed overwhelming, as well as a thoroughly disagreeable prospect.

Lawrence also spent the majority of January 1922 fighting the flu virus, which brought with it his usual low mood and a good deal of frustration. In the same month, he also learned that *The Lost Girl* had been awarded the James Tait Black Memorial prize for the best English novel of 1920. As well as the cachet of winning a literature award, the prize also included £100. This unexpected financial boost, along with his ill health – which was preventing the couple from travelling – gave Lawrence a chance to reconsider his options. He wrote to Mountsier in mid-January: 'Suddenly that I am on the point of coming to America I feel I *can't* come. Not yet. It is something almost stronger than I am. I would rather go to Ceylon, and come to America later, from the east.'[24]

And so to Ceylon they went first – driven by a sort of deep intuition that Lawrence often relied on when faced with a dilemma. And despite his insistence that he must leave Europe early in 1922, he did come to yearn for it, in his own contradictory way. The thought of 'breaking off' left Lawrence with a sinking feeling even before they had departed. 'I long for Europe', he wrote a few months into their travels, having found that he missed the 'old civilization' with a 'burning nostalgia'.

But for now, at least, Ceylon was beckoning. Lawrence booked two berths on the *S. S. Osterley*, a 12,000-ton Orient Line steamer, sailing from Naples for Colombo on 26 February. The journey would last more than two weeks, but they found the steamer to be comfortable, roomy, and most importantly mostly empty of other travellers. They felt positively jolly.

But Frieda's sense of joy at becoming 'detached' was not matched by Lawrence. Sailing through the Straits of Messina, Lawrence had a pang of regret as he watched Mount Etna slowly disappearing over the horizon. He 'wept inside with pain – pain of parting'. For Lawrence, feeling emotional pain meant truly living – his need to wrench himself out of places that had become staid, thus forcing the agony of separation, was a necessary part of feeling alive again. Going to Ceylon might have offered him the opportunity to revive himself emotionally, but neither Lawrence nor Frieda had considered the physical impact of arriving in Ceylon in the hottest month of the year...

Chapter 14

'I look forwards, mustn't look back'

Life is a travelling to the edge of knowledge, then a leap taken.
We cannot know beforehand. We are driven from behind,
always as over the edge of the precipice.[1]

'It is all very wonderful', Lawrence wrote from the Brewsters' bungalow overlooking Kandy Lake, 'but we are almost too dazed yet to know what we feel'.[2] Lawrence and Frieda arrived in Colombo on 13 March, and the following day travelled onwards to Kandy, where the Brewsters were living on a half-wild estate surrounded by jungle trees. Their senses were immediately assaulted by their exotic location (Frieda claimed she knew they had arrived because she could smell cinnamon from the ship) and their arrival also coincided with the 28-year-old Prince of Wales's visit to see the Perahera Pageant, an annual procession to pay homage to the Sacred Tooth Relic of the Buddha. Lawrence was fascinated by the spectacle, and the ancient rituals, describing 'flaming torches of cocoanut blazing, and the great elephants in their trappings'. It was so 'wild and strange and perfectly fascinating' in the 'hot, still, starry night'.

Frieda too was thoroughly caught up in the mystique of her surroundings, even the primeval cries and howls from the jungle and the noises of creatures in the darkness didn't faze her. For Frieda it was 'like living in a fairy-tale', but for Lawrence it was akin to living in a strange, unfamiliar furnace, which was lovely to look at 'but very hot'. He didn't feel himself at all and was beginning to regret travelling to the East.

But it was more than just a physical malaise brought about by the intense heat and the inability to do *anything* without breaking a sweat. Lawrence also found the insouciance of the place and indifference of the people intolerable as well. As Catherine Carswell commented in her personal reflections on Lawrence: 'The carelessness of Italy was one thing, but the immense not-caring of the Orient was another'.[3] It was an apathy that he rejected outright – and as was often the case with Lawrence, his physical health reflected his state of mind. The very things that had enticed him to go to Ceylon – the heady tropical scents, the 'horrid' sounds of the jungle – now made him feel 'sick in the stomach'. Yet it did bring into sharp focus how he felt about England. 'I do think, still more now I am out here', he wrote, 'that we make a mistake forsaking England and moving out into the periphery of life…' And so he made up his mind to return to England.

Lawrence and Frieda lasted just over six weeks in Ceylon. But they didn't go back to England – not yet anyway. Instead, Lawrence booked them both a berth on the RMS *Orsova* to West Australia ('heaven knows why', he commented humorously). He was glad to have seen Ceylon, but he was equally glad to leave it behind now he didn't have to imagine it from afar. It was a very clear case of reality not living up to expectation. The couple landed in Perth, Western Australia on 4 May 1922, and had agreed that should they dislike it, they would travel on to San Francisco. Lawrence's approach was simple: 'Once started, best keep going till one is sure'.[4] Lawrence's first impression was that Perth was a 'queer godforsaken place' – which was less than encouraging – but the 'marvellous air' was welcome following the oppressive heat of Ceylon. He found the bush fascinating, and 'somewhat like a dream', and where Ceylon had offered nothing but the choking density of the jungle, here was a vast expanse of openness. But the awe-inspiring landscape of the bush wasn't enough to hold Lawrence's attention and just two weeks later he and Frieda boarded another boat, the *Malwa*, bound for Sydney in New South Wales.

The couple spent just over three months in total in Australia – but they were fruitful months. They found Sydney too expensive and so retreated forty miles south to Thirroul – 'the weirdest place you ever saw', Lawrence remarked. Their home for the next eleven weeks was a dilapidated bungalow, yet here at last he was able to write, and after just six and a half weeks he had written *Kangaroo* (1923), a semi-autobiographical account of Lawrence's impressions of Australia, which he depicts through the eyes of the hero – the slight, bearded Richard Lovat Somers, and his German wife Harriet. Alongside Lawrence's lyrical descriptions of the Australian landscape, and his portrayal of his and Frieda's daily experiences, he also explores Sydney's fringe politics through the eponymous 'Kangaroo' of the story, leader of the right-wing Digger movement Benjamin Cooley. During their stay in Australia, Lawrence was also gifted the story that would eventually become *The Boy in the Bush* (1924) via a manuscript given to him by writer Mollie Skinner, whom he had met at a guesthouse in Darlington on the first leg of their Australian adventure.

But Lawrence still found himself liking Australia 'less and less', despite the peace, the open landscape and (best of all) the fact no one knew them. He felt cleansed by the 'crashingly noisy' Pacific and it's 'very seaey water' but it was time to move on again. On 11 August, Frieda's forty-third birthday, they again boarded a ship – this time the *Tahiti* – bound for San Francisco. Their voyage was broken up by two brief stops; first on the volcanic island of Rarotonga ('tropical *almost* but not at all sweltering', Lawrence noted) and then on to Tahiti ('lovely island – but town spoilt') where they were joined on board by the crew and cast of the film 'Captain Blackbird' (the working title of *Lost and Found on a South Sea Island* (1923)) who had been shooting on the island.

On 4 September they arrived in San Francisco 'penniless' according to Lawrence, although they did manage to put up in the Palace Hotel, which Lawrence complained 'costs very much'. After four days in which Lawrence did much lamenting of the noise, the couple left for Santa Fe and their destination of Taos, New Mexico. It would take two days by train and a further 100km by motorcar – a journey that was 'very hot' according to Frieda and left Lawrence feeling 'dazed and vague'. When they were met at Lamy station by Mabel Dodge Sterne, wearing a turquoise blue dress and bedecked in silver and turquoise Indian jewellery, and her lover Tony Luhan, a handsome Indian who was draped in a blanket and had a large silver belt strapped across his chest, they must have seemed like a desert mirage.

But they had arrived, on what was Lawrence's thirty-seventh birthday, 11 September. And once they had stopped feeling hot and bothered from their long journey, they were able to fully appreciate the beauty of the landscape around them. In 1922, Taos was a village populated by a mixture of Pueblo Indians, Spanish-speaking mestizos and European bohemians, and was surrounded by breathtaking scenery. Lawrence was impressed.

As for his opinion of Mabel, the barbed comments – although small to begin with – were evident from the start. Lawrence referred to her as a 'sort of queen with various houses scattered around', and her artist friends as her 'dependents'. They were now in 'Mabel-town' as Frieda accurately dubbed it. This 'dependency' would prove to be a sticking point, but for now Lawrence and Frieda were grateful for their adobe house on the Indian reservation. The house had four large rooms, a kitchen and furniture that had been made in the village. It was known as 'Tony's house', despite being built by Mabel. 'Tony is the Indian "husband" – nice too, but silent', Lawrence remarked. Mabel was 'very generous' and 'nice' according to Lawrence, but what did she want in return? Mabel's renowned generosity was now, in essence, holding them captive. Lawrence rapidly grew tired of being 'arranged' by Mabel as though he were a 'retainer or protégé': 'But I won't be bullied, even by kindness', he resolved. Mabel expected Lawrence to spend time with her, be at her beck and call (especially when there were guests to whom she could show off the resident 'genius'), but most of all, she required Lawrence to write about *her* version of New Mexico with *her* as the central character. Mabel remembered (or perhaps misremembered) Lawrence approaching her, rather than the reverse: 'He said he wanted to write an American novel that would express the life, the spirit, of America and he wanted to write it around me – my life from the time I left

New York to come out to New Mexico; my life, from civilization to the bright, strange world of Taos; my renunciation of the sick old world of art and artists, for the pristine valley and the upland Indian lakes. I was thrilled at the thought of this.'[5] This was to become one of several sticking points.

As Catherine Carswell observed in *The Savage Pilgrimage*: 'Lawrence had quickly recognised what perhaps did not surprise him, that Mrs. Sterne wanted of him what he had made Gudrun want of Gerald in *Women in Love* – to use him as an instrument for the furthering of her own ideas and purposes – spiritual, political, artistic.'[6] From Mabel's perspective, Lawrence's presence in New Mexico was all her own doing. She believed that the sheer force of her will had brought him there: 'I leaped through space, joining myself to the central core of Lawrence, where he was in India, in Australia. Not really speaking to him, but *being* my wish, I became that action that brought him across the sea.'[7] But it was that 'will' that Lawrence came to resent. Mabel embodied all that Lawrence hated about America – a sense of knowingness that brokered no discussion: 'everybody seems to be trying to enforce his, or her, *will*, and trying to see how much the other person or persons will let themselves be overcome…I dislike that: and I despise it.'[8]

Mabel's smothering influence and the nature of her commune ('Mabel Sterne and suppers and motor drives and people dropping in') was problematic but it was her attempt to come between Lawrence and Frieda that eventually drove them both away. Reflecting on the situation after Lawrence's death, Mabel wrote that from their first meeting, 'I sensed Lawrence's plight and that the womb in me roused to reach out to take him',

> …*for I remember thinking: He is through with that – he needs another kind of force to propel him…the spirit…." The womb behind the womb – the significant, extended, and transformed power that succeeds primary sex, that he was ready, long since, to receive from woman. I longed to help him with that – to be used – to be put to his purpose.*[9]

It was veiled in flowery language, but the message was clear – Mabel felt Lawrence needed saving from Frieda. Frieda couched her account of the incident in more straightforward terms:

> *Mabel and Lawrence wanted to write a book together: about Mabel, it was going to be. I did not want this. I had always regarded Lawrence's genius as given to me. I felt deeply responsible for what he wrote. And there was a fight between us, Mabel and myself: I think it was a fair fight. One day Mabel came over and told me she didn't think I was the right woman for Lawrence and other things*

equally upsetting and I was thoroughly roused and said: 'Try it then yourself, living with a genius, see what it is like and how easy it is, take him if you can.'[10]

Relations were strained enough by November for Lawrence to have written to Mabel reminding her that his relationship with Frieda was with 'the best thing in my life' and 'the best thing in life'.

Whatever the truth of the matter, by the middle of December Frieda and Lawrence couldn't tolerate the colony or Mabel anymore. They had no intention of leaving America and it's remarkable, mountainous landscape, and so they arranged to rent a couple of log cabins on the Del Monte ranch, which was owned by the Hawk family. They took with them two young Danish painters, Kai Gótzsche and Knud Merrild, who had come from New York and needed somewhere to stay. Mabel was still nearby but too far away to exert any real influence, and most importantly they were no longer dependent on her financially or for their accommodation. 'We were friends no more', Mabel concluded. 'There was nothing but antagonism between us, scarcely veiled, and Frieda was triumphant and glad.'[11]

It was a 'real mountain winter' in 1922 according to Frieda with snow, ice and 'knifey cold' temperatures. Initially there was practical work to be undertaken to prepare the cabins for habitation and the coming winter weather. It was hard, physical labour, but Lawrence, Frieda and their two new Danish friends lived and worked together in harmony – and with the practical tasks completed they were able to enjoy horse riding and walks together, eat together, spend evenings together playing cards, singing and talking into the night for a blissful three and a half months. Was this the feted 'Rananim' Lawrence had so frequently spoke of and fantasised about? If it was, it had come about by accident rather than design. Yet Lawrence still longed for Europe. 'I know now I don't want to live anywhere very long. But I belong to Europe', he wrote to Catherine Carswell.

The new year of 1923 brought new visitors to Del Monte – Lawrence's American publisher Thomas Seltzer and his wife, followed by Lawrence's agent Robert Mountsier. But it also brought sad news from a former literary adversary. Katherine Mansfield had died in Fontainebleu, France, from a pulmonary haemorrhage brought about by the simple act of running up a flight of stairs. Lawrence heard the news from a note that had come from John Middleton Murry via Koteliansky. Despite their problematic relationship, Lawrence was dignified in his response – honouring his former attachment to the couple and expressing genuine regret for not just the loss of Katherine but for the loss of their friendship. 'I always knew a bond in my heart', he replied to Murry. 'Feel a fear where the bond is broken now...I wish it needn't all have been as it has been: I do wish it.'[12]

Lawrence had reestablished a connection with Murry – albeit tentatively – but at the same time his relationship with Mountsier was beginning to break down. Agent and author were finding it increasingly difficult to work together – exacerbated by frosty relations between Seltzer and Mountsier – and Lawrence finally decided to end their partnership in early February 1923, prompting him to transfer his American business over to the Curtis Brown agency.

Frieda remained the one, constant fixture in Lawrence's life. As others came and went – dismissed by Lawrence either in a fury or allowed to quietly drift away – Frieda was the exception, no matter how violently they quarrelled or how often they threatened to abandon each other. Loyalty was now more important to Lawrence than romantic love, and Frieda embodied that – regardless of her earlier indiscretions. But more importantly she never lost sight of who she was, even when Lawrence's ego threatened to overshadow her. Their fulfilment as a couple came from acknowledging each other as individuals, as well as husband and wife.

In the spring of 1923, Lawrence started longing to write another book. But, according to Frieda, he could only write in places where his imagination could have 'space and free play'. Feeling that life in Taos wasn't conducive to a creative vision (Lawrence remarked that he found the USA 'sterile') – and with their six-month visas almost up – Lawrence decided Mexico *proper* was the place he needed to be. And if he didn't have to spend time with any Americans, so much the better. However, this would prove difficult. Two friends of Mabel Sterne's, Witter Bynner and his lover Willard 'Spud' Johnson, whom Lawrence and Frieda had taken under their wing (much to Mabel's annoyance) – and who were also American – accompanied them. This, Lawrence could just about tolerate, but he wanted no more Americans for now. Mabel had thoroughly put him off the idea.

Lawrence's first impression of Mexico was encouraging. He found the atmosphere 'easy' and 'alive', but most importantly he felt he had found the emotional release he needed to write. In Taos he had finished the *Studies in Classic American Literature* (1923) and written seven poems, one of which completed the volume *Birds, Beasts and Flowers*, but what he desired most was to lose himself in another novel. The work he had begun at the commune in Taos, the fledgling 'American novel' that centred on Mabel Sterne, was now tainted by the lady herself, so Lawrence would need to look somewhere else for inspiration. Fortunately, Mexico did not disappoint – although out of all the cultural sights Lawrence experienced in Mexico, it was predominantly those that shocked or had the most impact on him that were relived in his fiction. Lawrence didn't like the 'gruesome Aztec carvings', and found the continent 'sub-cruel, a bit ghastly', but he did enjoy the Pyramid of the Sun at Teotihuacan ('very impressive there – far more than Pompeii or the Forum') and found the Indians 'attractive', but it was the hideous experience of a bull-fight that sickened Lawrence enough to a) want to include the spectacle in his fiction; and b) want to leave Mexico. The incident was fictionalised in *The Plumed Serpent* (1926) – Lawrence's political novel set in contemporary Mexico during the Mexican Revolution. The novel opens with a group of tourists experiencing a bullfight, from which the protagonist, Kate Leslie, departs in disgust before becoming embroiled in a religious movement to revive pre-Christian religion in Mexico. Lawrence's description of the event reflects both their shock at witnessing something so inhumane and the visceral brutality of the fight:

> *Kate had never been taken so completely by surprise in all her life. She had still cherished some idea of a gallant show. And before she knew where she was, she was watching a bull whose shoulder's trickled blood goring his horns up and down inside the belly of a prostrate and feebly plunging old horse. The shock almost overpowered her.*[13]

It was unpleasant and upsetting, but in some respects it was what Lawrence needed. Shortly after the experience, Lawrence left Mexico City for Chapala – initially on his own, to do a reconnaissance, with Frieda following a few days later – and it was here that he finally felt able to lose himself in his fictional world. Chapala was on the north shore of the vast Lake Chapala, Mexico's largest freshwater lake, twenty-eight miles south of the city of Guadalajara. The couple took a house, surrounded by trees and flowers, by the lake; and although they couldn't see the water because of the dense trees, they were close enough to be able to bathe in it regularly – although the novelty soon wore off after Frieda encountered a snake while bathing. Lawrence singled out a spot by the lake under a pepper tree for the purposes of writing. 'I shall begin a novel now', Lawrence wrote in early May, 'as soon as I can take a breath.' He made two false starts but a month later he reported to Catherine Carswell, 'we are still here':

> *I felt I had a novel simmering in me, so came here, to this big Lake, to see if I could write it. It goes fairly well. I shall be glad if I can finish the first draft by the end of this month. Then we shall pack up at once, go to Mexico City and sail from Vera Cruz for New York. Hope to be in England by early August. Where will you be then? I shall be glad to be back. But wanted to get this novel off my chest.*[14]

Lawrence turned out to be over-optimistic in his estimation as to how long it would take him to finish the first draft of his new work, 'Quetzalcoatl', named after the feathered serpent-god of the Aztecs. Latterly, this title was discarded in favour of *The Plumed Serpent*, much to Lawrence's annoyance ('Must one really discard such a fascinating word?' he asked his publisher – offering in the same letter the tongue-in-cheek 'Men in Big Hats' as a suitable substitute title). Lawrence made it clear he didn't wish to leave until 'Quetzalcoatl' was completed. Yet Frieda longed to return to Europe – to England to see her children, and then Germany to see her mother.

Lawrence wasn't keen – not just because he felt the 'undigested' novel needed to be expurgated from his system before he moved on again, but because thinking of England made him mistrust his own feelings. There is a grim resignation to Lawrence's letters between June and August 1923 – he acknowledges that he 'ought' to come to England, but he struggles to hide his displeasure at the idea. Nevertheless, the couple began to make their way to New York so that they could cross the Atlantic. But Lawrence's mind was still on Mexico.

The issue came to a head on 7 August. Frieda got Lawrence as far as the quay, but his mind was made up – he would not be travelling to England. 'I feel I can't come to England yet – though I came here on purpose', he wrote to Kot. 'But it's no good, I shall have to put it off'.[15] After a blazing row, Frieda sailed back to Southampton on the *RMS Orbita* on her own. They parted on bad terms – Frieda feeling very much aggrieved at Lawrence's failure to master his feelings towards England, and Lawrence no doubt irritated by her disloyalty to him and loyalty to her children. 'F. wants to see her children', Lawrence wrote to Murry after the scene at the quay. 'And you know, wrong or not, I can't stomach the chasing of those Weekley children'.[16]

According to Catherine Carswell it was 'one of the worst quarrels – perhaps the very worst – of their life'. Frieda even expressed her desire to never see Lawrence again in a letter from the *Orbita* to Seltzer's wife Adele:

> *I feel so cross with Lawrence, when I hear him talk about loyalty – Pah, he only thinks of himself – I am glad to be alone and I will not go back to him […] I will not stand his bad temper any more if I never see him again – wrote him so.*[17]

Yet it quickly became clear that neither were happy without the other. Lawrence travelled around restlessly, getting very little writing done, and Frieda wasn't happy alone in a Hampstead flat. But Lawrence would come when he was ready. Accompanied by one of 'the Danes', Kai Götzsche, he returned to Mexico and made his way back to Guadalajara where they stayed for a month, and where Lawrence rewrote Mollie Skinner's story, 'The House of Ellis', into *The Boy in the Bush*. He hoped that Frieda would eventually capitulate and return to Mexico to be with him, although in his usual contradictory style his letters also suggest he was prepared to offer Frieda a 'regular arrangement' to support her financially if their temporary separation became permanent. Frieda didn't want to go back to Mexico – at least not yet – and Lawrence 'didn't want much to go to England'. It was, quite literally, a Mexican standoff.

Surprisingly, it was eventually broken by Lawrence – and only then because he had exhausted all the places he wanted to travel to. '[I] suppose it is the next move in the battle which never ends and in which I never win', he wrote resignedly in November.

Lawrence sailed with Götzsche on the *S.S Toledo* on 22 November and arrived in London on 12 December. Frieda later remarked that 'I think he was right; I should have gone to meet him in Mexico, he should not have come to Europe; these are the mistakes we make, sometimes irreparable'.[18] She offers no additional insight into why it was the wrong decision (although one incident that happened later perhaps throws some light on the comment). Yet on the face of it, Lawrence's European profile had never been so high – the second half of 1923 saw more of Lawrence's books published in such a short period than ever before, or indeed since. August saw the publication of *Studies in Classic American Literature* by Seltzer and in September, *Kangaroo* and *Fantasia of the Unconscious* were published by Secker in London. The American edition of *Kangaroo* was also released by Seltzer in September, followed by *Birds, Beasts and Flowers* and *Mastro-don Gesualdo* in October. In November, Secker brought out the English version of *Birds, Beasts and Flowers* and Seltzer published *The Captain's Doll* in New York. But there is little reference to any joy this brought Lawrence in his letters. England made him ill – physically and emotionally. He quickly caught a cold and within a week of arriving was already complaining that he 'loathed' every minute he had to spend in London.

He did, however, organise a 'welcome home' supper, which was held in a private room at the Café Royal. The guest list included Don and Catherine Carswell, Koteliansky, Murry, Mary Cannan, Mark Gertler, and artist the Honourable Dorothy Brett – all potential recruits for Lawrence's longed-for 'Rananim' community. The evening started well – Lawrence was on top form, performing the role of the charming and entertaining host with aplomb, and Frieda was delighted. But a little worse for wear from the constant flow of wine, the conviviality of the evening quickly descended into chaos. Kot began to make drunken speeches 'in praise and love' for Lawrence, which were punctuated by him smashing wine glasses on the floor, and then Lawrence decided to make an appeal. He was among his true friends, and he wanted their support. He was going back to New Mexico – would they accompany him? Lawrence went around the table asking each guest in turn, testing their loyalty. There were some vague affirmatives but a lot of ambiguity, but all the guests – except Dorothy Brett –

would eventually make their excuses. Lawrence went deathly silent and 'without uttering a sound, fell forward with his head on the table, was deadly sick, and became at once unconscious'.[19] Lawrence had to be carried to a cab, and then carried from the cab up to his first-floor flat and put to bed. Whether Lawrence felt he might never return to England, and thus it was his last opportunity to rally some spiritual companionship, or whether Frieda's presence alone was no longer enough to sustain him emotionally, physically and creatively, is unclear. But the incident was profound enough for him to comment later: 'That is what coming home means to me. Never again, pray the Lord'.[20]

Lawrence went to Derbyshire to be with his family for New Year 1924, although even that was with reluctance. He couldn't seem to muster the enthusiasm to go and claimed he felt the 'dead hand of the past' weighing down on him like the 'stone lid of a tomb'.

Late January brought a trip to Paris, where the couple stayed into the first week of February, before travelling onwards to Baden-Baden to spend time with Frieda's mother. Lawrence had done what he set out to do – he had seen his English friends, visited his family, travelled on the continent and settled some of his business affairs in London. In some respects he had won his 'battle' over Europe, but at the expense of his physical and mental health. He was ready to leave.

On 5 March 1924 Lawrence, Frieda and Dorothy Brett sailed for America on the *Aquitania*, arriving in New York on 11 March in 'half a blizzard, snow and rain'.[21] New York looked 'vile' according to Lawrence, but the weather was the least of his problems. Thomas Seltzer met the trio on the wharf, looking 'very diminished' according to Lawrence. His publishing business had had a very bad winter and Seltzer had been suffering from sleepless nights. 'So, it seems, might I', Lawrence predicted ominously.

Chapter 15

Return to Taos

There is now no smooth road into the future: but we go round, or scramble over the obstacles. We've got to live, no matter how many skies have fallen.[1]

Lawrence was right to be concerned about Seltzer. He was headed for ruin and all Lawrence could do was hope that he could extract from Seltzer the money that was owed to him (more than $4,000 in 1923) before he went under completely. Yet again, Lawrence's finances were in peril. The situation was dire, but Seltzer was at least prepared to cover the train fare to Taos, where Lawrence and Frieda could live simply – although, as before, they would have to do so within the orbit of the incorrigible Mabel Sterne (now Luhan).

They also had their recruit in tow – the Honourable Dorothy Brett. The daughter of Lord Esher, Dorothy (always known as just 'Brett') was an unmarried, Slade-trained artist. She was deaf, but fiercely independent and didn't mind getting her hands dirty, despite her aristocratic origins. She was also the former lover of John Middleton Murry and had a strong propensity for idolising the men in her life – which to anyone who knew the potential outcome of competing with Frieda for Lawrence's attention, probably looked like a disaster waiting to happen. And she wasn't just competing with Frieda either – Mabel was now ready to stake another claim on the prodigal genius. The dynamics of three spirited and headstrong women sharing just one Lorenzo had all the hallmarks of a disaster-in-waiting. Mabel regarded the usurper and her ear-trumpet 'Toby' with suspicion: '…it was not a jolly, sociable ear-trumpet that longed to be a part of everything else. No. I soon saw that it was an eavesdropper. It was a spy upon any influence near Lorenzo'.[2] And Frieda recalled,

> *Lawrence said to me: 'You know, it will be good for us to have the Brett with us, she will stand between us and people and the world.' I did not really want her with us, and had a suspicion that she might not want to stand between us and the world, but between him and me.*[3]

Brett's later eulogy to Lawrence, *Lawrence and Brett: A Friendship*, gives an indication of just how frosty the relationship between the three women was:

Suddenly Mabel walks in. She had asked me to supper over at her place but I would not go. In she walks, without speaking or looking at us, and sits down on the day-bed. Not a word is spoken by any of us. She leans back, silent, like a stone monument. We look at each other. What is it all about? Frieda's eyes are blazing, and you look down at your plate, entirely withdrawn. All through the meal we sit silently; we can neither speak to each other nor to Mabel; and she says nothing to us...I feel an undercurrent of emotional strain.[4]

Written in the form of a present-tense letter to Lawrence, Brett's recreation of her time with him makes it very clear how she viewed their relationship – using Lawrence's own words to illustrate the importance of that 'friendship' as an opening quote: 'Friendship is as binding/ As the Marriage Vow –/ As important – as Eternal'.[5]

All three women from this period in Lawrence's life published their reflections of him within five years of his death – Mabel in 1932, Brett in 1933 and Frieda in 1934. There is a sense that they needed to justify their relationships with him – to themselves and the outside world – as much as they needed the cathartic process of writing about him to make sense of their feelings. Yet that is where the similarities end. Dorothy Brett's is the most Lawrence-centric. Where Frieda and Mabel put much of themselves into their portraits of Lawrence – particularly Mabel – Brett's account reveals very little of who she was, and much about Lawrence. She writes as though she is in conversation with Lawrence, remembering with him the things they did together, and what she has thought or done when they were apart. It's a snapshot of memories painted in words. Frieda called it 'hero-worship', but to Brett it was the kind of adoration one gave to a soulmate.

Whatever Frieda and Mabel thought of Brett, she did at least prove her usefulness. Frieda openly admitted Brett 'did her share of the work', which was most evident when Mabel made over to Frieda a near-derelict ranch on Lobo mountain for the trio to inhabit. It was a surprising but generous gesture, although it was not totally unconditional; it may not have been explicit, but Mabel still expected Lawrence to write about 'her' New Mexico. To mitigate this obligation, and with full confidence in her husband's worth, Frieda presented Mabel with the original manuscript of *Sons and Lovers* – prescient now with the benefit of time, but of very little value in 1924. Lawrence and Brett worked alongside the Native American labourers and a Mexican carpenter for five weeks to make the three-roomed cabin that Lawrence and Frieda would live in, and a smaller cabin for Brett, clean and habitable. She could also type, and her artistry enabled her to design cover-jackets for Lawrence's books – two of which were subsequently used (on the Seltzer edition of *The Boy in the Bush* and the Knopf edition of *The Plumed Serpent*).

The summer of 1924 was a period of relative harmony, despite the inhospitable nature of their location. Barring one particularly awkward incident in which a soiree at the Lawrence's cabin turned oddly violent during an episode of drunken dancing, it was a 'wonderful summer' according to Frieda. Brett painted and helped Lawrence; Lawrence baked, painted furniture, mended things and wrote; Frieda cooked for everyone, read books and sewed; and in the evenings when the temperature dropped they rode to Del Monte for the post and fresh milk. 'I myself find a good deal of satisfaction living like this alone in this unbroken country',[6] Lawrence wrote that summer.

It all sounded idyllic but for one troubling incident involving Lawrence's health – which had been relatively good all year. In early August, Lawrence began to go down with a cold. It was nothing unusual given his medical history, but this time he began to cough up blood. He spent the next few days in bed, but when Frieda called a doctor in, Lawrence turned on her with 'wild fury' and threw an egg cup at her head, declaring in a temper, 'How *dare* you…You *know* I dislike doctors. You *know* I wouldn't have him or you wouldn't have sent for him behind my back. I *won't* see him – I *won't!*'[7] Lawrence was no doubt aware of what the blood signified. He was in the third (active) stage of the pulmonary tuberculosis that would ravage his lungs over the next five years. But he refused to have it pointed out to him – he was too proud to admit his vulnerability. And so the doctor (reading the situation, and the testiness of his patient) told Frieda and Lawrence it was nothing more than 'a touch of bronchial trouble'. Lawrence did recover this time, but it marked the start of his ongoing mistrust of doctors and medical workers. He preferred to trust his own internal voice – which always told him what he wanted to hear.

During Lawrence's convalescence, news came from Eastwood that his father, Arthur Lawrence, had died on 10 September. It was unexpected: Lawrence was surprised by his feelings, commenting that 'it upsets one…makes a strange break.' Whatever bitterness Lawrence had once felt towards his father had dissipated – helped no doubt by time and distance. Lawrence had regularly sent money back to Ada over the years to assist with the care of their father and he now sent a financial contribution for the funeral, and to help with any other expenses. 'I hate to think of that Eastwood cemetery', Lawrence commented. 'I hate to think of Eastwood anyhow.' Arthur Lawrence was laid to rest in the 'hateful' cemetery, alongside Lydia and Lawrence's elder brother William Ernest with the simple inscription 'Rest After Weariness'.

Back in New Mexico, as autumn approached and the weather began to turn, so too did Frieda's attitude towards Brett. Things came to a head in Oaxaca,

Mexico, where the trio had de-camped in November for the winter and new year of 1924–25. 'There is trouble; the air is heavy and disturbed', Brett recorded of a long walk she took with Lawrence. They returned to find Frieda 'sitting smoking in a rocking-chair – she looks at us. Our joyousness radiates out of us, permeates the air of the patio. Frieda's eyes begin to dart about, her mouth tightens, but she says nothing to me.'[8]

Fortunately, it began (eventually) to dawn on Brett that there had been a 'change in atmosphere' and Frieda gave voice to her emotions 'in a rage', telling Brett that she spoiled all her fun. In early January 1925, Lawrence himself intervened by letter, telling Brett that the three of them didn't make a 'happy combination'. His solution was simple – he told Brett she should 'go her own way', ideally back to the ranch, while they stayed in Oaxaca. Lawrence was trying to work on *The Plumed Serpent*, and it was all becoming a strain – the intensity of writing at his usual fever-pitch, mediating Frieda's anger towards Brett, and finally having to tell Brett that she was no longer welcome.

Less than a month later, Lawrence once again succumbed to illness – but this time it was more serious. At the end of January 1925 he finished the novel, but only a few days later in early February he suffered a near-fatal physical collapse. Lawrence called it 'malaria, 'flu and tropical fever' according to Catherine Carswell, and although it could have been a combination of any or all the above, the most probable cause was the active tuberculosis in his lungs. 'This the doctor told Frieda privately but plainly, and she knew from what he said that Lawrence would never be the same man again',[9] Carswell wrote. Frieda was certain he would die. She felt that he 'couldn't or wouldn't live on'. His death was unthinkable, although she also conceded that the worst part of it was the 'emotional depression and the *nerves*' (his and hers) as it drove her to despair.

Lawrence was moved to the Hotel Francia, and plans were tentatively conceived for a return to Europe in March. The couple then embarked on a torturous and highly uncomfortable (not to mention risky) train journey back to Mexico City at the end of February, where they checked in to the Hotel Imperial. 'I am pale green and no longer fat', Lawrence wrote just before he suffered another relapse that set their travel plans back by another month. Frieda attempted to put on a brave face, but knew Lawrence was 'doomed' and would 'never be well again'. She too had also succumbed to influenza, and nursing Lawrence had taken a heavy toll on her emotional health too.

During their time in Mexico City, Lawrence was forced to face the truth. Frieda recalled how she had been out one morning and when she returned to the hotel, the doctor was there. He told her 'brutally' when she entered Lawrence's room that he had tuberculosis, and that Lawrence had looked at her with 'unforgettable eyes'. Frieda was also told privately that his only chance of any kind of recovery was to return to the ranch, but that he had a year or two at the most. They were advised against the journey back to Europe by the doctor, so at the end of March they travelled north again and into New Mexico – although the already challenging ordeal was made even more difficult by the American border authorities, who were reluctant to let a sickly consumptive into the country. With the American embassy in Mexico behind them, and Frieda's sheer pig-headedness, they were eventually allowed in, but not before Lawrence was subjected to a physical examination and forced to strip.

They finally made it back to Del Monte and the additional two miles to their own ranch, where Lawrence initially slept for much of the time. But he did improve little by little. 'I am just gathering myself together, the last bits of me, as it were, struggling in from the long journey', Lawrence wrote. Frieda was helped by a young Native American couple, Trinidad and Rufina Archuleta and she proudly announced that 'Lawrence needn't do a thing and I am developing into a "chef".'[10] To begin with, Lawrence did little more than 'lie in the sun', but he soon realised it was his writing that gave him a reason to be alive and *feel* alive. He had started a biblical play in Mexico City called 'Noah's Flood', which explored the end of the 'old world', and by early May he had finished it and re-christened it *David*. He also compiled a book of essays, which became *Reflections on the Death of a Porcupine and Other Essays* (1925). But he still yearned for the escapism that only novel writing could provide. Being able to live so intensely with his characters and the experience he was fictionalising was a life in itself to Lawrence – and a far better use of time than 'jazzing and motoring', he thought.

Lawrence and Frieda's time in New Mexico was limited by their visa and as Lawrence approached the age of 40 on 11 September 1925, their six-month stay was up. Lawrence didn't want to leave but they had no choice. They left the ranch on 10 September, travelling by train to New York via Denver, knowing that they might never come back – unless Lawrence's tuberculosis went into extended remission, it was unlikely they would be allowed into the country.

By 21 September they were on the *SS Resolute* bound for Europe. 'I feel now I rather want to go for a bit, to England',[11] Lawrence wrote to Brett back in New Mexico. Lawrence had been forced to face his own mortality and had ample time during his recovery to reflect on his life and how he felt about the country of his birth. It is likely that his need to go back was prompted by a longing for the England of his youth – Lawrence certainly felt an intense nostalgia for the Midlands, amplified by the wholly different landscapes and circumstances he had been living in abroad. 'One's native land has a sort of hopeless attraction, when one is away', he remarked the following month. His deep affection for the English countryside had never wavered; in his own words it was the 'country of my heart'. But after so many journeys to England that had ended in disappointment and disillusion, would this trip be any different?

Lawrence still felt indifferent when he arrived in London, but he looked on 'with wonder instead of exasperation'. He was shocked by the sheer number of people who were unemployed and on 'the dole' and his 'wonder' soon turned into his usual frustration towards the populace's grim acceptance of the status quo. 'There's no *kick* in the people: they're about as active as seaweed', he bemoaned. Lawrence felt a 'terrible feeling everywhere' – London was 'not very cheering…the people very depressed'. To make matters worse, his friends had also disappeared. Koteliansky was nowhere to be seen; Murry had holed himself up to work on *The Life of Jesus* (1926); Mark Gertler was in a sanatorium; and Catherine Carswell was 'buried alive in a hole of a horrid little cottage in damp and dismal Bucks'. His reaction to being back in England was no different from his previous visits. London particularly came in for criticism for being 'almost gruesome' and he concluded that there was 'no life in anybody'.

Lawrence and Frieda escaped London for the Midlands, visiting his sister Emily in Nottingham for a week before travelling to Ripley to see Ada, where he spent a further week. He immediately caught a cold, and the weather was awful: 'we simply hate it up here', he commented grumpily. Even the 'motoring' they did around Derbyshire, which should have stirred up Lawrence's nostalgia for the place, did nothing to raise his spirits. He decided he didn't want to be reminded of the past and that he was weary of it; 'the spirit seems to have flown', he concluded.

Lawrence and Frieda returned to London but with their eyes very firmly set on the continent. On 29 October they left England for Baden-Baden where 'peasants were still peasants', and the Rhine villages were still 'untouched and lovely'. They visited Frieda's mother, who was older and slower, but still active enough to walk uphill to their hotel to visit them, and Lawrence found himself playing whist with the German old guard of 'Barons, Baronesses, Counts and Excellencies' – all friends of Frieda's mother and the living remnants of a time of grandeur long since passed.

They stayed in Germany long enough to celebrate Anna von Richthofen's seventy-fourth birthday, but Italy was where they really desired to be, and so in mid-November they followed Martin Secker and his wife Rina to Sportorno – a coastal village forty miles from Genoa. Within three days of arriving they took the Villa Bernada, a pink, friendly looking villa. But crucially – for Frieda's future at least – they became well-acquainted with their landlady, Serafina Ravagli, and her husband Angelo. Angelo was an officer in the Italian Bersaglieri, and when Frieda first met him he was in uniform with 'gay plumes' and a 'blue sash'. Frieda was attracted to him from the start, and the two would become intermittent lovers over the final three to four years of Lawrence's life. It is probable Lawrence knew of the affair, either through guessing or from Frieda's own mouth – but their relationship was always notable for their tolerance of each other's indiscretions. Neither Lawrence nor Frieda were easy people to live with – as many of their friends found out over the years – but as a couple they lived in the belief that loyalty and honour transcended the 'pledged word' of a promise and was embodied instead in 'a feeling faithfully followed'.[12] It was something intangible and undefined, but it was the bedrock of their marriage.

Lawrence was far more likely to object to Frieda's children than he was to any lover – a reaction that was put to the test when Frieda's daughter Barbara (Barby) came to stay. Now a 21-year-old woman, Barby was staying at Alassio, not far from Spotorno, during the winter of 1925 to 1926 and Frieda was, naturally, keen to spend as much time with her as possible. Lawrence resented this, not only because she represented an unwelcome intrusion into their relationship but also because he now had competition for Frieda's attention. He had already written of his dislike of Frieda's children in a letter to Brett from Baden-Baden. Barby, he told Brett, was engaged to an 'absolute nothingness of a fellow', Elsa was 'too bouncy' and 'the boy' (Monty) was full of 'loftiness'. Privately, Lawrence admitted that he couldn't bear Frieda's children. Lawrence's letters from the end of 1925 only reveal Barby's intermittent presence in Sportorno, but Frieda later divulged that a fierce quarrel had taken place on at least one occasion, in which Lawrence had said to Barby, 'Don't imagine your mother loves you…she doesn't love anybody, look at her false face',[13] before throwing half a glass of red wine in her mother's face. It was a deliberately cruel act, designed to set Frieda and Barby against each other, and taunt Barby into some sort of retaliation.

Things appeared to settle down. Lawrence and Barby gradually warmed to each other and often painted together – Lawrence even went as far as to encourage his sister Ada to buy one of Barby's paintings to 'help her on'. Lawrence suffered another bronchial haemorrhage in early February 1926, and it was during his convalescence that Frieda's other daughter, Elsa, also came to stay. But her visit coincided with a visit to Lawrence from Ada and a friend from England.

Frieda assumed this was Lawrence's attempt to counterbalance the presence of the Weekley daughters, and they soon split off into hostile camps with Frieda complaining that 'Ada felt he [Lawrence] belonged to her and the past'. The weather was dreadful, which put both parties in a bad mood, but it was an argument over Lawrence's care, or lack thereof from Frieda, that prompted Lawrence to moan in a letter that everything was a 'great muddle', 'with daughters that are by no means mine, and sister who doesn't see eye to eye with F. What a trial families are!' Ada told Frieda that she hated her and locked Lawrence in his room and wouldn't give Frieda the key. Frieda doesn't reveal her verbal reaction to this incident in her memoir, but it can probably be assumed that cross words were said on both sides. Then she walked out and went to stay in the hotel where Barby and Elsa were staying. Once well enough, Lawrence decided to go with Ada to Monte Carlo and Nice, before she headed back to England, and after they had left, Frieda moved back into the villa with her daughters. She remembered how a picture arrived from Lawrence with a sketch of Jonah on it, about to be swallowed by the whale. Lawrence had written underneath: 'Who is going to swallow whom?' But Frieda was still too angry to find it amusing.

After Ada left for England – with Lawrence's apologies for 'the bust-up' – he didn't go back to Spotorno. Instead he sent a telegram to Brett to tell her he was on his way to Capri. Brett was spending time with the Brewsters, whom she had grown fond of over the five months she had been in Capri. She was shocked when Lawrence finally arrived by 'how frail, how delicate and collapsed'[14] his appearance was. In his own words he was 'so tired of it all…Oh, so tired!" and his restlessness seemed to be catching up with him; he told Brett that,

My life is unbearable. I feel I cannot stand it any longer. Chopping and changing is not my way, as you know; but I get so tired of it all. It makes me ill, too.

Lawrence was still smarting from the 'bust-up' with Frieda, but he did at least have a sympathetic ear in his adoring disciple, Brett. While Lawrence poured out his misery to Brett, they painted, explored, hiked and had long conversations lying in the grass under the shade of the trees.

It was during Lawrence's time away from Frieda, and reconnection with Brett, that Lawrence and Brett had some sort of awkward sexual encounter that has never been clearly explained. The two companions travelled from Capri to Ravello, and it was here that, according to Brett, over two consecutive nights Lawrence came into her room and made a tentative sexual approach, but on both occasions it was ended abruptly by either one or both of them, and nothing of note happened. It was all a bit hopeless – and Lawrence was probably relieved when the two parted ways soon afterwards, telling her via a letter that he was glad she was 'mooning' amongst friends and that she ought to forget whatever had passed between them.

Perhaps the encounter brought into sharp focus what was important to Lawrence – and that, whether Lawrence could acknowledge it openly, was Frieda. The situation was eased by a mollifying letter from Frieda, and after an absence of seven weeks, Lawrence meandered his way back to Spotorno via Florence. While he was away, he'd had two unlikely supporters working on his wife. 'The children tried like wise elders to talk me round', Frieda recorded.

'"Now Mrs. L." (so they called me) "be reasonable, you have married him, now you must stick with him." So Lawrence came back.'[15] In some respects, Barby and Elsa provided the buffer between Lawrence and Frieda that they so needed, and that Brett had failed to provide in New Mexico. 'F's daughters are really very funny', Lawrence wrote to Kot, 'they sit on their mother with ferocity, simply won't stand her cheek, and fly at her very much in her own style. It leaves her a bit flabbergasted, and is very good for her, as you'll guess.'[16]

Lawrence was welcomed back on 3 April, like the 'Easter lamb', and he reported in a letter that everybody was pleased to see him. A change of scene was decided on – the term of the rent on the Villa Bernarda was almost up and new surroundings would help to cement their new start. On 20 April they left for Florence. On their arrival they based themselves at the Pensione Lucchesi and spent May looking for somewhere more permanent. Lawrence liked the idea of having a 'pied à terre' at their disposal so they could come and go as they pleased – lending it to friends when they were away. The Tuscan landscape was dotted with villas, but the impressive Villa Mirenda crowned a hilltop and even though the weather was terrible ('a May long remembered in France and Italy for the cold ferocity of its rains',[17] Catherine Carswell recalled) the Lawrences were captivated: 'My heart went out to it. I wanted that villa',[18] Frieda remembered.' There were three peasant families living and working on the estate, and the spacious villa came with six rooms and 'service included' – it was the antithesis to the ranch and must have seemed the height of luxury in comparison. It was exactly what Lawrence needed – not just because his health would gradually deteriorate over the following years, but because it gave him the environment he needed to write and paint. Whether he acknowledged it, his illness was now arbitrarily dictating where the Lawrences based themselves. Lawrence told himself and others that he was no longer interested in going back to America: 'every week seems to alienate my soul further from America',[19] he wrote, but the reality was, he wouldn't have been allowed back into the country. And despite quipping to Frieda's mother that 'an Englishman of 40 is almost always bronchial',[20] the intermittent haemorrhages and his weakening strength would have made him all too aware that he was not going to recover.

The Mirenda, with its 'two gardens' and 'lovely slopes of vines and olives', provided Lawrence with the nearest thing he would get to a home in the final few years of his life – and a space in which he could write. During the spring of 1926 he typed out Frieda's translation of *David* and wrote essays about Florence, as well as some shorter fictional pieces based on observations and conversations he had had in Capri. But as a wet spring transitioned into a hot summer, they knew the heat would become too stifling; and although Lawrence conceded that leaving again was a 'bit of a bore' and the thought of travelling filled him with dread, they needed to escape the 'real Italian summer'.

They travelled to Baden-Baden first, to celebrate Anna von Richthofen's seventy-fifth birthday – spending a fortnight in the Black Forest landscape, where Lawrence claimed he 'always felt well' – before leaving Germany for London at the end of July. Lawrence was keen to see the early rehearsals of *David* that the Stage Society were performing but had no desire to stay holed up in the city for long. Frieda stayed in London – she could easily see her children while there – but Lawrence struck out on his own, determined that this visit to 'the same old England' would be different. He caught his usual cold within days of arriving but was well enough to travel to Scotland – a place Lawrence had never been – and he found it 'very nice' but 'rather cold'. It was, he concluded, '*too* northern for me'. His reaction to the weather perhaps reminded him of the precarious state of his health; it was here that Lawrence revealed in a letter that he intended to return to Baden-Baden to take a twenty-day inhalation cure for his condition. It was the first time Lawrence openly admitted to seeking medical assistance for his tuberculosis, although the procedure didn't actually take place on that occasion.

Lawrence broke up his return journey from Scotland by meeting his sisters, Ada and Emily, in Mablethorpe, Lincolnshire, a small seaside town with 'great sweeping sands, that take the light'. It clearly agreed with him: 'England seems to suit my health – I feel very well here', he commented in a letter to Brett, who was now back at the Del Monte ranch. Frieda joined them before Lawrence's sisters departed, and the couple stayed on for another fortnight in a bungalow in Sutton-on-Sea. 'I rather like being back in my own country, the Midlands', Lawrence remarked to Earl Brewster. Although he still didn't care for London, he was willing to admit that his 'own regions' gave him 'something' – was that 'something' a sense of belonging? He himself wasn't even sure. 'Curiously, I like England again...', he wrote. It was almost as if the feeling had crept up on him, nurtured by a sense of nostalgia for the place he 'knew as a boy'. For the first time in many years, Lawrence seemed to be *enjoying* England, or at least Mablethorpe, where the people were 'alive'. He felt at home.

The weather eventually turned dreary, and the sea grey and 'unsightly' according to Lawrence, so they left Mablethorpe – Lawrence to Ripley to briefly see Ada, and to help take his old friend and fellow tuberculosis sufferer Gertie Cooper for a lung X-ray, and Frieda went to London. Once Lawrence was reunited with Frieda in London they visited some of the 'old people' (Koteliansky, Enid Hopkin, Richard Aldington, the Carswells et al) and Frieda saw her son Monty. Lawrence also met Aldous Huxley and his wife Maria for the first time since 1915, and the two men went on to enjoy a close friendship for the rest of Lawrence's life. Catherine Carswell, who saw him that autumn, remarked that on his return to London the 'old weariness was upon him', and he was longing for the 'rich and glowing autumn of the Mirenda vineyards'.[21] Lawrence was certainly keen to return to Italy by the end of September so that they could enjoy the *vendemmia* (grape harvest). They arrived back at the villa just in time for the final few days of the ancient celebrations in early October. 'We are all festooned with grapes', Lawrence commented to Frieda's sister Else. Initially, they kept their arrival back in Florence quiet – Lawrence was enjoying the quiet and stillness of the villa after the noise and social whirlwind of London and the Midlands. 'No traffic and no bothers', he commented. It was the perfect environment for writing another novel.

With his recent trip to England still fresh in his mind, and a renewed sense of it being his 'home', he was inspired to set his new work in the Midlands. He also used the ongoing coal-strike back in England, and his views on class divisions as inspiration.

Around 22 October 1926 he put pen to paper and began to write the first sentences of what would become *Lady Chatterley's Lover*.

Chapter 16

Lawrence and the Lady

People without minds may go on being shocked, but they don't matter.
People with minds realize that they aren't shocked, and never really were:
and they experience a sense of relief.[1]

Lady *Chatterley's Lover* did not come to Lawrence in a short, sharp burst of creative genius like so many of his previous novels, although the first draft was written quickly. Yet it changed our perception of Lawrence the writer forever – not just because of its overt sexuality, but because it became the best-selling book of his writing career, thus securing his literary legacy well beyond his own lifetime.

It began life as what Frieda referred to as 'a short long story', and by the end of November 1926, Lawrence had finished the first version of what would grow into the full-length novel. He wrote outdoors whenever he could, taking his 'book and pen and cushion, and followed by John the dog…go into the woods behind the Mirenda and come back to lunch with what he had written'.[2] But as was customary with Lawrence, he started a complete rewrite almost immediately, but this time it 'comes out of me slowly', he remarked, allowing the story, which Lawrence thought was 'good' to flow, although he also worried it was 'too deep' in certain sections. He was certainly engrossed in the project – Frieda remembered him sitting 'almost motionless except for his swift writing'. So much so that the local wildlife would crawl over him unnoticed. He was concerned it was becoming '*absolutely* improper', but he pressed on and by late February 1927 he had written the second version. He had already predicted that Martin Secker would probably hate it, and it would be 'impossible to print', but he would call it 'Lady Chatterley's Lover', which he felt was 'nice and old-fashioned sounding'.

The second version was indeed 'improper' for 1927 – and was the first sexually explicit book Lawrence had written. It not only described sexual encounters but also gave Parkin (the gamekeeper, who would become 'Mellors' in the final version) a sexual vocabulary. In an age of literary repression, even words such as 'phallus', or the nouns 'penis' and 'vagina' were considered too risqué to appear in print. Lawrence's use of 'cunt', 'fuck', 'fucker', and 'fucking' was offensive in the extreme.

Lawrence laid the rewritten manuscript aside for a few weeks and spent more time at his easel instead. Painting was something that he had always taken pleasure in, and he now threw himself into his other creative outlet with gusto and intensity. His paintings began to reflect the physicality of his novel. He wrote to Brett that, 'Even my pictures, which seem to me absolutely innocent, I find people *can't even look* at them. They glance, and look quickly away.'[3] The paintings Lawrence completed while he was writing *Lady Chatterley's Lover* were later exhibited in 1929 by the Dorothy Warren Gallery, but of the twenty-five on display, thirteen were confiscated several days later by Scotland Yard on the grounds that they were 'gross, coarse, hideous, unlovely and obscene'.[4] By then, the novel had made Lawrence an artistic pariah as well as a literary one.

But back in March 1927, he began to think he ought to go over the manuscript again. He wasn't entirely sure what to do with it – it was wholly unpublishable as it was, yet he was adamant he wouldn't alter it. It was a dilemma he couldn't really afford to dwell on – the exchange rate in Italy was falling, and he couldn't afford to spend time writing works that would never appear in print.

So while Lawrence considered what to do with his unpublishable manuscript, he wrote the short stories 'The Lovely Lady', 'None of That!' and 'Things'. He also embarked on a project about the ancient Etruscan civilisation, for which he undertook scholarly research and a tour of Etruscan sites. From this he produced a set of essays, which he was able to sell to magazines, and although he never finished the book he was planning to publish them in, the essays were eventually published together posthumously in *Sketches of Etruscan Places and other Italian Essays* (1932). But the Etruscan walking tour Lawrence enjoyed – more so because he was accompanied by his friend Earl Brewster – was to be the last of its kind. In July, Lawrence suffered his worst bronchial haemorrhage to date. It was a hot day and he had been gathering peaches in the garden. Once inside, he collapsed in his room, crying out to Frieda in a 'strange, gurgling voice'. She rushed to his side to find a slow stream of blood coming from his mouth. She could do nothing but hold him and try to make him calm until the doctor arrived.

Lawrence was advised that a move to the fresher air of the pine-wooded mountains would be beneficial to his recovery, preferably 2,000-feet above sea level. By the end of July he was up and 'creeping feebly about', but better, if weak. So for three weeks in August they went to Villach in Austria – hoping that a cooler climate would revive the flagging Lawrence. 'It is heaven to be cool again', Lawrence wrote, 'really cool, and a deep green river from the ice, and a bit of rain.'[5] It was 'like a new life'.

Although Lawrence's health improved marginally, and he was able to 'go on little wallks', he still felt 'only about a third' of him had come back.

Understandably, he was despondent, and not very pleased with himself. He felt he had lost something of his old vitality, referring to his emotional vitality, rather than how he felt physically. From Austria, Lawrence and Frieda returned to Else's little wooden house on the edge of a forest overlooking a valley in Irschenhausen, Bavaria – a place they hadn't visited since 1913. Lawrence was delighted to find the little wooden house on the edge of the forest unaltered, and he began to feel better.

With his spirits raised, and Frieda keen to go back to the Villa Mirenda, the couple decided to wind their way back to Italy via Baden-Baden so that Lawrence could try the inhalation cure that was mooted eighteen months previously. Lawrence described it as sitting 'in a white shroud and hood in the steam, or vapor rather, and look at other dim shrouded figures sitting across the room! – but I think it does me good'.[6] He was also advised to go into the sanatorium to aid his recovery, but Lawrence had no intention of following that piece of advice: 'I shan't go into any sanatorium. Why should I?' he wrote to his sister, Emily. For Lawrence it was all a question of spirits – he knew a sanatorium would depress him further, and with Gertie Cooper's recent operation to have her lung, six ribs and a gland removed, discouraging him even more, he was adamant. 'I'm just beginning to get back a bit of my real self, and my appetite, why should I stick myself in a German sanatorium? I won't!' he reiterated.

By 20 October, Lawrence and Frieda were back at the Mirenda. Frieda was 'blissfully happy', but Lawrence felt oddly about the place. He found it 'alien, bare and empty'. It was almost as if he had never known it and he confided to Frieda's mother that he didn't feel at home there.

But there was something else bothering Lawrence. His long period of ill-health and subsequent convalescence had had a profound impact on his financial situation. During his illness he had been too unwell to start anything new, and except for some translations of Verga – which he often turned to when he was lacking in physical and creative energy – he had written nothing of note. The money came in 'slowly' and even if he had been well enough to travel, they hadn't the financial security to do so. 'Nothing goes very well – money dwindles – the govt. takes 20 per cent off what I do get – and Curtis Brown [his agent] 10 per cent. *Pax!* What does one exist for, but to be made use of, by people with money?'[7] he commented to Don Carswell. With some degree of unwillingness, Lawrence embarked on some new projects: a volume of short stories, a new collection of poems, and a piece of time-slip fiction that turned Eastwood into an ancient agricultural community, which remained unfinished until his death. And, of course, there was always *Lady Chatterley*.

The manuscript had been languishing in an 'old chest' during Lawrence's convalescence. According to Frieda, Lawrence had asked, 'Shall I publish it, or will it only bring me abuse and hatred again?' to which she responded, 'You have written it, you believe in it, all right, then publish it.'[8]

But how could Lawrence make the unpublishable publishable without compromising the integrity of his work? Fortunately, an ideal solution that would mitigate the need for Lawrence to use a traditional publisher had just presented itself. Lawrence had recently been reconciled with Norman Douglas, the essayist and literary executor to the late Maurice Magnus, whom Lawrence had a long-standing feud with over the unflattering depiction of Magnus in an introduction he wrote to *Memoirs of the Foreign Legion* (1924). Douglas had been reintroduced to Lawrence via Lawrence's friend Giuseppe 'Pino' Orioli, a bookseller who already acted as Douglas's private publisher. In mid-November 1927 Lawrence began to see the sense in a similar arrangement. It would bring in the 'badly needed shekels' and avoid the inevitable bad publicity.

Cutting out the middlemen was extremely appealing to Lawrence. Alongside Orioli, who was already a close friend, they could do all the work themselves – Lawrence would have more control over the process and the cost of production would be dramatically reduced. With a new plan of action to self-publish the manuscript, Lawrence now embarked on the third and final rewriting of *Lady Chatterley's Lover*. He wrote with astonishing speed given his precarious health. From 26 November 1927 to 8 January 1928 he wrote between 2,000 and 4,000 words a day, transforming the manuscript into a hard-hitting comment on the failure of society and the female sexual experience. Parkin was rewritten as Mellors and given more intellect, and the class divide was subtly widened by enhancing Clifford's egotism and by adding a new character – the cad, Michaelis. But more importantly, Lawrence wanted the end of the novel to reflect a different future – one where Connie and Mellors can escape the expectations of society and plan a world of their own. It was, in Lawrence's words, 'a very pure and tender novel', but also 'shocking, the most improper novel in the world!'

The beginning of 1928 was an exciting but troubled time. Once Lawrence had completed the final version of the novel, he needed it typed up. It was well known that Lawrence 'loathed' typing himself, and so he had to send the manuscript out. Only Frieda had been privy to *Lady Chatterley* thus far, and so it was the first test of how the wider public would react to this, his 'most improper' novel.

Initially, it didn't go well. The first typist, a novelist friend called Nellie Morrison, refused to go any further than chapter five because it was too 'indecent'. But his old London friend Catherine Carswell managed to recruit several friends, and between them and Aldous Huxley's wife Maria, who typed the final seven chapters while the Lawrences and Huxleys holidayed together in Switzerland, the manuscript, and two expurgated duplicates (one for Curtis

Brown in New York, and one for Secker in case commercial sale *was* possible) were eventually ready for the printer by 5 March.

Four days later, Lawrence met Orioli in Florence, and the two of them carried the unexpurgated typescript (Lawrence rather accurately referred to it as a 'bomb' to Secker) to the Tipografia Giuntina, an old-fashioned print shop where the typesetters still worked by hand. The fact none of them could read English was probably a blessing. Lawrence chose the paper, the mulberry-coloured binding and even drew the phoenix printed on the cover – a symbol that has become synonymous with Lawrence ever since. While printing was in progress, Lawrence, with a decisiveness and energy that belied his frail physical health, went on a marketing crusade. Now, there was no holding him back: he wanted to publish 1,000 copies of the unexpurgated edition, and 'fling them in the face of the world'.

He enlisted his friends – literary and other – to the cause. Mabel Dodge Luhan was charged with encouraging the American literati to buy copies, and Lawrence sent her some 'little order-forms', asking, 'do please send them out for me.' As any self-published writer knows, Lawrence's extensive network of contacts and prolific correspondence over the years would now, he hoped, pay dividends. During the spring and early summer of 1928, Lawrence was thought to have written to at least fifty close friends and associates, old and new, including Lady Cynthia Asquith, Earl Brewster, the Huxleys, Catherine Carswell and Idella Purnell. The exception was his sisters, Ada and Emily, who were kept in the dark. This was probably to alleviate them both of any unnecessary worrying they might do on his behalf, rather than concern around their reaction to the content – although it's likely they would have found it distasteful. He also continued to implore Secker, Curtis Brown and Alfred Knopf to consider commercial publication, but even as early as the end of March he had decided that Secker was 'himself an expurgated edition of a man',[9] because he had told Lawrence it would be impossible to make the novel fit for public presentation. There was a slightly more favourable review from Knopf, who didn't find it 'too much of an abomination', but Curtis Brown was thoroughly unimpressed that Lawrence had published his own novel. 'Damn them all', was Lawrence's response.

Lawrence would need a thick skin. Although it became clear very quickly that he had at least covered his costs, a large proportion of British booksellers cancelled their orders, or declined to take them on arrival (Lawrence's London friends collected them and redistributed them). He wrote: '…the London people have all been trying to make me feel tremendously in the wrong, and holding up pious hands afraid of touching pitch: which I don't forgive 'em, and shan't.'[10] A handful of the first British press reviews were favourable, commenting on the 'high literary quality', but that opinion, overall, turned hostile come the autumn.

On the other side of the Atlantic, the situation was more dire. Copies that had been mailed to American subscribers were frequently confiscated by customs authorities – so much so that Lawrence declared in August 1928 that it was 'useless' trying to mail copies to America. 'Damn the Americans – damn and damn them', Lawrence wrote to Orioli. The risk was enhanced even more – ironically, by a stunning review. On 1 September the *New York Sun* published a review by Herbert J. Seligmann, in which he declared the novel to be 'magnificent' and of 'great beauty and strength'. Such a glowing endorsement put *Lady Chatterley's Lover* on the hit list for literary pirates looking to make some fast cash. In 1928, a book that was judged 'indecent' was not protected by international copyright laws. This meant that anyone could photograph the text, or typeset it again, and sell it as the genuine article. Lawrence was aware that James Joyce's *Ulysses* (1922) had been pirated due to its suppression and didn't want *Lady Chatterley's Lover* to suffer the same fate.

Domestically, it was during the summer of 1928 that Frieda gradually began to distance herself emotionally from Lawrence. While Lawrence busied himself with the publishing process – an experiment that Frieda wholly supported – Frieda busied herself around the villa but was beginning to feel increasingly trapped by Lawrence's illness. Inevitably she looked elsewhere for the physical and emotional attachment she no longer felt she had with Lawrence, and she began an affair with Angelo Ravagli, the husband of her and Lawrence's former landlady. In April 1928 she had managed to visit Angelo Ravagli – who was stationed in the north-eastern town of Gradisca – while travelling with her sister Else to visit Barby in Alassio. In the same month, Lawrence had decided to give up the Mirenda and leave Italy, but Frieda had been so upset by the idea, Lawrence had capitulated and paid another six months' rent. He hadn't the strength to fight his corner and was heavily preoccupied with *Lady Chatterley* at the time. Frieda's reaction was significant, not just because it indicated how attached she was to the Mirenda, but because leaving northern Italy would have cut her off from Ravagli. In some respects, life was beginning to imitate Constance Chatterley's fictional struggle to free herself from her wheelchair-bound husband, Sir Clifford.

In a letter to her mother she admitted she felt her life was now ruled and dictated by Lawrence's illness. She was no longer living her own life – and although she never admitted to resenting Lawrence for the situation, even when she was clearly exasperated by his bad health and irritability – she needed to claim back something of the person she was before Lawrence's diagnosis. Ravagli was part of this process, and from 1928 onwards she maintained a relationship with her Italian lover, while honouring her implicit bind to Lawrence.

The summer and early autumn of 1928 were an astonishingly frenetic time for Lawrence. Not only was he going through the publication and distribution process of *Lady Chatterley*, but his health dictated that Lawrence and Frieda leave the Mirenda during the hotter summer months and travel to a more comfortable climate. From the second half of June they were in Switzerland, staying in several different locations depending on Lawrence's needs, and in mid-September they left for Baden-Baden, before heading to France in early October. Lawrence felt himself a 'stray individual' – a sentiment that proved accurate when the Lawrences made the decision to leave the Mirenda permanently while they were staying in Baden-Baden.

By early September Lawrence claimed to have sold 'something like 600 copies' of his privately printed *Lady Chatterley's Lover* in England, making him more than £700 profit (approximately £45,000 today) despite rumours of the novel's total suppression – which came to nothing. But that didn't stop some of the more intransigent newspapers from trying to instigate a wholescale public denouncement of the 'shameful book', which was a 'Landmark in Evil':

> *There has been brought to our notice within the last few weeks a book which we have no hesitation in describing as the most-evil outpouring that has ever besmirched the literature of our country. The sewers of French pornography would be dragged in vain to find a parallel in beastliness...'Lady Chatterley's Lover' defies reproduction in any manner whatever that would convey to our readers the abysm of filth into which D. H. Lawrence has descended...The circulation in this country of 'Lady Chatterley's Lover' must be stopped.*[11]

In the same article, the newspaper also claimed that an Oxford Street bookseller maintained outwardly that it did not stock the novel, but the salesman had whispered to the customer that 'he could get a copy privately and purely as a personal favour if twelve guineas were paid on the spot and no receipt was asked for!' If anything, the scandal instigated by the press only served to heighten the novel's appeal and infamy.

But either way, it didn't matter. Lawrence had sold all his copies and was, compared to his previous standard of living, wealthy. As his health deteriorated in the final year of his life, the success of *Lady Chatterley's Lover* and the work he secured because of it helped Lawrence immeasurably. He had the flexibility of working when he felt able without the pressure of writing out of necessity. He could afford to stay in hotels, travel if his health allowed, and pay medical bills. But most importantly, he left a financial legacy that would benefit Frieda for the rest of her life.

In early October 1928, Frieda began to pack up the Villa Mirenda with the help of the local peasants. She had left Lawrence in Toulon, and so said her final goodbyes to the villa she had loved alone. She describes poignantly how she parted with it: 'When I gave a last look from the two cypress trees along the road there stood the Mirenda upon its hill in the evening sun, with its shutters closed, old and solid, it seemed as if its eyes had closed for sleep, to dream of the life that had been and gone.'[12] Frieda travelled back to Toulon, and then the couple accepted an invitation from Richard Aldington and Dorothy 'Arabella' Yorke to stay with them on the French-Mediterranean island of Port-Cros. The island was 'all green pine forest', Lawrence described, '– umbrella pines – then the blue sea, and the other isles, and the mainland. There are no people on the island, only a few fishermen and the hotel on the little bay, an hours walk.'[13]

Lawrence bemoaned in a letter that the Mirenda was bad for his health and that he hoped Port-Cros would be 'a nice place to winter', which was prophetic. The result of Frieda's trip to pack up the Mirenda was a nasty dose of influenza, which she brought back with her and passed on to Lawrence, who had only been writing a mere day or two previously that he was 'feeling very well'. He spent several days in bed and two of those suffering from bronchial haemorrhages and feeling 'rotten'. During his convalescence Lawrence began writing some short poems, which he originally called 'Pensées' but which would be published in a collection named *Pansies* (1929). He also took on some journalistic work, primarily short articles on contemporary subjects that didn't take long to write but were well paid.

By November Lawrence had decided the island 'wasn't good enough' and the weather had turned for the worse, so they decided to go to Bandol, west of Toulon, staying in the Hotel Beau Rivage. Just before they left, Lawrence had an unexpected letter that brought a rush of nostalgia. It was from David Chambers – younger brother of Jessie. Lawrence's life had changed immeasurably since his youthful days at the Haggs – he was now famous (or 'infamous' to many) and had spent most of his adult life avoiding any reminders of his past. Yet now, just over a year from his death, he wanted to remember again. 'Whatever I forget, I shall never forget the Haggs – I loved it so', he wrote in reply. 'I loved to come to you all, it really was a new life began in me there...Because whatever else I am, I am somewhere still the same Bert who rushed with such joy to the Haggs.'[14]

Chapter 17

Towards Darkness

I have always wanted to be as the flowers are
so unhampered in their living and dying,
and in death I believe I shall be as the flowers are.
I shall blossom like a dark pansy, and be delighted
there among the dark sun-rays of death.[1]

Bandol was pleasant enough. It was 'pretty', and Lawrence felt it 'suited him well', but what Frieda really wanted was a house. She was bored, and restless, and fidgety, but Lawrence didn't know where he wanted to settle: 'Why can't women be peaceful?' Lawrence complained, somewhat hypocritically. For once, it was Frieda who was desperate to travel onwards rather than Lawrence, who had clearly forgotten all the occasions Frieda had been forced to leave a place on his insistence.

Lawrence's peace was destined to be shattered though. Just before Christmas 1928, Lawrence heard from a contact in New York that there were at least two pirated editions of *Lady Chatterley's Lover* in circulation that had been photographed from his edition, and given forged signatures. Lawrence derived nothing financially from the pirated copies, despite being the copyright holder. *Lady Chatterley* was also inadvertently causing Lawrence problems with one of his other works. In early January 1929, Lawrence sent a registered package to Laurence Pollinger – his literary agent at Curtis Brown in London – containing two typed copies of his collection of poems, *Pansies*, which he had almost completed. But as soon as the package arrived on English soil, it was opened by the postal authorities. The official line was that it was part of a random search to ensure the correct postage had been paid for the contents. But in truth, anything from Lawrence sent through the post was now regarded as highly suspect.

On 21 January Lawrence received the news that six copies of the second edition of *Lady Chatterley's Lover* sent to Pollinger had been confiscated and that two Scotland Yard detectives had been 'making enquiries'. But more troubling was the news from Pollinger that the two copies of *Pansies* had indeed been seized as they were considered 'obscene' and 'indecent', and that he [Pollinger] feared that all their joint correspondence was now being intercepted and read by the police. The matter of whether *Pansies* should be published was debated in the

House of Commons on 28 February by the Home Secretary, Sir William Joynson Hicks. Joynson Hicks admitted he 'did not exercise any literary censorship',[2] while also claiming that the package had been sent by 'open post' – thus giving the impression its contents were discovered as part of normal postal procedure. This was a clever piece of misdirection. Lawrence had sent a sealed package by registered post, not the open post, which at the time could only have been opened by a direct warrant from the Home Secretary. So either the postal authorities had stepped outside of their remit and opened the package without authority, or the Home Secretary had directed them in advance to seize and open anything Lawrence was sending into the country. Questions were rightly raised as to who had made the decision about the book's 'indecency' and what qualification they had 'to make a literary discrimination of this kind?'[3] Joynson Hicks was clear that his action was the right one: 'I am advised there is no public doubt whatever that this contained indecent matter, and as such was liable to be seized. I have given instructions for the book to be detained for two months, to enable the author to establish to the contrary if he desires to do so.'[4]

Just two days later the press were reporting that, 'The solicitors for Mr D. H. Lawrence have asked the Post-Master General to surrender the manuscripts', and that 'Mr. Michael Joseph, a director of Messrs. Curtis Brown the firm of publishers, said tonight that the solicitors had been instructed to test the action of the authorities.'[5]

Lawrence found the whole thing farcical as well as downright hypocritical. It only served to enrage him and give him an additional reason to persist in his campaign against hypocrisy and censorship – which was given added impetus in the summer of 1929 when Lawrence's paintings were exhibited publicly. But in the interim Frieda and Lawrence had their usual discussions (and usual indecision) regarding where they should live. Lawrence also had another pressing matter – trying to outsmart the literary pirates who were making money from *Lady Chatterley*. Aldous Huxley and his wife Maria wrote from Paris to suggest that it might be a suitable location to bring out a cheap English-language edition to undercut the pirates. There was certainly a market for it in Paris due to the large numbers of English and Americans living there as expatriates.

Frieda and Lawrence had been considering Spain for their next move, but Lawrence decided to go to Paris first. Paris also had the benefit of being home to Sylvia Beach's infamous but celebrated 'Shakespeare and Company' bookshop and publishing house, who had been responsible for publishing Joyce's *Ulysses* when it had been suppressed on the grounds of its obscenity. If Lawrence could convince Beach to publish an edition of *Lady Chatterley* then it had the potential to be an extremely fruitful partnership. As early as December 1928 he asked

Aldous to sound out Sylvia Beach, although both men had an aversion to the American-born expatriate. Now, he wanted to go and scope Paris out himself.

Frieda took the opportunity to travel to Baden-Baden, ostensibly to see her mother, but probably to visit Ravagli too – although there is no record of this. Lawrence arrived in Paris on 11 March with one of his newer friends, Welsh writer Rhys Davies, and ended up staying a month. His negotiations with Sylvia Beach were unsuccessful – Lawrence was in many respects a rival to Joyce and so there was a conflict of interest – but he managed to secure an arrangement for 3,000 copies with the little-known publisher Edward Titus. The visit was a success in literary terms but was disastrous for his health. The entire visit was punctuated with bouts of irritability and fury from Lawrence as his illness took its toll – exacerbated by the noise and traffic of the city. 'I get so sick of cities',[6] he wrote, calling it his 'Paris grippe'. 'I haven't been well in Paris', he wrote to Lady Ottoline Morrell, who he had recently patched up a relationship with. 'Sometimes one feels as if one were drifting out of life altogether – and not terribly sorry to go.'[7]

Lawrence was unwell enough for the Huxleys to arrange a medical assessment, and they made some in-roads where Frieda had failed. They managed to convince him to have a lung X-ray, but as soon as Frieda arrived in Paris he refused to have any more medical interventions and the couple set off to Majorca – much to the despair of the Huxleys, who couldn't understand Lawrence's flippancy towards the disease that was slowly killing him. It was a classic case of Lawrence endeavouring to convince himself that his illness wasn't going to define the rest of his life. And Frieda knew that the best remedy for Lawrence was to humour him and allow him to think he was still in control of his own mind and body. Her modus operandi was to keep his spirits up, because if his mind weakened to the extent of his body, then he would surely succumb to his illness even quicker. Lawrence knew he was going to die prematurely; he just didn't know when or where – little wonder he sought to maximise every moment of his condemned existence. And it was this knowledge that affected his mood so dramatically in Paris. He railed against his illness and the feeling manifested itself in anger rather than melancholy: 'he preferred to be angry',[8] Aldous Huxley wrote of his final months. The Huxleys may not have approved of his approach to his illness, but his courage was without question. Even Aldous admitted that in the last year of his life, Lawrence's vitality 'went on welling up in him, leaping, now and then, into a great explosion of bright foam and iridescence, long after the time when, by all the rules of medicine, he should have been dead'.[9]

But in the spring of 1929, that vitality was rapidly diminishing due to Lawrence's surroundings. Paris was making him sicker in mind as well as body, so in early April Frieda and Lawrence left for Majorca, which Lawrence commented was a 'wonderful place for doing nothing'. They stayed for two months until mid-June when the couple parted again – Lawrence to go and stay with the Huxleys in Forte dei Marmi on the Tuscan coast, and Frieda to act as Lawrence's representative at an exhibition of his paintings at the Warren Gallery in London. The exhibition marked another aspect of Lawrence's ongoing battle with the English authorities over censorship of art and literature – a situation that dogged him throughout the remainder of his life.

Lawrence met the owner of the gallery, Dorothy Warren, in 1915 at Ottoline Morrell's country house, Garsington. Lawrence's paintings – the majority of which had been at the Villa Mirenda and had therefore been packed up when the couple left – arrived in London in the summer of 1928 and a book of reproductions was published privately to accompany the exhibition, with an introduction written by Lawrence (which also underwent postal scrutiny when Lawrence sent it to England to be typed). After some delays, and much anxiety from Lawrence over Dorothy's organisational skills, the Warren Gallery finally opened its doors for a private viewing on 14 June 1929, and was opened to the public soon afterwards. An early review by a London art critic praised the 'force of conviction' in the paintings and singled out 'Boccaccio Story' as worthy of specific mention for being 'lovely in colour and convincing in drawing'.[10] Critic Gwen John, reviewing the exhibition for the journal *Everyman*, commented that several paintings were 'pictures of real beauty and great vitality'.[11] Lawrence wasn't strong enough to attend, but he had also been advised by his London agent that he might face arrest if he arrived in England.

The authorities couldn't arrest Lawrence, but they could imprison his paintings – and they did just that on 5 July. Following a complaint from a member of the public, thirteen of the twenty-five paintings on display were judged by a police officer to be obscene. The press wrote, 'The raid was carried out quietly after the public had left the galleries. The officers arrived about six o'clock, produced a search warrant, and examined the pictures and books on show in the galleries. They quickly took possession of 12 pictures [sic] and five books, which they took to Marlborough Street police station.'[12]

Lawrence later opined that it was the fragments of pubic hair that were visible on the paintings that had led to their confiscation. He was, understandably, furious, but was also concerned that his pictures would be burnt. Dorothy Warren had suggested they fight in court for a complete vindication of Lawrence's work, but he preferred to compromise. He wrote to Dorothy, 'No, no, I want you to accept the compromise. I do not want my pictures to be burned under any circumstance or for any cause…There is something sacred to me about my pictures, and I will not have them burnt, for all the liberty of England.'[13]

On this occasion, Lawrence wasn't prepared to sacrifice his work on the altar of censorship.

On 8 August the matter was brought to court. The proceedings were reported in the press under several colourful headlines, one of those being 'Novelist's Coarse, Hideous & Unlovely Pictures'. Dorothy was summoned to explain why the artworks should not be destroyed 'in the interests of public morality'.[14] Acting in Lawrence's best interests, Dorothy suggested that she would remove any offensive pictures and promise never to exhibit them again. Two were to go into private collections anyway, and the rest were returned to Lawrence. The books were destroyed, Dorothy was ordered to pay court costs, and Lawrence's original paintings were never exhibited in Britain again.

The other excitement that summer was the publication of *Pansies* – one unexpurgated edition printed privately by London bookshop owner Charles Lahr and one that had been censored by Martin Secker as a trade edition. The Secker edition received favourable reviews and was credited for 'not transgressing the bounds of conventional respectability' – which given the climate of anti-Lawrence sentiment that summer, probably came as a shock to everyone. 'He is a rebel', one review noted, 'one discerns kinship with John Donne, in more ways than one. There is much fine, even great, poetry in "Pansies", and much rubble.'[15]

In July, Lawrence went from the Huxleys' villa on the Tuscan coast to Florence, where he immediately caught a cold. When Frieda arrived from London, he was well enough to take a train to Baden-Baden where Frieda's mother was turning seventy-seven. But the visit was a disaster. Frieda's mother was a living embodiment of old-age vitality that Lawrence himself would never attain. He also accused her in a letter to Ada of purposefully staying at a high altitude in the Black Forest to get her daily dose of 'mountain air', even though the climate was making him feel miserable and ill. 'It's the most ghastly state of almost inane selfishness I ever saw – and all comes of her hideous terror of having to die. At the age of seventy-eight! May god preserve me from ever sinking so low.'[16]

From Baden-Baden they went to Bavaria, where Lawrence thought the altitude would be better for his lungs, but he encountered the same challenges as before – this time exacerbated by several dubious pieces of medical advice he had picked up on his travels such as eating a no-salt diet, and taking arsenic and phosphorus – which predictably, made him feel worse. He just wanted to find somewhere he wouldn't feel ill – but he was chasing ghosts. There was no such place.

In September, they committed to returning to Bandol – it had suited Lawrence the previous winter, and he hoped it would have the same soothing effect this time. Initially, it did – he felt 'nearly himself' and that he could finally breathe again. The couple rented a six-roomed villa named Beau Soleil overlooking the sea, where they would end up staying four months. 'Here I feel much better', he relayed to Kot in early October. They had a 'nice little house on the sea' and Lawrence was able to sit on the terrace in the sun. But just a few days later, Lawrence was bed-ridden again, feeling 'too rotten' to do anything. He felt so ill that he finally conceded that perhaps he did need medical intervention: 'I'll have to go into a sanatorium', he admitted reluctantly.

The Brewsters arrived and visited every day and the Huxleys were often in the area to provide friendship and support. November brought a slight improvement to Lawrence's health, and he was able to get up and take short walks. Remarkably, he continued to work intermittently – producing poetry, magazine articles, and expanding his essay 'A Propos of *Lady Chatterley's Lover*'. He also promised to write an introduction for artist and astrologer Frederick Carter, but he turned this into his own standalone piece, *Apocalypse* (1931), and wrote a separate piece for Carter. Much of his work was completed propped up in bed with pillows behind him and a writing pad on his knees.

'The flesh is very weak', Lawerence wrote in late November. 'My health is *very* tiresome, and I don't feel like doing a thing: unusual for me.' It shows something of Lawrence's absolute conviction that he would carry on living just as he had before that even four months before his death he was telling friends, 'I believe I'd get better in no time in New Mexico, because I'm not really weak…Now I have really come to this conclusion, I shall try all my might to arrange getting back, in the New Year.'[17]

They passed a quiet Christmas, although Lawrence complained of a 'bit of extra bronchitis', but it was to be Lawrence's last. From January 1930 onwards, Lawrence was in a great deal of pain – but still, he made plans as though his recovery was just a matter of time. 'We could sail Dollar Line from Marseille', he told Dorothy Brett, 'and land either in New York or San Francisco: I wouldn't mind a long sea trip.'[18] Imagining a future for himself was helping to sustain him. He knew that the moment he stopped making plans then the game was up, and death was the only conclusion.

On 17 January, Lawrence allowed an English tuberculosis specialist to examine him. Dr Andrew Morland was travelling in the south of France and was asked by Kot and Mark Gertler to visit Lawrence. His prognosis was grave and he immediately recommended complete bed rest. He was to see no one and do nothing – including work, which was of course anathema to Lawrence. Morland also suggested that if he didn't improve his only option was to go into a sanatorium.

In early February it was very clear that Lawrence was not better, and neither had he put any weight on to his already wasted frame. In pain and desperation – for nothing else would have compelled him to go – he agreed to Morland's suggestion and entered the unfortunately named Ad Astra Sanatorium in Vence (meaning *to the stars* in Latin). He put all his papers in order before he left Beau Soleil, destroying some and keeping others. He asked Frieda whether he ought to make a will – to which Frieda told him not to 'bother about wills'. She was worried that to answer 'yes' would only confirm that he was going to die. This would have profound consequences for Lawrence's family later. At the Ad Astra he had a balcony and view of the pretty mimosa in the garden, and friends brought him flowers and fruit, but it was 'dull', and he quickly lapsed into a torpor that he never recovered from. His letters became short and perfunctory as he was overtaken by pain and bodily weakness.

On 26 February, American sculptor Jo Davidson visited Ad Astra to take a clay model of Lawrence's head – an idea suggested by H. G. Wells. The finished result shows how emaciated Lawrence had become. Yet there is a hardness to his expression: Lawrence was resolute to the end. His final (underwhelmed) opinion on someone else's interpretation of art would be the last words the great writer ever wrote, which would probably have pleased Lawrence had he realised: 'Joe Davidson (?) came and made a clay head of me – made me tired – result in clay mediocre.' Davidson would go on to model President Franklin D. Roosevelt, Albert Einstein and Mahatma Gandhi.

On Saturday, 1 March, Lawrence did something typically Lawrence. With Frieda's assistance, he broke out of the Ad Astra and travelled with Frieda in a taxi to a rented house in Vence called the Villa Robermond. The effort Lawrence would have exerted performing this last, great rebuff to the 'institution' shows not only the strength of his determination but also, crucially, his acceptance of what would be his final fight. And there would only be one winner.

The next day after lunch, Lawrence's condition deteriorated rapidly, and he cried out for morphine. Aldous and Maria Huxley were there, so Aldous went to find a doctor while Frieda, Maria and Barby took it in turns to hold Lawrence in their arms as he became insensible, muttering, 'Hold me, hold me, I don't know where I am, I don't know where my hands are…where am I?'[19] Lawrence was eventually given morphia by the superintendent of Ad Astra whom Barby had pleaded with to help them. Following this, Lawrence grew quiet and said, 'I am better now', so Aldous and Barby went out again to try to arrange additional treatment to get Lawrence through to the morning. But before they returned, Lawrence's breathing became shallower and the gaps between his breaths grew larger – just as his mother's had twenty years before. At about 10.15 pm Lawrence breathed his last and slipped away. Frieda wrote, 'he was no longer in life with me':

There had been the change, he belonged somewhere else now, to all the elements; he was the earth and sky, but no longer a living man. Lawrence, my Lorenzo who had loved me and I him...he was dead...[20]

Two days later, Lawrence was buried in Vence, overlooking the Mediterranean. It was a simple occasion, without ceremony, in which his friends and loved ones said a final goodbye and put flowers into his grave.

It was exactly how Lawrence would have wanted it.

Epilogue: Unconquered

Lawrence's death was not the conclusion of his story. His literary legacy went on to cause conflict decades after his death – not only for those he held most dear but also in the establishment that he has spent his life condemning. From the first, and to the last, he was a disruptor.

The first conflict took place in the years immediately following his death. With Lawrence's final wish to return to New Mexico still in her thoughts, Frieda travelled back to the ranch with Angelo Ravagli, who would stay with Frieda until her death in 1956. Lawrence had died intestate – there was allegedly a will from 1914 but no one knew where it was – and so his estate had to be administered jointly by Frieda and Lawrence's brother George, whom Frieda openly disliked. Frieda was adamant that Lawrence wished her to have the income *and* copyrights from his estate so that she could continue to benefit from them during her lifetime and beyond, but George, backed by Lawrence's sister Emily, argued that while Frieda should have the income of the estate during her lifetime, on her death the copyrights should revert to the Lawrence family. This seemed a reasonable approach – Frieda would benefit all the time she needed financial support, but that income stream wouldn't automatically pass to her children by Ernest Weekley, or to Angelo Ravagli – none of whom were blood relations of Lawrence. Frieda didn't agree.

In November 1932, the dispute culminated in a hearing in London. 'The lost or mislaid will of Mr David Herbert Lawrence the author, who died in March last year [sic] at Vence, France, was the subject of a settled action before Lord Merrivale in the Probate Court yesterday',[1] the *Daily Mirror* reported.

Mrs. Lawrence, the widow, explained how the will was made. In 1914 at the outbreak of the war, she and her husband were staying in Buckinghamshire. With them were Miss Katherine Mansfield and Mr. Middleton Murry, the author.

The men were expecting to have to serve, and were discussing their finances. They then each made a will, the documents being executed in identical language.

Mr. Middleton Murry had kept his will, and it was produced in court and could be regarded as a draft of Mr. Lawrence's which had been lost before Mr. Lawrence's death.

Lord Merrivale pronounced for the contents of the document executed in 1914, remarking that the terms of the settlement were generous.[2]

The 'generous' settlement consisted of the entire estate in perpetuity: capital, future income, copyrights, manuscripts, paintings – essentially everything that had been Lawrence's was now Frieda's. She was the sole beneficiary, so when she died in 1956, it was divided between her three children by Weekley, and her third husband Angelo Ravagli, whom she had married in 1950. The Lawrence family were given a token sum of money, along with some manuscripts and paintings – but none of them would ever earn money from the ongoing sales of his published works.

The second slightly dubious incident concerned the actions of Ravagli and was revealed via a throwaway comment he made after Frieda's death. In 1935, Frieda decided that she wanted Lawrence's ashes to join her in New Mexico, where she could have a shrine built for him on the ranch. She arranged for Lawrence's body to be exhumed and cremated, and Ravagli was charged with travelling to Vence to oversee the process and bring the ashes back to Taos. This directive was followed to the letter, as far as Frieda was concerned, but following her death, Ravagli confessed that he had 'thrown away the D. H. cinders' in the Mediterranean before boarding the boat back to America with an empty urn. When the ship docked in New York, Ravagli filled the urn with wood ashes and passed them off as Lawrence's once he returned to the ranch. His motive for doing this is unclear if the story is true. It has been suggested it was to avoid paying tax to transport the ashes, but contrary to that is a document bearing an official consulate seal. The document is displayed in Lawrence's shrine at the ranch and appears to provide the provenance for what is buried there. It states that 'the box bearing the seal…contains an urn which contains only the remains after cremation of David Herbert Lawrence, which are being taken to the United States on board the SS Conte Di Savoia.' Perhaps Ravagli simply decided that Lawrence would have preferred to let the warm Mediterranean breeze decide where he should go rather than be trapped inside a concrete block. 'Not I, not I, but the wind that blows through me', Lawrence wrote in 'The Song of a Man Who Has Come Through'. Incidentally, Frieda used this quote in abbreviated form for the title of her memoir, so perhaps Ravagli was more perceptive than he was given credit for.

The ashes, whether they were Lawrence's or not, *were* sealed into a block of concrete inside Lawrence's shrine (which, incidentally, Ravagli *did* construct) to prevent them being removed – not just by future fans of Lawrence but by Frieda's unruly neighbour Mabel Luhan, who Frieda was convinced wanted to steal Lawrence's ashes. Frieda was buried just outside the shrine she believed she was sharing with Lawrence, under a stone bearing the von Richthofen crest, in total ignorance of Ravagli's alleged deception.

Lawrence's original gravestone also has its own story to tell. At Frieda's request, Lawrence's exhumation was attended by her friend and English resident of Vence, Martha Gordon Crotch. After the exhumation, Martha retrieved

Lawrence's gravestone – a simple rising phoenix mosaic, made from pebbles from the beaches of Bandol, and set in plaster. It was designed by Dominique Matteucci, an Italian artisan who had been living in a cottage at the Villa Robermond where Lawrence died.

Martha told Frieda she would keep it safe, and so when war broke out in Europe in 1939, Martha returned to England with the headstone in tow. It is not known whether Frieda had given permission for Martha to do as she wished with the headstone, but knowing it had value as a literary souvenir, she tried to sell it to Vivian de Sola Pinto, Professor of English at the University of Nottingham, for £200. Professor Pinto was keen for the headstone to come to Nottingham, to acknowledge its most famous literary son, but could not (or would not, depending on differing accounts) raise the funds to purchase it. Martha then abandoned the headstone in a London hotel before returning to Vence. Fortunately the hotel had the foresight to contact Professor Pinto and the headstone was removed to Nottingham before being given to Eastwood Council in 1957, who after forgetting its existence for several years, finally displayed it in the local library. It was eventually given permanent residency in the D. H. Lawrence Birthplace Museum in 2008.

Yet it was the trial of *Lady Chatterley's Lover* in 1960 that would have the biggest impact, and finally put to rest Lawrence's most long-standing conflict. *Regina Vs Penguin Books Ltd.* was the public prosecution in October 1960 of Penguin's decision to publish an unexpurgated version of *Lady Chatterley* in August of the same year – although what the trial really amounted to would be the most expansive and expensive lecture ever delivered on Lawrence's work. The 'not guilty' verdict resulted in a far greater degree of freedom for publishing explicit material in the UK, and the novel went from the sort of book the chief prosecutor, Mervyn Griffith-Jones, 'wouldn't wish his wife or servants to read', to a book that became admired, accepted and, more importantly, published as Lawrence intended it to be. Indeed, all the trial really established is that the novel contained nothing more salacious than some swear-words that Lawrence sought to cleanse of their indecent connotations – words that have since become commonplace in both speech and text in the twenty-first century. In *Lawrence Vs Censorship*, Lawrence had finally won.

D. H. Lawrence was everything that society wished he wasn't: infuriatingly stubborn; intransigent; frequently prophetic, and far too contradictory; an enemy of mediocrity; intensely intellectual to the point of obscurity; and, of course, so very impossible and full of anger. But he lived the life that was right for him – and in doing so, laid a path for others. As one critic wrote so succinctly on 3 March 1930, 'D. H. Lawrence is dead, but the new living of which he was the interpreter has only just begun.'

Notes

Introduction

1. The Obscene Publications Act, 1959. Cited in Rolph, C. H. (1961) (Eds.) *The Trial of Lady Chatterley: Regina V. Penguin Books Limited.* Penguin, London.
2. Rolph, C. H. (1961) (Eds.) *The Trial of Lady Chatterley: Regina V. Penguin Books Limited.* Penguin, London.
3. *Berks and Oxon Advertiser,* 15 November 1915.
4. Ibid.
5. *The Sphere,* 23 October 1915.
6. Lawrence, D. H. 'Morality and the Novel'.
7. Rolph, C. H. (1961) (Eds.) *The Trial of Lady Chatterley: Regina V. Penguin Books Limited.* Penguin, London.
8. Ibid.
9. Ibid.
10. Ibid.
11. Lawrence, D. H. (1960) *Lady Chatterley's Lover.* Penguin, London.
12. Lawrence, D. H. (1929) 'A Propos of Lady Chatterley's Lover', in Lawrence, D. H. (2000) *Lady Chatterley's Lover.* Edited by Michael Squires, Penguin Books, London.
13. Ibid.
14. Rolph, C. H. (1961) (Eds.) *The Trial of Lady Chatterley: Regina V. Penguin Books Limited.* Penguin, London.

Chapter 1

1. McDonald, E. D. (1936) (Eds.) *Phoenix: The Posthumous Papers of D. H. Lawrence.* William Heinemann Ltd., London.
2. *The Guardian,* 12 September 1960.
3. Cox, J. C. (1912) *The Churches of Nottinghamshire.* George Allen & Co., London.
4. Worthen, J. (2005) *D. H. Lawrence: The Life of an Outsider.* Allen Lane, London.
5. McDonald, E. D. (1936) (Eds.) *Phoenix: The Posthumous Papers of D. H. Lawrence.* William Heinemann Ltd., London.
6. Ibid.
7. Lawrence, A. and Stuart Gelder, G. (1932) *Early Life of D. H. Lawrence.* Martin Secker, London.
8. Lawrence, D. H. (1913) *Sons and Lovers.* Gerald Duckworth & Co. Ltd., London.
9. Lawrence, A. and Stuart Gelder, G. (1932) *Early Life of D. H. Lawrence.* Martin Secker, London.
10. Lawrence, D. H. (1918) 'Piano' from *New Poems.* Martin Secker, London.
11. Lawrence, A. and Stuart Gelder, G. (1932) *Early Life of D. H. Lawrence.* Martin Secker, London.
12. *The Guardian,* 12 September 1960.
13. Lawrence, D. H. (1913) *Sons and Lovers.* Gerald Duckworth & Co. Ltd., London.

14. Lawrence, A. and Stuart Gelder, G. (1932) *Early Life of D. H. Lawrence*. Martin Secker, London.
15. Ibid.
16. Lawrence, D. H. (1913) *Sons and Lovers*. Gerald Duckworth & Co. Ltd., London.
17. McDonald, E. D. (1936) (Eds.) *Phoenix: The Posthumous Papers of D. H. Lawrence*. William Heinemann Ltd., London.
18. *The Guardian*, 12 September 1960.
19. Ibid.
20. McDonald, E. D. (1936) (Eds.) *Phoenix: The Posthumous Papers of D. H. Lawrence*. William Heinemann Ltd., London.
21. Lawrence, D. H. (1913) *Sons and Lovers*. Gerald Duckworth & Co. Ltd., London.
22. Ibid.
23. Boulton, J. T. (1979) (Eds.) *The Letters of D. H. Lawrence, Volume I, September 1901 – May 1913*. Cambridge University Press, Cambridge.
24. Lawrence, D. H. (1913) *Sons and Lovers*. Gerald Duckworth & Co. Ltd., London.
25. Ibid.
26. E. T. (Chambers, Jessie) (1935) *D. H. Lawrence: A Personal Record*. Frank Cass & Co. Ltd., London.
27. Lawrence, D. H. (1913) *Sons and Lovers*. Gerald Duckworth & Co. Ltd., London.
28. Lawrence, D. H. (1913) *Sons and Lovers*. Gerald Duckworth & Co. Ltd., London.
29. Ibid.
30. Neville, G. H. (1981) *A Memoir of D. H. Lawrence: The Betrayal*. Cambridge University Press, Cambridge.
31. Ibid.
32. Lawrence, A. and Stuart Gelder, G. (1932) *Early Life of D. H. Lawrence*. Martin Secker, London.
33. Ibid.
34. McDonald, E. D. (1936) (Eds.) *Phoenix: The Posthumous Papers of D. H. Lawrence*. William Heinemann Ltd., London.
35. Lawrence, D. H. (1913) *Sons and Lovers*. Gerald Duckworth & Co. Ltd., London.
36. Worthen, J. (2005) *D. H. Lawrence: The Life of an Outsider*. Allen Lane, London.
37. *The Guardian*, 12 September 1960.
38. Roberts, W. and Moore, H. T. (1968) (Eds) *Phoenix II: Uncollected, Unpublished, and Other Prose Works by D. H. Lawrence*. The Viking Press, New York.
39. Neville, G. H. (1981) *A Memoir of D. H. Lawrence: The Betrayal*. Cambridge University Press, Cambridge.
40. *The Guardian*, 12 September 1960.
41. *Nottingham Journal*, 1932. Cited in Neville, G. H. (1981) *A Memoir of D. H. Lawrence: The Betrayal*. Cambridge University Press, Cambridge.
42. *Ripley and Heanor News and Ilkeston Division Free Press*, 30 March 1900.
43. Ibid.
44. Ibid.
45. *Derby Daily Telegraph*, 29 March 1900.
46. *Nottinghamshire Guardian*, 14 July 1900.

Chapter 2

1. Lawrence, D. H. (1913) *Sons and Lovers*. Gerald Duckworth & Co. Ltd., London.
2. Lawrence, A. and Stuart Gelder, G. (1932) *Early Life of D. H. Lawrence*. Martin Secker, London.

3. Lawrence, D. H. (1913) *Sons and Lovers*. Gerald Duckworth & Co. Ltd., London.
4. Ibid.
5. Ibid.
6. Neville, G. H. (1981) *A Memoir of D. H. Lawrence: The Betrayal*. Cambridge University Press, Cambridge.
7. E. T. (Chambers, Jessie) (1935) *D. H. Lawrence: A Personal Record*. Frank Cass & Co. Ltd., London.
8. *Eastwood and Kimberley Advertiser*, 18 October 1901.
9. Lawrence, D. H. (1913) *Sons and Lovers*. Gerald Duckworth & Co. Ltd., London.
10. *Eastwood and Kimberley Advertiser*, 18 October 1901.
11. Lawrence, D. H. (1913) *Sons and Lovers*. Gerald Duckworth & Co. Ltd., London.
12. Boulton, J. T. (1979) (Eds.) *The Letters of D. H. Lawrence, Volume I, September 1901 – May 1913*. Cambridge University Press, Cambridge.
13. Ibid.
14. Lawrence, D. H. (1913) *Sons and Lovers*. Gerald Duckworth & Co. Ltd., London.
15. E. T. (Chambers, Jessie) (1935) *D. H. Lawrence: A Personal Record*. Frank Cass & Co. Ltd., London.
16. Ibid.
17. Ibid.
18. E. T. (Chambers, Jessie) (1935) *D. H. Lawrence: A Personal Record*. Frank Cass & Co. Ltd., London.
19. Worthen, J. (2005) *D. H. Lawrence: The Life of an Outsider*. Allen Lane, London.
20. *The Guardian*, 12 September 1960.
21. E. T. (Chambers, Jessie) (1935) *D. H. Lawrence: A Personal Record*. Frank Cass & Co. Ltd., London.
22. Ibid.
23. Ibid.
24. Ibid.
25. Neville, G. H. (1981) *A Memoir of D. H. Lawrence: The Betrayal*. Cambridge University Press, Cambridge.
26. Roberts, W. and Moore, H. T. (1968) (Eds) *Phoenix II: Uncollected, Unpublished, and Other Prose Works by D. H. Lawrence*. The Viking Press, New York.
27. Neville, G. H. (1981) *A Memoir of D. H. Lawrence: The Betrayal*. Cambridge University Press, Cambridge.
28. E. T. (Chambers, Jessie) (1935) *D. H. Lawrence: A Personal Record*. Frank Cass & Co. Ltd., London.
29. Lawrence, D. H. (1913) *Sons and Lovers*. Gerald Duckworth & Co. Ltd., London.
30. Ibid.
31. Ibid.
32. Ibid.
33. Boulton, J. T. (1979) (Eds.) *The Letters of D. H. Lawrence, Volume I, September 1901 – May 1913*. Cambridge University Press, Cambridge.
34. Lawrence, D. H. (1918) *New Poems*.
35. E. T. (Chambers, Jessie) (1935) *D. H. Lawrence: A Personal Record*. Frank Cass & Co. Ltd., London.

Chapter 3

1. E. T. (Chambers, Jessie) (1935) *D. H. Lawrence: A Personal Record*. Frank Cass & Co. Ltd., London.

2. Worthen, J. (2005) *D. H. Lawrence: The Life of an Outsider.* Allen Lane, London.
3. Roberts, I. D. (1983) 'D. H. Lawrence and Davidson Road School: An Institutional Viewpoint', in *The D.H. Lawrence Review,* Vol. 16, No. 2, pp.195-210.
4. Lawrence, D. H. (1908) 'Lessford's Rabbits'. *The Mortal Coil and Other Stories* (Eds.) Sagar, K. (1971) Penguin, London.
5. Lawrence, D. H. (1909) 'A Lesson on a Tortoise'. *The Mortal Coil and Other Stories* (Eds.) Sagar, K. (1971) Penguin, London.
6. Ibid.
7. Roberts, I. D. (1983) 'D. H. Lawrence and Davidson Road School: An Institutional Viewpoint', in *The D.H. Lawrence Review,* Vol. 16, No. 2, pp.195-210.
8. Lawrence, D. H. (1908) 'Lessford's Rabbits'. *The Mortal Coil and Other Stories* (Eds.) Sagar, K. (1971) Penguin, London.
9. E. T. (Chambers, Jessie) (1935) *D. H. Lawrence: A Personal Record.* Frank Cass & Co. Ltd., London.
10. Ibid.
11. Ibid.
12. Ibid.
13. Roberts, I. D. (1983) 'D. H. Lawrence and Davidson Road School: An Institutional Viewpoint', in *The D.H. Lawrence Review,* Vol. 16, No. 2, pp.195-210.
14. E. T. (Chambers, Jessie) (1935) *D. H. Lawrence: A Personal Record.* Frank Cass & Co. Ltd., London.
15. Boulton, J. T. (1979) (Eds.) *The Letters of D. H. Lawrence, Volume I, September 1901 – May 1913.* Cambridge University Press, Cambridge.
16. Corke, H. (1971) 'D. H. Lawrence: The Early Stage', in *The D.H. Lawrence Review,* Vol. 4, No. 2, pp. 111-121.
17. E. T. (Chambers, Jessie) (1935) *D. H. Lawrence: A Personal Record.* Frank Cass & Co. Ltd., London.
18. Ford, F. M. (1938) *Mightier Than the Sword: Memories and Criticisms.* George Allen & Unwin Ltd., London.
19. Ford, F. M. (1938) *Mightier Than the Sword: Memories and Criticisms.* George Allen & Unwin Ltd., London.
20. Ibid.
21. E. T. (Chambers, Jessie) (1935) *D. H. Lawrence: A Personal Record.* Frank Cass & Co. Ltd., London.
22. Roberts, W. and Moore, H. T. (1968) (Eds) *Phoenix II: Uncollected, Unpublished, and Other Prose Works by D. H. Lawrence.* The Viking Press, New York.
23. Worthen, J. (2005) *D. H. Lawrence: The Life of an Outsider.* Allen Lane, London.
24. E. T. (Chambers, Jessie) (1935) *D. H. Lawrence: A Personal Record.* Frank Cass & Co. Ltd., London.
25. Roberts, W. and Moore, H. T. (1968) (Eds) *Phoenix II: Uncollected, Unpublished, and Other Prose Works by D. H. Lawrence.* The Viking Press, New York.
26. Lawrence, D. H. (1913) *Love Poems and Others.* Duckworth & Co., London.
27. E. T. (Chambers, Jessie) (1935) *D. H. Lawrence: A Personal Record.* Frank Cass & Co. Ltd., London.
28. Corke, H. (1971) 'D. H. Lawrence: The Early Stage', in *The D.H. Lawrence Review,* Vol. 4, No. 2, pp. 111-121.
29. Boulton, J. T. (1979) (Eds.) *The Letters of D. H. Lawrence, Volume I, September 1901 – May 1913.* Cambridge University Press, Cambridge.
30. Ibid.

31. Boulton, J. T. (1979) (Eds.) *The Letters of D. H. Lawrence, Volume I, September 1901 – May 1913.* Cambridge University Press, Cambridge.
32. Corke, H. (1971) 'D. H. Lawrence: The Early Stage', in *The D.H. Lawrence Review,* Vol. 4, No. 2, pp. 111-121.
33. Corke, H. (1975) *In Our Infancy: An Autobiography.* Cambridge University Press, Cambridge.
34. Ibid.
35. Ibid.
36. Ibid.
37. Ibid.
38. Lawrence, D. H. (1913) *Love Poems and Others.* Duckworth & Co., London.
39. Ibid.
40. Boulton, J. T. (1979) (Eds.) *The Letters of D. H. Lawrence, Volume I, September 1901 – May 1913.* Cambridge University Press, Cambridge.
41. Worthen, J. (2005) *D. H. Lawrence: The Life of an Outsider.* Allen Lane, London.
42. E. T. (Chambers, Jessie) (1935) *D. H. Lawrence: A Personal Record.* Frank Cass & Co. Ltd., London.
43. Ford, F. M. (1938) *Mightier Than the Sword: Memories and Criticisms.* George Allen & Unwin Ltd., London.

Chapter 4

1. Lawrence, D. H. (1913) *Sons and Lovers.* Gerald Duckworth & Co. Ltd., London.
2. Neville, G. H. (1981) *A Memoir of D. H. Lawrence: The Betrayal.* Cambridge University Press, Cambridge.
3. E. T. (Chambers, Jessie) (1935) *D. H. Lawrence: A Personal Record.* Frank Cass & Co. Ltd., London.
4. Ibid.
5. Lawrence, D. H. (1913) *Sons and Lovers.* Gerald Duckworth & Co. Ltd., London.
6. Ibid.
7. Ibid.
8. Boulton, J. T. (1979) (Eds.) *The Letters of D. H. Lawrence, Volume I, September 1901 – May 1913.* Cambridge University Press, Cambridge.
9. Worthen, J. (2005) *D. H. Lawrence: The Life of an Outsider.* Allen Lane, London.
10. E. T. (Chambers, Jessie) (1935) *D. H. Lawrence: A Personal Record.* Frank Cass & Co. Ltd., London.
11. Lawrence, D. H. (1913) *Sons and Lovers.* Gerald Duckworth & Co. Ltd., London.
12. Lawrence, D. H. (1916) *Amores.* Gerald Duckworth & Co. Ltd., London.
13. Ibid.

Chapter 5

1. *The Daily News,* 14 February 1911.
2. *Southwark and Bermondsey Recorder,* 24 February 1911.
3. *The Gentlewoman,* 4 March 1911.
4. *Westminster Gazette,* 13 February 1911.
5. E. T. (Chambers, Jessie) (1935) *D. H. Lawrence: A Personal Record.* Frank Cass & Co. Ltd., London.
6. *The Daily News,* 14 February 1911.
7. Ford, F. M. (1938) *Mightier Than the Sword: Memories and Criticisms.* George Allen & Unwin Ltd., London.

8. Cobau, W. & Hopkin, O. (1976) 'A View From Eastwood: Conversations With Mrs. O. L. Hopkin'. *The D.H. Lawrence Review 9*, No. 1, pp. 126–36.
9. Neville, G. H. (1981) *A Memoir of D. H. Lawrence: The Betrayal*. Cambridge University Press, Cambridge.
10. Boulton, J. T. (1979) (Eds.) *The Letters of D. H. Lawrence, Volume I, September 1901 – May 1913*. Cambridge University Press, Cambridge.
11. E. T. (Chambers, Jessie) (1935) *D. H. Lawrence: A Personal Record*. Frank Cass & Co. Ltd., London.
12. Delavenay, E. (1969) *D. H. Lawrence: U Homme et la Genese de son Oeuvre* (2 vols.), Libraire C. Klincksieck, Paris. Referenced in: Neville, G. H. (1981) *A Memoir of D. H. Lawrence: The Betrayal*. Cambridge University Press, Cambridge.
13. Ludwig, R. (1965) (Eds.) *Letters of Ford Madox Ford*. Princeton University Press. Referenced in: Jefferson, G. (1982) *Edward Garnett: A Life in Literature*. Jonathan Cape, London.
14. Goldring, D. (1943) *South Lodge: Reminiscences of Violet Hunt, Ford Madox Ford and The English Review Circle*. Constable, London. Referenced in: Jefferson, G. (1982) *Edward Garnett: A Life in Literature*. Jonathan Cape, London.
15. Ford, F. M. (1907) 'Literary Portraits: XII. Mr. Edward Garnett', *Tribune 2*. Quoted in Harvey, D. D. (1962) *Ford Madox Ford: A Bibliography of Works and Criticism*. Princeton University Press.
16. Garnett, E. (1934) Introduction to D. H. Lawrence, *A Collier's Friday Night*. Martin Secker, London.
17. Grice, A. (2021) *D. H. Lawrence and the Literary Marketplace: The Early Writings*. Edinburgh University Press, Edinburgh.
18. Boulton, J. T. (1979) (Eds.) *The Letters of D. H. Lawrence, Volume I, September 1901 – May 1913*. Cambridge University Press, Cambridge.
19. Ford, G. (1973) 'Jessie Chambers' Last Tape on D. H. Lawrence', in *Mosaic: An Interdisciplinary Critical Journal*, Vol. 6, No. 3: Literature and Ideas: A Miscellany of Opinions and Analysis (Spring, 1973), pp. 1-12.
20. Ibid.

Chapter 6
1. Lawrence, D. H. (1913) *Sons and Lovers*. Gerald Duckworth & Co. Ltd., London.
2. Lawrence, D. H. (1914) 'The Shades of Spring', in *The Prussian Officer and Other Stories*. Duckworth & Co., London.
3. 'Introduction to The Collected Poems of D. H. Lawrence', in McDonald, E. D. (1936) (Eds.) *Phoenix: The Posthumous Papers of D. H. Lawrence*. William Heinemann, London.
4. Boulton, J. T. (1979) (Eds.) *The Letters of D. H. Lawrence, Volume I, September 1901 – May 1913*. Cambridge University Press, Cambridge.
5. E. T. (Chambers, Jessie) (1935) *D. H. Lawrence: A Personal Record*. Frank Cass & Co. Ltd., London.
6. Ibid.
7. Ibid.
8. Ibid.
9. Ibid.
10. Lawrence, D. H. (1913) *Sons and Lovers*. Gerald Duckworth & Co. Ltd., London.
11. E. T. (Chambers, Jessie) (1935) *D. H. Lawrence: A Personal Record*. Frank Cass & Co. Ltd., London.

12. Ibid.
13. Ibid.
14. Lawrence, F. (1935) '*Not I, But the Wind…*' Heinemann, London.

Chapter 7

1. Huxley, A. (1932) (Eds.) *The Letters of D. H. Lawrence*. Viking Press, New York.
2. Ibid.
3. Lawrence, F. (1935) '*Not I, But the Wind…*' Heinemann, London.
4. Boulton, J. T. (1979) (Eds.) *The Letters of D. H. Lawrence, Volume I, September 1901 – May 1913*. Cambridge University Press, Cambridge.
5. Ibid.
6. Boulton, J. T. (1979) (Eds.) *The Letters of D. H. Lawrence, Volume I, September 1901 – May 1913*. Cambridge University Press, Cambridge.
7. Tedlock, E. W. (1964) (Eds.) *Frieda Lawrence: The Memoirs and Correspondence*. Alfred A. Knopf, New York.
8. Ibid.
9. Ibid.
10. Boulton, J. T. (1979) (Eds.) *The Letters of D. H. Lawrence, Volume I, September 1901 – May 1913*. Cambridge University Press, Cambridge.
11. E. T. (Chambers, Jessie) (1935) *D. H. Lawrence: A Personal Record*. Frank Cass & Co. Ltd., London.
12. Ibid.
13. *Westminster Gazette*, 22 June 1912.
14. *The Bystander*, 24 July 1912.
15. *Westminster Gazette*, 13 July 1912.
16. Boulton, J. T. (1979) (Eds.) *The Letters of D. H. Lawrence, Volume I, September 1901 – May 1913*. Cambridge University Press, Cambridge.
17. Ibid.
18. Garnett, D. (1954) *The Golden Echo*. Harcourt, New York, in Nehls, E. (1957) (Eds.) *D. H. Lawrence: A Composite Biography, Volume One, 1885-1919*. University of Wisconsin Press, Madison.
19. Boulton, J. T. (1979) (Eds.) *The Letters of D. H. Lawrence, Volume I, September 1901 – May 1913*. Cambridge University Press, Cambridge.
20. Lawrence, D. H. (1934) 'Mr Noon', in *A Modern Lover*. Martin Secker, London.
21. Ibid.
22. Ibid.
23. Lawrence, F. (1935) '*Not I, But the Wind…*' Heinemann, London.
24. Nehls, E. (1957) (Eds.) *D. H. Lawrence: A Composite Biography, Volume One, 1885-1919*. University of Wisconsin Press, Madison.
25. Ibid.
26. Ibid.
27. Boulton, J. T. (1979) (Eds.) *The Letters of D. H. Lawrence, Volume I, September 1901 – May 1913*. Cambridge University Press, Cambridge.

Chapter 8

1. Corke, H. (1965) *D. H. Lawrence: The Croydon Years*. University of Texas Press, Austin.
2. Boulton, J. T. (1979) (Eds.) *The Letters of D. H. Lawrence, Volume I, September 1901 – May 1913*. Cambridge University Press, Cambridge.

3. Ibid.
4. Lawrence, D. (1917) *Look! We have come through!* Chatto & Windus, London.
5. Boulton, J. T. (1979) (Eds.) *The Letters of D. H. Lawrence, Volume I, September 1901 – May 1913*. Cambridge University Press, Cambridge.
6. Nehls, E. (1957) (Eds.) *D. H. Lawrence: A Composite Biography, Volume One, 1885-1919*. University of Wisconsin Press, Madison.
7. *The Scotsman*, 24 February 1913.
8. Worthen, J. (2005) *D. H. Lawrence: The Life of an Outsider*. Allen Lane, London.
9. Ibid.
10. Ibid.
11. Lawrence, D. H. (1915) *Twilight in Italy*. Duckworth & Co., London.
12. Boulton, J. T. (1979) (Eds.) *The Letters of D. H. Lawrence, Volume I, September 1901 – May 1913*. Cambridge University Press, Cambridge.
13. Nehls, E. (1957) (Eds.) *D. H. Lawrence: A Composite Biography, Volume One, 1885-1919*. University of Wisconsin Press, Madison.
14. Nehls, E. (1957) (Eds.) *D. H. Lawrence: A Composite Biography, Volume One, 1885-1919*. University of Wisconsin Press, Madison.
15. An advert printed in the *Westminster Gazette*, 11 July 1913.
16. An advert printed in the *Pall Mall Gazette*, 27 June 1913.
17. Zytaruk, G. J. and Boulton, J. T. (1981) (Eds.) *The Letters of D. H. Lawrence, Volume II, June 1913 – October 1916*. Cambridge University Press, Cambridge.
18. *The Illustrated London News*, 5 July 1913.
19. *The Clarion*, 25 July 1913.
20. Zytaruk, G. J. and Boulton, J. T. (1981) (Eds.) *The Letters of D. H. Lawrence, Volume II, June 1913 – October 1916*. Cambridge University Press, Cambridge.
21. Ibid.
22. Woolf, V. (1924) *The Hogarth Essays: Mr. Bennett and Mrs. Brown*. Hogarth Press, London.
23. Ibid.
24. Zytaruk, G. J. and Boulton, J. T. (1981) (Eds.) *The Letters of D. H. Lawrence, Volume II, June 1913 – October 1916*. Cambridge University Press, Cambridge.
25. Scott-James, R. A. (1937) 'Edward Garnett', in the *Spectator*.
26. Moore, H. T. (1962) (Eds.) *The Collected Letters of D. H. Lawrence: Volume II*. Heinemann, London.
27. *Lynn Advertiser*, 31 July 1914.

Chapter 9

1. Lawrence, D. H. (1922) *England, My England, and Other Stories*. Thomas Seltzer, New York.
2. Lawrence, F. (1935) '*Not I, But the Wind...*' Heinemann, London.
3. Zytaruk, G. J. and Boulton, J. T. (1981) (Eds.) *The Letters of D. H. Lawrence, Volume II, June 1913 – October 1916*. Cambridge University Press, Cambridge.
4. Tedlock, E. W. (1963) *D. H. Lawrence, Artist and Rebel: A Study of Lawrence's Fiction*. University of New Mexico Press, Albuquerque.
5. Steele, B. (1985) (Eds.) *Study of Thomas Hardy and Other Essays – D. H. Lawrence*. Cambridge, Cambridge University Press.
6. Ibid.
7. Lawrence, D. H. (1925) *Reflections on the Death of a Porcupine*. Willian Heinemann, London.
8. Ibid.

9. Lawrence, D. H. (1922) 'England, My England', in *England, My England*. Thomas Seltzer, United States.
10. *The Globe*, 5 October 1915.
11. *The Sphere*, 23 October 1915.
12. *Berks and Oxon Advertiser*, 19 November 1915.
13. Ibid.
14. Huxley, A. (1932) (Eds.) *The Letters of D. H. Lawrence*. The Viking Press, New York.
15. Ibid.

Chapter 10

1. Lawrence, D. H. (1923) *Kangaroo*. Thomas Seltzer, New York.
2. Zytaruk, G. J. and Boulton, J. T. (1981) (Eds.) *The Letters of D. H. Lawrence, Volume II, June 1913 – October 1916*. Cambridge University Press, Cambridge.
3. Lawrence, D. H. (1916) *Amores*. B. W. Huebsch, New York.
4. Tedlock, E. W. (1964) (Eds.) *Frieda Lawrence: The Memoirs and Correspondence*. Alfred A. Knopf, New York.
5. Kinkead-Weekes, M. (1996) *D. H. Lawrence: Triumph to Exile*. Cambridge University Press, Cambridge.
6. Ibid.
7. Tedlock, E. W. (1963) *D. H. Lawrence, Artist and Rebel: A Study of Lawrence's Fiction*. University of New Mexico Press, Albuquerque.
8. Ibid.
9. Gathorne-Hardy, R. (1974) (Eds.) *Ottoline at Garsington: Memoirs of Lady Ottoline Morrell, 1915-1918*. Faber and Faber, London.
10. *Civil and Military Gazette (Lahore)*, 25 June 1933.
11. Ibid.
12. Lawrence, D. H. (1923) *Studies in Classic American Literature*. Thomas Seltzer, New York.
13. Ibid.
14. *Sunday Mirror*, 8 April 1917.

Chapter 11

1. Moore, H. T. (1962) *The Collected Letters of D. H. Lawrence*. Heinemann, London.
2. *The Sketch*, 12 December 1917.
3. *Times Literary Supplement*, 22 November 1917.
4. Boulton, J. T. and Robertson, A. (1984) (Eds.) *The Letters of D. H. Lawrence, Volume III, October 1916 – June 1921*. Cambridge University Press, Cambridge.
5. Ibid.
6. Tedlock, E. W. (1964) (Eds.) *Frieda Lawrence: The Memoirs and Correspondence*. Alfred A. Knopf, New York.
7. Boulton, J. T. and Robertson, A. (1984) (Eds.) *The Letters of D. H. Lawrence, Volume III, October 1916 – June 1921*. Cambridge University Press, Cambridge.
8. Kinkead-Weekes, M. (1996) *D. H. Lawrence: Triumph to Exile*. Cambridge University Press, Cambridge.

Chapter 12

1. Carswell, C. (1932) *The Savage Pilgrimage: A Narrative of D. H. Lawrence*. Harcourt, Brace and Co., New York.
2. *Derby Daily Telegraph*, 13 February 1919.
3. Ibid.

4. Lawrence, D. H. (1920) *Women in Love.* Thomas Seltzer Inc., New York.
5. Tedlock, E. W. (1964) (Eds.) *Frieda Lawrence: The Memoirs and Correspondence.* Alfred A. Knopf, New York.
6. Foster Damon, S. (1935) *Amy Lowell: A Chronicle.* Houghton Mifflin Co., Boston, Massachusetts.
7. Ibid.
8. Carswell, Catherine (1932) *The Savage Pilgrimage: A narrative of D. H. Lawrence.* Harcourt, Brace and Company, New York.
9. Lawrence, D. H. (1920) *The Lost Girl.* Martin Secker, London.
10. Ibid.
11. Squires, M. (2008) *D. H. Lawrence and Frieda: A Portrait of Love and Loyalty.* André Deutsch, London.
12. Weintraub, S. (1965) *Reggie: A Portrait of Reginald Turner.* New York. Cited in Kinkead-Weekes, M. (1996) *D. H. Lawrence: Triumph to Exile.* Cambridge University Press, Cambridge.
13. Lawrence, D. H. (1920) 'David', published in McDonald, E. D. (1936) (Eds.) *Phoenix: The Posthumous Papers of D. H. Lawrence.* William Heinemann Ltd., London.
14. Lawrence, D. H. (1922) *Aarons Rod.* Thomas Seltzer, New York.
15. Carswell, Catherine (1932) *The Savage Pilgrimage: A narrative of D. H. Lawrence.* Harcourt, Brace and Company, New York.
16. Ibid.
17. Boulton, J. T. and Robertson, A. (1984) (Eds.) *The Letters of D. H. Lawrence, Volume III, October 1916 – June 1921.* Cambridge University Press, Cambridge.
18. Lawrence, F. (1935) '*Not I, But the Wind…*' Heinemann, London.
19. Roberts, W., Boulton, J. T. and Mansfield, E. (1987) (Eds.) *The Letters of D. H. Lawrence, Volume IV, June 1921 – March 1924.* Cambridge University Press, Cambridge.
20. Boulton, J. T. and Robertson, A. (1984) (Eds.) *The Letters of D. H. Lawrence, Volume III, October 1916 – June 1921.* Cambridge University Press, Cambridge.
21. Ibid.
22. Ibid.

Chapter 13

1. Lawrence, D. H. (1923) 'Medlars and Sorb-Apples' from *Birds, Beasts and Flowers.* Thomas Seltzer, New York.
2. Kinkead-Weekes, M. (1996) *D. H. Lawrence: Triumph to Exile.* Cambridge University Press, Cambridge.
3. Ibid.
4. Dodge Luhan, M. (1932) *Lorenzo in Taos: D. H. Lawrence and Mabel Dodge Luhan.* Alfred A. Knopf, New York.
5. Lawrence, D. H. (1922) *Aarons Rod.* Thomas Seltzer, New York.
6. Lawrence, D. H. (1934) 'Mr Noon', in *A Modern Lover.* Martin Secker, London.
7. *Daily News*, 29 December 1920.
8. *The Sketch*, 5 January 1921.
9. *The Scotsman*, 17 January 1921.
10. *Weekly Dispatch*, 5 December 1920.
11. *The Aberdeen Daily Journal*, 17 January 1921.
12. Ibid.
13. Ibid.
14. *Pall Mall Gazette*, 3 December 1920.

15. Lawrence, D. H. (1921) *Sea and Sardinia*. Thomas Seltzer, New York.

16. Lawrence, D. H. (1922) *Fantasia of the Unconscious*. Thomas Seltzer, New York.

17. *Sunday Illustrated*, 4 September 1921.

18. *Pall Mall Gazette*, 5 August 1921.

19. *Nation and Athenaeum*, 14 August 1921.

20. Ibid.

21. Ibid.

22. *John Bull*, 17 September 1921.

23. Roberts, W., Boulton, J. T. and Mansfield, E. (1987) (Eds.) *The Letters of D. H. Lawrence, Volume IV, June 1921 – March 1924*. Cambridge University Press, Cambridge.

24. Ibid.

Chapter 14

1. Roberts, W. and Moore, H. T. (1968) *Phoenix II: Uncollected, Unpublished, and Other Prose Works by D. H. Lawrence*. The Viking Press, New York.

2. Roberts, W., Boulton, J. T. and Mansfield, E. (1987) (Eds.) *The Letters of D. H. Lawrence, Volume IV, June 1921 – March 1924*. Cambridge University Press, Cambridge.

3. Carswell, C. (1932) *The Savage Pilgrimage: A Narrative of D. H. Lawrence*. Harcourt, Brace and Co., New York.

4. Ibid.

5. Dodge Luhan, M. (1932) *Lorenzo in Taos*. Alfred A. Knopf, New York.

6. Carswell, C. (1932) *The Savage Pilgrimage: A Narrative of D. H. Lawrence*. Harcourt, Brace and Co., New York.

7. Dodge Luhan, M. (1932) *Lorenzo in Taos*. Alfred A. Knopf, New York.

8. Roberts, W., Boulton, J. T. and Mansfield, E. (1987) (Eds.) *The Letters of D. H. Lawrence, Volume IV, June 1921 – March 1924*. Cambridge University Press, Cambridge.

9. Dodge Luhan, M. (1932) *Lorenzo in Taos*. Alfred A. Knopf, New York.

10. Lawrence, F. (1935) '*Not I, But the Wind…*' Heinemann, London.

11. Dodge Luhan, M. (1932) *Lorenzo in Taos*. Alfred A. Knopf, New York.

12. Roberts, W., Boulton, J. T. and Mansfield, E. (1987) (Eds.) *The Letters of D. H. Lawrence, Volume IV, June 1921 – March 1924*. Cambridge University Press, Cambridge.

13. Lawrence, D. H. (1926) *The Plumed Serpent*. Martin Secker, London.

14. Carswell, C. (1932) *The Savage Pilgrimage: A Narrative of D. H. Lawrence*. Harcourt, Brace and Co., New York.

15. Ibid.

16. Ibid.

17. Squires, M. (2008) *D. H. Lawrence and Frieda: A Portrait of Love and Loyalty*. André Deutsch, London.

18. Ibid.

19. Carswell, C. (1932) *The Savage Pilgrimage: A Narrative of D. H. Lawrence*. Harcourt, Brace and Co., New York.

20. Boulton, J. T. and Vasey, L. (1989) (Eds.) *The Letters of D. H. Lawrence, Volume V, March 1924 – March 1927*. Cambridge University Press, Cambridge.

21. Ibid.

Chapter 15

1. Lawrence, D. H. (1934) *Lady Chatterley's Lover*. Grosset & Dunlap, New York.

2. Dodge Luhan, M. (1932) *Lorenzo in Taos*. Alfred A. Knopf, New York.

3. Lawrence, F. (1935) '*Not I, But the Wind…*' Heinemann, London.

4. Brett, D. (1933) *Lawrence and Brett: A Friendship*. J. B. Lippincott Co., Philadelphia.
5. Ibid.
6. Boulton, J. T. and Vasey, L. (1989) (Eds.) *The Letters of D. H. Lawrence, Volume V, March 1924 – March 1927*. Cambridge University Press, Cambridge.
7. Brett, D. (1933) *Lawrence and Brett: A Friendship*. J. B. Lippincott Co., Philadelphia.
8. Brett, D. (1933) *Lawrence and Brett: A Friendship*. J. B. Lippincott Co., Philadelphia.
9. Carswell, C. (1932) *The Savage Pilgrimage: A Narrative of D. H. Lawrence*. Harcourt, Brace and Co., New York.
10. Boulton, J. T. and Vasey, L. (1989) (Eds.) *The Letters of D. H. Lawrence, Volume V, March 1924 – March 1927*. Cambridge University Press, Cambridge.
11. Ibid.
12. Lawrence, D. H. (1923) *Kangaroo*. Thomas Seltzer, New York.
13. Lawrence, F. (1935) *'Not I, But the Wind...'* Heinemann, London.
14. Brett, D. (1933) *Lawrence and Brett: A Friendship*. J. B. Lippincott Co., Philadelphia.
15. Lawrence, F. (1935) *'Not I, But the Wind...'* Heinemann, London.
16. Boulton, J. T. and Vasey, L. (1989) (Eds.) *The Letters of D. H. Lawrence, Volume V, March 1924 – March 1927*. Cambridge University Press, Cambridge.
17. Carswell, C. (1932) *The Savage Pilgrimage: A Narrative of D. H. Lawrence*. Harcourt, Brace and Co., New York.
18. Lawrence, F. (1935) *'Not I, But the Wind...'* Heinemann, London.
19. Boulton, J. T. and Vasey, L. (1989) (Eds.) *The Letters of D. H. Lawrence, Volume V, March 1924 – March 1927*. Cambridge University Press, Cambridge.
20. Ibid.
21. Carswell, C. (1932) *The Savage Pilgrimage: A Narrative of D. H. Lawrence*. Harcourt, Brace and Co., New York.

Chapter 16

1. Lawrence, D. H. (1929) 'A Propos of Lady Chatterley's Lover', in Lawrence, D. H. (2000) *Lady Chatterley's Lover*. Edited by Michael Squires, Penguin Books, London.
2. Lawrence, F. (1935) *'Not I, But the Wind...'* Heinemann, London.
3. Boulton, J. T. and Vasey, L. (1989) (Eds.) *The Letters of D. H. Lawrence, Volume V, March 1924 – March 1927*. Cambridge University Press, Cambridge.
4. *Daily Mirror*, 9 August 1929.
5. Boulton, J. T., Boulton, M. H., and Lacey, G. M. (1991) (Eds.) *The Letters of D. H. Lawrence, Volume VI, March 1927 – November 1928*. Cambridge University Press, Cambridge.
6. Ibid.
7. Huxley, A. (1932) (Eds.) *The Letters of D. H. Lawrence*. The Viking Press, New York.
8. Lawrence, F. (1935) *'Not I, But the Wind...'* Heinemann, London.
9. Boulton, J. T., Boulton, M. H., and Lacey, G. M. (1991) (Eds.) *The Letters of D. H. Lawrence, Volume VI, March 1927 – November 1928*. Cambridge University Press, Cambridge.
10. Ibid.
11. *John Bull*, 20 October 1928.
12. Lawrence, F. (1935) *'Not I, But the Wind...'* Heinemann, London.
13. Boulton, J. T., Boulton, M. H., and Lacey, G. M. (1991) (Eds.) *The Letters of D. H. Lawrence, Volume VI, March 1927 – November 1928*. Cambridge University Press, Cambridge.
14. Ibid.

Chapter 17

1. Aldington R. and Orioli, G. (Eds.) (1933) *Last Poems by D. H. Lawrence.* The Viking Press, New York.
2. *Sunderland Daily Echo and Shipping Gazette,* 28 February 1929.
3. *Western Daily Press,* 1 March 1929.
4. *Sunderland Daily Echo and Shipping Gazette,* 28 February 1929.
5. *Leeds Mercury,* 2 March 1929.
6. Sagar, K. and Boulton, J. T. (1993) (Eds.) *The Letters of D. H. Lawrence, Volume VII, November 1928 – February 1930.* Cambridge University Press, Cambridge.
7. Ibid.
8. Huxley, A. (1932) (Eds.) *The Letters of D. H. Lawrence.* The Viking Press, New York.
9. Ibid.
10. *The Scotsman,* 17 June 1929.
11. John, G. (1929) 'The Eve of a Poets Mind', in *Everyman,* 27 June 1929. Cited in Levy, M. (1964) (Eds.) *The Paintings of D. H. Lawrence.* The Viking Press, New York.
12. *Yorkshire Evening Post,* 6 July 1929.
13. Sagar, K. and Boulton, J. T. (1993) (Eds.) *The Letters of D. H. Lawrence, Volume VII, November 1928 – February 1930.* Cambridge University Press, Cambridge.
14. *The Leicester Mail,* 8 August 1929.
15. *Aberdeen Press and Journal,* 4 July 1929.
16. Sagar, K. and Boulton, J. T. (1993) (Eds.) *The Letters of D. H. Lawrence, Volume VII, November 1928 – February 1930.* Cambridge University Press, Cambridge.
17. Ibid.
18. Ibid.
19. Lawrence, F. (1935) *'Not I, But the Wind…'* Heinemann, London.
20. Ibid.

Epilogue

1. *Daily Mirror,* 4 November 1932.
2. Ibid.

Bibliography

Books

Aldington R. and Orioli, G. (Eds.) (1933) *Last Poems by D. H. Lawrence*. The Viking Press, New York.

Boulton, J. T. (1979) (Eds.) *The Letters of D. H. Lawrence, Volume I, September 1901 – May 1913*. Cambridge University Press, Cambridge.

Boulton, J. T. and Robertson, A. (1984) (Eds.) *The Letters of D. H. Lawrence, Volume III, October 1916 – June 1921*. Cambridge University Press, Cambridge.

Boulton, J. T. and Vasey, L. (1989) (Eds.) *The Letters of D. H. Lawrence, Volume V, March 1924 – March 1927*. Cambridge University Press, Cambridge.

Boulton, J. T., Boulton, M. & Lacy, G. M. (1991) (Eds.) *The Letters of D. H. Lawrence, Volume VI, March 1927 – November 1928*. Cambridge University Press, Cambridge.

Boulton, J. T., Boulton, M. H., and Lacey, G. M. (1991) (Eds.) *The Letters of D. H. Lawrence, Volume VI, March 1927 – November 1928*. Cambridge University Press, Cambridge.

Brett, D. (1933) *Lawrence and Brett: A Friendship*. J. B. Lippincott Co., Philadelphia.

Carswell, C. (1932) *The Savage Pilgrimage: A Narrative of D. H. Lawrence*. Harcourt, Brace and Co., New York.

Corke, H. (1965) *D. H. Lawrence: The Croydon Years*. University of Texas Press, Austin.

Cox, J. C. (1912) *The Churches of Nottinghamshire*. George Allen & Co., London.

Dodge Luhan, M. (1932) *Lorenzo in Taos: D. H. Lawrence and Mabel Dodge Luhan*. Alfred A. Knopf, New York.

E. T. (Chambers, Jessie) (1935) *D. H. Lawrence: A Personal Record*. Frank Cass & Co. Ltd., London.

Ford, F. M. (1938) *Mightier Than the Sword: Memories and Criticisms*. George Allen & Unwin Ltd., London.

Foster Damon, S. (1935) *Amy Lowell: A Chronicle*. Houghton Mifflin Co., Boston, Massachusetts.

Garnett, D. (1954) *The Golden Echo*. Harcourt, New York.

Garnett, E. (1934) Introduction to D. H. Lawrence, *A Collier's Friday Night*. Martin Secker, London.

Gathorne-Hardy, R. (1974) (Eds.) *Ottoline at Garsington: Memoirs of Lady Ottoline Morrell, 1915-1918*. Faber and Faber, London.

Goldring, D. (1943) *South Lodge: Reminiscences of Violet Hunt, Ford Madox Ford and the The English Review Circle*. Constable, London.

Grice, A. (2021) *D. H. Lawrence and the Literary Marketplace: The Early Writings*. Edinburgh University Press, Edinburgh.

Harvey, D. D. (1962) *Ford Madox Ford: A Bibliography of Works and Criticism*. Princeton University Press.

Huxley, A. (1932) (Eds.) *The Letters of D. H. Lawrence*. The Viking Press, New York.

Jefferson, G. (1982) *Edward Garnett: A Life in Literature*. Jonathan Cape, London.

Kinkead-Weekes, M. (1996) *D. H. Lawrence: Triumph to Exile*. Cambridge University Press, Cambridge.

Lawrence, A. and Stuart Gelder, G. (1932) *Early Life of D. H. Lawrence*. Martin Secker, London.

Lawrence, D. (1917) *Look! We have come through!* Chatto & Windus, London.

Lawrence, D. H. (1913) *Love Poems and Others*. Duckworth & Co., London.

Lawrence, D. H. (1913) *Sons and Lovers*. Gerald Duckworth & Co. Ltd., London.

Lawrence, D. H. (1914) *The Prussian Officer and Other Stories*. Duckworth & Co., London.

Lawrence, D. H. (1915) *Twilight in Italy*. Duckworth & Co., London.

Lawrence, D. H. (1916) *Amores*. B. W. Huebsch, New York.

Lawrence, D. H. (1916) *Amores*. Gerald Duckworth & Co. Ltd., London.

Lawrence, D. H. (1918) *New Poems*. Martin Secker, London.

Lawrence, D. H. (1920) *The Lost Girl*. Martin Secker, London.

Lawrence, D. H. (1920) *Women in Love*. Thomas Seltzer Inc., New York.

Lawrence, D. H. (1921) *Sea and Sardinia*. Thomas Seltzer, New York.

Lawrence, D. H. (1922) *Aarons Rod*. Thomas Seltzer, New York.

Lawrence, D. H. (1922) *England, My England*. Thomas Seltzer, United States.

Lawrence, D. H. (1922) *Fantasia of the Unconscious*. Thomas Seltzer, New York.

Lawrence, D. H. (1923) *Birds, Beasts and Flower*. Thomas Seltzer, New York.

Lawrence, D. H. (1923) *Kangaroo*. Thomas Seltzer, New York.

Lawrence, D. H. (1923) *Studies in Classic American Literature*. Thomas Seltzer, New York.

Lawrence, D. H. (1925) *Reflections on the Death of a Porcupine*. Willian Heinemann, London.

Lawrence, D. H. (1926) *The Plumed Serpent*. Martin Secker, London.

Lawrence, D. H. (1929) 'A Propos of Lady Chatterley's Lover', in Lawrence, D. H. (2000) *Lady Chatterley's Lover*. Edited by Michael Squires, Penguin Books, London.

Lawrence, D. H. (1929) *Pansies*.

Lawrence, D. H. (1934) *A Modern Lover*. Martin Secker, London.

Lawrence, D. H. (1960) *Lady Chatterley's Lover*. Penguin, London.

Lawrence, D. H. (1960) *Love Among the Haystacks and Other Stories*. Penguin, London.

Lawrence, D. H. (1978) *The First Lady Chatterley (The first version of 'Lady Chatterley's Lover')*. Heinemann, London.

Lawrence, F. (1935) *'Not I, But the Wind…'* Heinemann, London.

Ludwig, R. (1965) (Eds.) *Letters of Ford Madox Ford*. Princeton University Press.

McDonald, E. D. (1936) (Eds.) *Phoenix: The Posthumous Papers of D. H. Lawrence*. William Heinemann Ltd., London.

Moore, H. T. (1962) (Eds.) *Collected Letters of D. H. Lawrence*. Heinemann, London.

Moore, H. T. (1962) (Eds.) *The Collected Letters of D. H. Lawrence: Volume II*. Heinemann, London.

Nehls, E. (1957) (Eds.) *D. H. Lawrence: A Composite Biography, Volume One, 1885-1919*. University of Wisconsin Press, Madison.

Neville, G. H. (1981) *A Memoir of D. H. Lawrence: The Betrayal*. Cambridge University Press, Cambridge.

Roberts, W. and Moore, H. T. (1968) (Eds) *Phoenix II: Uncollected, Unpublished, and Other Prose Works by D. H. Lawrence*. The Viking Press, New York.

Roberts, W., Boulton, J. T. and Mansfield, E. (1987) (Eds.) *The Letters of D. H. Lawrence, Volume IV, June 1921 – March 1924*. Cambridge University Press, Cambridge.

Rolph, C. H. (1961) (Eds.) *The Trial of Lady Chatterley: Regina V.* Penguin Books Limited. Penguin, London.

Sagar, K. and Boulton, J. T. (1993) (Eds.) *The Letters of D. H. Lawrence, Volume VII, November 1928 – February 1930*. Cambridge University Press, Cambridge.

Squires, M. (2008) *D. H. Lawrence and Frieda: A Portrait of Love and Loyalty*. André Deutsch, London.

Steele, B. (1985) (Eds.) *Study of Thomas Hardy and Other Essays – D. H. Lawrence*. Cambridge, Cambridge University Press.

Tedlock, E. W. (1963) *D. H. Lawrence, Artist and Rebel: A Study of Lawrence's Fiction*. University of New Mexico Press, Albuquerque.

Tedlock, E. W. (1964) (Eds.) *Frieda Lawrence: The Memoirs and Correspondence*. Alfred A. Knopf, New York.

Woolf, V. (1924) *The Hogarth Essays: Mr. Bennett and Mrs. Brown*. Hogarth Press, London.

Worthen, J. (2005) *D. H. Lawrence: The Life of an Outsider*. Allen Lane, London.

Zytaruk, G. J. and Boulton, J. T. (1981) (Eds.) *The Letters of D. H. Lawrence, Volume II, June 1913 – October 1916*. Cambridge University Press, Cambridge.

Journals

Cobau, W. & Hopkin, O. (1976) 'A View From Eastwood: Conversations With Mrs. O. L. Hopkin'. *The D.H. Lawrence Review 9*, No. 1, pp. 126–36.

Corke, H. (1971) 'D. H. Lawrence: The Early Stage', in *The D.H. Lawrence Review*, Vol. 4, No. 2, pp. 111-121.

Delavenay, E. (1969) *D. H. Lawrence: U Homme et la Genese de son Oeuvre* (2 vols.), Librarie C. Klincksieck, Paris.

Ford, F. M. (1907) 'Literary Portraits: XII. Mr. Edward Garnett', *Tribune 2*.

Ford, G. (1973) 'Jessie Chambers' Last Tape on D. H. Lawrence', in *Mosaic: An Interdisciplinary Critical Journal*, Vol. 6, No. 3: Literature and Ideas: A Miscellany of Opinions and Analysis (Spring, 1973), pp. 1-12.

John, G. (1929) 'The Eve of a Poets Mind', in *Everyman*, 27 June 1929. Cited in Levy, M. (1964) (Eds.) *The Paintings of D. H. Lawrence*. The Viking Press, New York.

Roberts, I. D. (1983) 'D. H. Lawrence and Davidson Road School: An Institutional Viewpoint', in *The D.H. Lawrence Review*, Vol. 16, No. 2, pp.195-210.

Scott-James, R. A. (1937) 'Edward Garnett', in the *Spectator*.

Newspapers and Magazines

Aberdeen Press and Journal
Berks and Oxon Advertiser
Civil and Military Gazette (Lahore)
Daily Mirror
Derby Daily Telegraph
Eastwood and Kimberley Advertiser
John Bull
Leeds Mercury
Lynn Advertiser
Nation and Athenaeum
Nottinghamshire Guardian
Pall Mall Gazette
Ripley and Heanor News and Ilkeston Division Free Press
Southwark and Bermondsey Recorder
Sunday Illustrated
Sunday Mirror
Sunderland Daily Echo and Shipping Gazette
The Aberdeen Daily Journal
The Bystander

The Clarion
The Daily News
The Gentlewoman
The Globe
The Guardian
The Illustrated London News
The Leicester Mail
The Scotsman
The Sketch
The Sphere
Times Literary Supplement
Weekly Dispatch
Western Daily Press
Westminster Gazette
Yorkshire Evening Post

Archives

The University of Nottingham has an extensive and internationally renowned collection of
D. H. Lawrence texts and ephemera, including first editions, Lawrence's personal letters,
photographs, manuscripts, and original texts of his many works. There are also several smaller
collections in the UK such as those at Nottinghamshire Archives, the British Library and
the Museum of Croydon. Thousands of Lawrence's original letters have been published
by Cambridge University Press across seven volumes covering the period from 1901 to his
death in 1930, which are digitised at archive.org.

Lawrence's extensive travelling led to many collections being established overseas. A full
list can be viewed on the University of Nottingham Manuscript and Special Collections
website at nottingham.ac.uk/manuscriptsandspecialcollections.

Index

Ad Astra Sanatorium, 170
Aldington, Hilda. *See* H.D.
Aldington, Richard, 93, 112, 154, 163
Alps, the, 73, 88
America, 101, 108-109, 119-24, 129-134, 137-140, 144, 153, 173
Americans, 37-8, 54, 88, 109, 119, 131, 133, 140, 149, 160-61, 165
Andrews, Esther, 109
Arlen, Michael, 103
  see also Kouyoumdijan, Dikran.
Asquith, Herbert ('Beb') and Cynthia, 77, 80, 86, 90, 104, 113-14, 160
Atkinson, Frederick, 54
Athenaeum, 119-20, 124
Australia, 136, 138
Austria, 75, 93, 132, 157-58

Baden-Baden, 88, 92, 121, 127, 144 150-51, 154, 158, 162, 166-68
Baynes, Rosalind (*née* Thorneycroft), 126-28
Beach, Sylvia, 165-66
Beardsall, Lydia. *See* Lawrence, Lydia.
Beardsall family, 3-4, 8
Beau Soleil, Villa, 168-70
Beauvale Board School, 11
Beresford, J.D., 102
Berkshire, 112, 114, 128
Bernada, Villa, 150
Black Forest, 154, 168
Blackpool, 44
Breach, The. *See* Eastwood.
Brett, Dorothy, 143-48
  argues with Frieda, 145-46, 148
  artwork, 147
  disability, 145
  relationship with DHL, 146, 152
  intimate encounter with DHL, 152
  living in Mexico, 146-48, 153
  'Toby', 145

Brewster, Achsah and Earl, 131, 133, 135, 152, 157, 160, 169
Brinsley. *See* Mining.
Brontë sisters, 21
Buckinghamshire, 94, 98, 172
  suspicions directed at DHL and Frieda during the war, 95
Buddhism, 133
Burrows, Louie, 27-8
  break with DHL, 60
  engagement to DHL, 45, 47, 50-1
  making plans with DHL, 47-8
  tensions, 51, 53, 57-8
Bynner, Witter, 140

Café Royal, 143-44
Campbell, Gordon, 92
Cannan, Mary, 97, 123, 143
Cannan, Gilbert, 97
Capri, 121-25, 128, 131, 152-53
Carswell, Catherine, 111, 121-23, 135, 138-39, 141-43, 148, 150, 153-55, 159-60
Carwell, Don, 116, 158, 143
Cearne, the, 54-5, 57-9, 87
  DHL and Frieda visit, 83-5, 87
  DHL falls ill at, 58
  DHL's first visit, 55
Censorship, xi, 55, 100, 165, 167-68, 174
Ceylon (Sri Lanka), 133-36
Chambers, Alan, 19, 27
  DHL's friendship with, 17
Chambers, David, 163
Chambers, Jessie, 11, 33, 57, 59-62
  appearance, 18
  as Miriam, 23, 56-7, 61-2
  as Muriel, 42
  break with DHL, 42, 62, 70
  childhood and youth, 18, 20
  DHL's recreations of, 56, 61

final meeting with DHL, 62
finds out about Frieda, 70
friendship with Helen Corke, 42, 55
influence on DHL's writing, 17, 21, 35,
    47, 50, 52, 56
life after DHL, 71
Lydia Lawrence's dislike of, 23
relationship with DHL, 18, 20-8, 37, 39,
    42, 44-5, 51
teacher training and teaching, 25
The Rathe Primrose, 81
Chambers, May, *see* Holbrook, May.
Chambers family, 17-18
Channing, Minnie ('Puma'), 103
Chapel. *See* Eastwood.
Chapel Farm (Hermitage), 112-14, 119
Chesterton, G.K., 36
Clarke, Ada (DHL's sister). *See*
    Lawrence, Ada.
Clarke, Eddie (DHL's brother-in-law), 82
Collings, Ernest, 86
Colet Court School, 84-5
Collieries. *See* Mining.
Communism, 97
Conrad, Joseph, 32, 35, 54
Consumption. *See* tuberculosis.
Cooper, Gertrude ('Gertie'), 154, 158
  see also tuberculosis.
Copyright, 161, 164, 172-73
Corke, Helen, 34
    DHL's relationship with, 39-42,
      50-1, 53
    end of relationship with DHL, 53-4
    grief after loss of Herbert, 40-1
    relationship with Jessie Chambers,
      42, 55
    the Freshwater diaries, 40
    'The Saga' and *The Trespasser*, 40-2, 50
Cornwall, 48, 102, 111, 114, 117
    DHL and Frieda monitored by the
      authorities, 106 107
    DHL and Frieda move to, 102-104
    DHL and Frieda's expulsion from,
      107, 110
    with the Murry's in, 105-106
Crawford, Grace, 38
Croydon, 28, 44, 46, 51, 53, 58, 80
    Davidson Road School, 29-30, 33

DHL's life in, 29-43
DHL's thoughts on, 31
writing in, 30, 32, 34

Darlington (Australia), 136
'David' (Michaelangelo), 121-22,
    149, 153-54
Davidson Road School. *See* Croydon.
Davidson, Jo, 170
Davies, Rhys, 166
Dax, Alice, 26, 50
Dax, Harry, 26
Del Monte Ranch:
    DHL and Frieda living at, 139-40,
      147, 149
    Dorothy Brett at, 154
    setting and isolation, 139
Dennis, Louisa Lily Western, 15
Derby, 1, 12
Derbyshire, 1, 12, 32, 80, 89, 102, 117,
    144, 150
Dickens, Charles, 21
Doolittle, Hilda. *See* H.D.
Douglas, Norman:
    and Maurice Magnus, 121
    attacks Magnus's memoir, 159
Dover, 53, 66, 121
Duckworth & Co., 71-72, 75, 78, 80, 84,
    87, 91-93, 107, 114
Duckworth, Gerald, 59, 90, 92

Eastwood and surrounds, 1-32, 35, 44, 46,
    48-9, 64, 70, 82, 87, 158
    8a Victoria Street, 2, 11
    Annesley hills, 18
    Beauvale Board School, 11
    Breach, the, 5
    Brinsley, 4-5
    Brinsley Brook, 2
    Brinsley Colliery, 1
    British School, 20, 22
    cemetery, 15, 46, 147
    community, 48
      Congregational Literary Society, 26
      debating society, 26
    Congregational Chapel, 8, 17, 26-7, 31
    D. H. Lawrence Birthplace Museum,
      2, 174

High Park woods, 5, 18
St. Mary's Church, 1
Walker Street, 5, 7
Eastwood Council, 174
Edward, Prince of Wales, 135
Eliot, George, 21
England, 3, 10, 53, 61, 68, 71, 82-4, 109,
    133, 152, 167
    DHL's relationship with, 78, 80, 82, 85,
        98, 100-101, 105, 135-36
    DHL's desire to leave, 66, 87, 96, 101,
        107-108, 114, 116-121, 141-44
    DHL's desire to return, 149-50, 154-55
    the English, 82, 88, 98, 103, 121, 123,
        126, 129, 144, 165-67
English Review, the, 28, 35-7, 52-3, 119
Esher, Viscount (Dorothy Brett's
    father), 145
Etna, 134
Etruscan, 157

Farjeon, Eleanor, 126
Fiascherino, 88, 94
Fiesole, 128
Flaubert, Gustav, 21
Florence, Italy, 82, 127-28, 129, 152, 168
    DHL's and Frieda in, 121-22, 131-32,
        153, 155
    publishing of *Lady Chatterley's Lover*,
        160
    time with Rosalind Baynes in, 127-28
Florida, 100, 102
Fontana Vecchia (Taormina), 125, 130-31
Ford, Ford Madox. *See* Hueffer,
    Ford Madox.
Forster, E. M., 95, 97, 105
France, 2, 71, 99, 101, 105, 139, 172
    DHL and Frieda in, 162, 169
Francia, Hotel (Oaxaca), 148
Freiburg, 65
Freud, Sigmund, 132
Frick, Ernst, 66

Garda, Lago di, 73, 75
Garnett, Constance, 55, 83, 87
Garnett, David (Bunny), 73, 79
    feelings towards DHL and Frieda, 83
Garnett, Edward, 53-4, 75, 78, 80-1, 88, 92
    DHL visits, 54, 57-9, 83, 87

end of relationship with DHL, 91
introduction to Duckworth, 59
literary advice, 55, 83, 89-90
thoughts on DHL, 55, 91
Garsington Manor, 97, 101, 167
Germany and Germans, 60, 63, 65, 87,
    109, 120-21, 125-6, 114
    anti-German feeling in England,
        95, 107
    DHL and Frieda's visits to, 66-8, 73, 75,
        131-32, 150, 154
    DHL's attitude towards, 82, 95-6, 150
Gertler, Mark, 93, 97, 114, 143, 150, 169
Gissing, George, 32
Gotzsche, Kai, 139, 142-43
Gray, Cecil, 107
    incident with authorities in WWI, 107
Greatham, 98
Greiffenhagen, Maurice, 49
    DHL copies of 'An Idyll', 50
    DHL obsession with 'An Idyll', 49
Gross, Otto, 66
Guadalajara, 141-42

H.D. (Hilda Doolittle), 93, 111-12
Haggs Farm, 17-20, 25, 28, 31, 44, 52,
    63, 163
    DHL recreates in prose, 17, 33-4, 59
    visits from DHL, 11, 17-19, 22
Hall, Alice Beatrice, 21
    in *The White Peacock*, 49
Hampstead, 38, 66, 93, 111, 142
    DHL and Frieda live at 1 Byron Villas,
        100, 102
    Hampstead Heath, 95
Hardy, Thomas, 35
    DHL's 'Study of Thomas Hardy', 93, 96,
        98, 108
    influence on DHL, 34
Hobson, Harold, 73-4
Holbrook, May (*née* Chambers) 8, 18-19,
    22, 31, 62, 70
Harrison, Austin, 53
Hawk family, 139
Heinemann, William:
    attitude to 'Paul Morel', 72
    DHL's introduction to, 38
    publishing business, 47, 53-5, 58-9, 71

Hermitage, 112-14, 119
Heseltine, Philip, 103, 105, 107, 132-33
Higher Tregerthen (Zennor), 105, 117
Hocking, William Henry, 117
Holderness, George, 20
Holdich, White, 49
    see also Hall, Alice.
Holt, Agnes, 34, 37, 39, 50
    intimate with DHL, 37
Hopkin, Enid, 154
Hopkin, Sallie and Willie, 71, 73, 79, 97
    Eastwood intellectual group, 26
    recreation of Willie in DHL's prose, 49
House of Commons, 100, 165
Huebsch, Benjamin, 119-120
Hueffer, Ford Madox (later Ford), 35-6,
    43, 53-5, 81
    and 'The Saga of Sigmund', 43, 52-3
    and The White Peacock, 37
    description as DHL as a 'genius', 36-8
    first meeting with DHL, 36
    introduces DHL to literary world, 37
    publishes DHL's poems, 37
Hunt, Violet, 37, 47
Huxley, Aldous and Maria, 160, 165, 168
    DHL's death and funeral, 170
    DHL's illness, 166-67, 169
    friendship with DHL and Frieda,
        154-55, 169
    Maria and Lady Chatterley's Lover, 159

Icking, 70, 72
Idyll, An. See Grieffenhagen, Maurice.
Igea, Villa, 75, 82
Ilkeston, 12-13, 20-1
Influenza, 116, 118, 120, 148, 134, 163
Italy, 72, 81-2, 94, 124, 126, 152-53, 157
    DHL and Frieda in, 73-5, 121, 150, 155,
        158, 161
    see also Capri.
    see also Florence.
    see also Spotorno.
    see also Trieste.
    see also Tuscany.
    DHL's attitude towards, 82, 135
    DHL writes about, 80, 82, 103
    publication of Lady Chatterley's
        Lover, 160

Jaffe, Else (Frieda's sister), 64, 66, 70, 77,
    82, 87-8, 155, 158
Jaffe, Edgar, 66, 88
James, Henry, 35
James Tait Black Prize, 134
Jennings, Blanche, 31, 34, 39, 49
Johnson, Willard ('Spud'), 140
Joyce, James, 89, 120, 161, 165-66
Joynson Hicks, Sir William ('Jix'), 165

King, Emily née Lawrence, 21, 114, 117,
    150, 154, 158, 160
    caring for Arthur Lawrence, 114
    childhood, 4
    dispute over DHL's estate, 172-73
Kings Scholarship Exam, 22
Kiowa Ranch, 146, 149, 153, 172-73
Knopf, Alfred, 160
Koteliansky, Samuel Solomonovitch
    ('Kot'), 116, 118-19, 121, 132, 139,
    150, 153-54
    at the Café Royal, 143
    becomes acquainted with DHL, 97
Kouyoumdjian, Dikran (Michael
    Arlen), 103
Krenkow family, 44, 62, 66, 68, 70

Lahr, Charles, 168
Lake District, 93, 97
Lamy (New Mexico), 137
Lawrence, Ada, 50, 60, 81, 112, 116, 123,
    160, 168
    and Arthur Lawrence, 10, 48, 147
    argument with Frieda, 151-52
    attitude towards DHL's literary estate,
    early life, 4-7, 18, 21
    closeness to DHL, 18, 70, 102, 113, 150
    holidays with DHL, 53, 154
    nursing DHL, 58, 118
    nursing Lydia Lawrence, 46
    visits to DHL with her children, 114
    wedding, 82, 86-7
Lawrence, Arthur, 15
    alcohol, 4, 6, 10, 48
    appearance, 4, 39-40
    dancing, 4
    death, 147
    DHL's dislike of, 8-9

later years, 48

marriage and relationship with Lydia
    Lawrence, 3-4, 6-8

relationship with his children, 8-9

Walter Lawrence scandal, 12-13

working in the mines, 1, 6, 10

Lawrence, David Herbert:

affair with Rosalind Baynes, 126-28

appearance, 11, 36, 39-40, 152, 170

attitude to war and armistice,
    94-96, 114-15

    conscription and medical
        examinations, 101, 106, 114

behaviours and characteristics:

    anger, 9-10, 21, 76, 83, 113, 119, 122,
        124, 140, 147, 165-66, 174

    conflict, 52, 56, 77, 83, 90, 94, 130,
        172, 174

    contradiction, 12, 26, 51, 65, 101, 134,
        142, 174

    depression and hopelessness, 45, 57,
        101, 106, 119, 152

    detachment and isolation, 38, 61, 68,
        103, 113

    domestic abilities, 76

    genius, vii, 11, 22, 36-8, 47, 51, 62, 65,
        91, 99, 132, 137-39, 156

    idealism, 25, 66, 97

    intellectualism, x, 12, 21, 23, 28, 32,
        59, 93, 97, 174

    intensity, 50, 55, 60, 85, 130, 148-49,
        157, 174

    jealousy, 76, 78, 83

    love of nature and landscapes, 1-2,
        17-20, 33, 117-18, 126, 136-37,
        149, 154

    misogyny, 51, 76

    vitality, 18, 36, 87, 111, 158, 166

birth, 4

childhood, 4-13

common features of DHL's writing:

    autobiography, 2, 4-8, 136

    editing and revisions, 35, 56, 60-1, 72,
        80, 83, 87, 98, 108-109, 119, 159

    Realism, 34, 89

    recreations of familiar people, 2, 7-10,
        14-16, 23, 28, 30, 40, 48-9, 74,
        108, 132-33

recreations of real settings, 2, 14, 17,
    121, 136, 155, 158

use of accent and dialect, xii

use of explicit language, vii, x-xii, 156,

class, 3-4, 12-13, 16, 20, 30, 38, 51, 64,
    76, 82, 126

controversy, xi-xii, 100, 117, 130,
    157, 164-167

death, 170-71

DHL's feelings about Eastwood, 1, 17,
    27, 29-31, 48-9, 114, 147

education,
    Nottingham University College, 22,
        24-5, 27, 33, 63
    school, 11-12, 14, 17
    teacher training college, 20, 22

engagement to Louie Burrows, 45

faith and religion, xii, 26-27, 115-16

funeral, 171

Haywoods Factory, 14, 16, 20

health and illness, 8, 11, 16, 20, 55,
    57-9, 106-108, 118-19, 134, 147-49,
    153-54, 157-170

'Lawrence paradox', 20

location of ashes, 173

love of The Haggs. See Haggs Farm.

memorial, 173

painting and artworks, vi, xii, 49-50, 129,
    151, 157, 173
    confiscation of, 167-68
    exhibition at the Warren Gallery,
        165, 167

poverty, vi, 33, 91, 103, 113, 116, 123

relationship with Dorothy Brett,
    143-48, 152

relationship with Edward Garnett, 53-
    55, 57-59, 80, 83-5, 89-92

relationship with Ford Madox Hueffer,
    36-8, 43

relationship with Jessie Chambers. See
    Chambers, Jessie.

relationship with Lydia Lawrence, 6,
    9, 11, 16-18, 22-3, 31, 43, 47, 51, 56,
    61-2, 72
    death of Lydia Lawrence, 44-6
    see also Lawrence, Lydia.

relationship with Mabel Luhan,
    137-40, 145-46

see also Luhan, Mabel (Evans
  Dodge Sterne).
relationship with the Murrys, 84-5, 92-
  3, 97-8, 105-106, 120, 140
  breakdown of relationship, 120,
    124, 132
  see also Mansfield, Katherine.
  see also Middleton Murry, John.
teaching and being a teacher, 20, 22, 29-
  30, 32-3, 40, 47, 52, 55, 58, 60
  British School, the, 20, 22
  see also Croydon.
  see also Davidson Road Boys' School,
themes in DHL's writing:
  civilisation, 99, 101, 157
  class and society, 30, 34, 50, 85, 88, 96,
    98, 105, 126, 155, 159
  education, 30, 132
  England, 10, 78, 98, 105, 121,
    126, 155
  love, xii, 9, 23-4, 34, 39, 41, 50,
    56, 61, 74, 77, 80, 85, 108, 109,
    126-28, 132
  physicality, 50, 87, 157
  psychoanalysis, vi, 105, 108,
    125, 130-32
  sensuality, 6,
  sex and sexuality, x, 41, 80, 86, 99, 127,
    156, 159
  the body, xii, 41
  union of man and woman, 96,
    105, 132
Works:
  early manuscripts
    'Paul Morel' (Sons and Lovers),
      46, 50, 52-3, 56-8, 60-62, 70-72,
      77-8, 82-3
    'Laetitia' (The White Peacock),
      24-5, 33-4
    'Nethermere' (The White Peacock),
      34-5, 37-9, 43
    'The Insurrection of Miss
      Houghton' (The Lost Girl),
      80, 125
    'The Saga of Siegmund' (The
      Trespasser), 40-43, 50, 52-4, 58-9
    'The Sisters' (The Rainbow and
      Women in Love), 81, 84, 87-90, 92

'The Wedding Ring' (The Rainbow
    and Women in Love), 89-92, 94,
    96
'Mr Noon' (unfinished novel), 49,
    74, 126, 129-30
'Quetzalcoatl' (The Plumed
    Serpent), 141-42
non-fiction
  Study of Thomas Hardy and Other
    Essays, 93, 96, 98, 108
  Movements in European History, vi,
    117, 119
  Psychoanalysis and the Unconscious
    and Fantasia of the Unconscious,
    vi, 125, 132, 143
  Studies in Classic American
    Literature, 108, 140, 143
  Reflections on the Death of a
    Porcupine and Other Essays, 98,
    149
  A Propos of Lady Chatterley's Lover,
    xii, 169
  Apocalypse and the Writings on
    Revelation, 169
  Introduction to Memoirs of the
    Foreign Legion, 159
novels
  Aaron's Rod, 119, 122, 126,
    128-29, 132
  Kangaroo, 114, 136, 143
  Lady Chatterley's Lover, vii, ix-xii,
    155-57, 159, 161-62, 164,
    169, 174
  Sons and Lovers, 2, 4-12, 14-17, 44-
    6, 57, 61-3, 74, 77-8, 81-6, 90-
    91, 120, 132, 146
  The Boy in the Bush, 136, 142, 147
  The Lost Girl, 80, 121, 126,
    128-30, 134
  The Plumed Serpent,
    141-42, 147-48
  The Rainbow, x, 74, 81, 92, 96, 98-
    101, 104-105, 108, 119
  The Trespasser, 40, 43, 49, 59, 71, 75
  The White Peacock, 24, 34, 37,
    43-5, 47-52
  Women in Love, 32, 81, 96, 105,
    108, 107-109, 118-19, 124, 129,
    132, 138

plays
  The Daughter-in-Law, 81
  The Widowing of Mrs. Holroyd, 87
  Touch and Go, 49, 119
  David, 149, 153-54
  A Collier's Friday Night, 55
poetry collections
  Love Poems and others, 80,
  Amores, 103-104
  Look! We have come through!, 109,
    112
  New Poems, 5, 26
  Birds, Beasts and Flowers, 126, 128,
    140, 143
  Pansies, 163-64, 168
short story collections
  *The Prussian Officer and Other
    Stories*, 92, 96
  *England, My England and Other
    Stories*, 98
  *The Fox, The Captain's Doll, The
    Ladybird*, 119, 143
  *The Lovely Lady and Other
    Tales*, 157
travel writing
  Twilight in Italy and Other Essays,
    80, 82, 103
  Sea and Sardinia, 131
  *Sketches of Etruscan Places and Other
    Italian Essays*, 157
Lawrence, Emily *see* King, Emily.
Lawrence, Frieda (*née* von Richthofen,
  also Weekley):
  affair with Angelo Ravagli, 150-51, 161,
    166, 172
  and DHL's health, 118-19, 147-49, 157,
    163, 166, 170
  appearance, 92
  arguments with DHL, 71, 77, 83, 95,
    105-6, 118, 140, 142, 151-52
    violence and conflict, 69, 76, 83,
      106, 147
  as a reader of DHL's work, 80, 159
  attitude to DHL's writing, 77, 80,
    89, 128
  attitude to WWI, 94-5, 114-15
  attitude towards travelling, 75, 121
  behaviours,

anger, 106, 148, 152
instinctiveness, 64
jealousy, 106, 145-46
passion, 69
romantic and sexual freedom, 63, 73-4
birth and family, 62-3, 67-70, 87-8, 92,
  120, 127, 131-32, 150, 154, 168
children, 63, 65-6, 69, 71-2, 78-9, 82-5,
  87, 142
death and burial, 173
DHL's feelings for Weekley children,
  78-9, 83, 151-52
DHL's love for, 65, 67-9, 71, 73, 76-7, 140
DHL's verbal abuse of, 76, 75, 151
early affairs, 64, 66, 73
feelings towards DHL's friends,
  tension with Dorothy Brett, 145-48
  tension with Mabel Luhan,
    137-39, 146
  tension with Ottoline Morell, 104
influence on DHL's writing, 74, 83, 85,
  89, 109
life after Lawrence, 172
loss of children, 71-2, 78-9, 84, 95
love for DHL, 63, 76-7, 140
marriage to Angelo Ravagli, 173
marriage to DHL, 92
marriage to Ernest Weekley, 63, 65, 75-6
  see also Nottingham.
meets DHL for the first time, 63
reaction to DHL's death, 170-71
recreations in DHL's work, 74, 89,
  131, 136
relationship with DHL's family,
  quarrel with Ada, 151
  quarrel regarding literary estate, 172
reunited with her children, 151
separation and divorce from Ernest
  Weekley, 67-8, 71-2, 78-9, 81, 87,
  89, 92
Lawrence, Ernest (also known as William
  Ernest), 4, 7-8, 14, 20, 46
death, 15
DHL's recreation of, 15-16
illness, 15
importance to Lydia Lawrence, 7, 16
life, 7, 15
obituary, 15

Lawrence, George (DHL's brother), 4, 7, 55, 172

Lawrence, Lydia (*née* Beardsall):
appearance, 18
attitude to Jessie Chambers, 23, 61-2
death, 46-7, 49-51, 60, 170
early life, 4-5
faith and chapel, 17, 26-7, 31
final illness, 43-6
meets and marries Arthur Lawrence, 4
notions of class and 'getting on', vi, 3, 5, 8, 31
recreated in DHL's works, 4-6, 23, 28, 45-6, 56, 61
relationship with Arthur Lawrence, 4, 6-9, 85
relationship with children, 6-8, 31
closeness to DHL, 9, 11, 16-17, 31, 56, 61, 72

Limb, Mabel, 31
Lobo (New Mexico), 146
London, 7, 15, 35-7, 39-40, 79, 100, 104-105, 107, 123, 150, 160, 167-68, 172
Bloomsbury, 104, 112
Café Royal, 143-44
DHL visits, 29, 32, 54, 84, 92-3, 114, 154-55
Hampstead, 38, 66, 93, 100, 102, 110-12, 142
in the war, 95, 111-12
Kensington, 84, 92, 94
literary circles, 37-38, 93
Selwood Terrace, 92
Lowell, Amy, 93, 113, 120
Luhan, Mabel (Evans Dodge Sterne), 128, 160, 173
artists commune ('Mabeltown'), 137-38
break with DHL and Frieda, 139
DHL writes about, 140
feelings for DHL, 138, 146
gift of ranch to Frieda, 146
interference in DHL's life, 137, 145
invites DHL and Frieda to Taos, 133
Luhan, Tony, 137

'Mabeltown'. *See* Luhan, Mabel.
Mablethorpe, 24, 154
Macartney, Herbert Baldwin, 40-41

Mackenzie, Compton, 121, 123
Magnus, Maurice, 121, 159
Mansfield, Katherine, 172, 87, 92, 100, 117
breakdown of relationship with DHL, 124-25
death, 139
DHL's reaction to, 139
editor of *Rhythm*, 84
first meets DHL and Frieda, 84-85
illness and health, 116
living with the Lawrences, 105-106
rejection of communal life, 106
relationship with Murry, 84
Margate, 85
Marsh, Edward, 86, 101, 107
Mason, Agnes, 37, 39
McLeod, Arthur, 32, 34, 50, 60, 86
Merrild, Knud, 139
Methuen and Co., x, 91-4, 96, 99-100, 107
Metz, 64, 67-8, 90
Mexico, 97, 140-142
DHL and Frieda visit, 140, 148
DHL's reflections on, 140
recreated in DHL's writing, 141
Meynell, Viola, 98
Midlands, 1, 35, 44, 112-14, 149, 154
as a literary setting, 155
DHL's dislike of, 1, 150
DHL's nostalgia for, 149, 154
Milan, 127
Mirenda, Villa, 155-56, 158, 161-63, 167
DHL and Frieda discover, 153
DHL's illness at, 157-58
Monte Carlo, 152
Morland, Andrew, 169
Morrell, Lady Ottoline, 95, 100, 102, 105-106
anger over portrayal in *Women in Love*, 108
argument with Frieda, 104
DHL first meets, 97
in contact with DHL again, 166
visits to Garsington, 101, 167
Morrell, Philip, 100, 104, 108
Mountain Cottage, 113-14, 117-18
Mountsier, Robert, 109, 132, 134
and Esther Andrews, 109
as DHL's agent, 139

becomes acquainted with DHL, 109
  DHL's break with, 140
Munich, 70, 82, 126
Murry, John Middleton, 92, 97, 98, 121,
  139, 142, 145, 150, 172
  arguments with DHL, 106, 124
  attack on *Women in Love*, 132
  Café Royal, 143
  editor of *Rhythm*, 84
  edits the *Athenaeum*, 120
  meets DHL and Frieda, 84
  friendship with DHL and Frieda, 85,
    93, 105
  in Cornwall with DHL and Frieda,
    102, 105-106
  relationship with DHL, 85, 106, 124,
    132, 140
  relationship with Katherine
    Mansfield, 84
  thoughts on DHL's writing, 100, 120

Naples, 122-23, 134
Nation, the, 86, 132
Native Americans, 146, 149
  Pueblo, 133, 137
Neville, George, 12, 44, 49, 126
  memories of DHL, 9-10, 11, 19, 21-2
  recreated by DHL, 49, 126
New Age, 26
New Mexico, 137, 147-49, 153, 169, 172
  DHL invited to, 133
  DHL invites friends to, 143
  DHL shrine, 173
  DHL writes about, 137-38, 146
New South Wales, 136
New York, 101, 123, 129, 138-39, 140-41,
  143, 160, 164, 169, 173
  visit by DHL, 144, 149
New Zealand, 84
Nice, 152
Nietzsche, Friedrich, 32
Nottinghamshire, 1-2, 7, 10, 65-67, 69, 71,
  85-7, 89, 126
  Nottingham Castle Art Gallery, 60
  Frieda's life with Weekley in, 65, 67, 75
  Haywoods Factory, 14, 20
  Nottingham, 1, 3, 7, 75, 150, 174
  Nottingham High School, 12-14, 17, 20

Nottingham University College, 22,
  24, 63
  the Beardsall's in, 3

Oaxaca, 147-48
Orioli, Guiseppe ('Pino'), 159-60, 161
  publishes *Lady Chatterley's Lover*, 160
Oxford, xi, 84

Pangbourne, 126
Paris:
  as location to publish *Lady Chatterley's
    Lover*, 165
  DHL visits, 144, 165
Penguin Books:
  and the Obscene Publications Act, ix-x
  and the *Lady Chatterley's Lover* trial,
    ix-xii, 174
Perth, 136
Pfitscherjoch Pass, 73
Phoenix:
  as a symbol for DHL, 59, 97
  on DHL's headstone, 2, 174
  on book covers, 160
Pinker, J. B., 90, 94, 96, 100-101, 107, 113,
  119, 124
  advance offer and financial support,
    91, 120
  death and estate, 123
  DHL breaks with, 120, 123
Porthcothan, 102
Pound, Ezra, 37-8
Prestatyn, Wales, 53
Prosecutions, Director of Public, 99
Pueblo. *See* Native Americans.
'Puma'. *See* Channing, Minnie.

Radford, Dollie, 111-14
'Rananim':
  invented, 97
  DHL dreams of, 105, 139
  DHL's friends' rejection of, 143
Rathe Primrose, The. See Jessie Chambers.
Ravagli, Angelo, 172-73
  affair with Frieda, 161
  and DHL's ashes, 173
  first meets DHL and Frieda, 150
  Frieda's visits to, 161, 166
  see also Lawrence, Frieda.

Reid, Reverend Robert, 26-7
Rhine, 150
Rhineland, 62
Rhys, Ernest, 38
Rhythm, The, 84
Richthofen, Anna von (Frieda's
    mother), 64
    DHL and Frieda visit, 150, 154, 168
    DHL's anger at, 168
    introduced to DHL, 67
Richthofen, Else von *see* Jaffe, Else.
Richthofen, Friedrich von (Frieda's father),
    64, 69, 92, 95
    meets DHL, 68
    relationship with family, 64
Richthofen, Johanna (Frieda's sister), 64,
    67, 132
Ripley, 102, 118, 123, 150, 154
Riva, 75
Robermond, Villa (Vence), 170, 174
Rome, 122
Royal Literary Fund, 97
Russell, Bertrand, 97, 104

San Francisco, 136-37, 169
Santa Fe, 137
Sardinia, 130-31
Schmidt, Florence, 38
Scotland, 154
Scotland Yard, 157, 164
Secker, Martin, 52-3, 119, 150, 156, 160
    DHL annoyed at, 132-33
    publishes DHL, 74, 128-29, 143, 168
Seltzer, Thomas, 120, 140, 142, 147
    break with DHL,
    DHL and Frieda's visits to,
    DHL's trust in, 144-45
    publishes DHL, 129, 131, 143
    visits DHL and Frieda, 139
Seltzer, Adele, 139, 142
Selwood Terrace. *See* London.
Shakespeare, William, 23
Shanklin, 35
Sheerness, 4
Sicily, 129, 131
    DHL and Frieda move to, 125-28
Skegness, 20
Skinner, Mollie, 136, 142

'Spanish flu'. *See* Influenza.
Spotorno, 151-52
Sri Lanka. *See* Ceylon.
St Ives, 114
Strikes, 124, 155
Surrey, 32
Sussex. *See* Greatham.
Sutton-in-Ashfield, 4
Sutton-on-Sea, 154
Switzerland, 159, 162
Sydney, 136

Tahiti, 136-37
Taormina, 125, 128, 130, 132-33
Taos, 137, 173
    DHL and Frieda in, 138, 140, 145
    landscape of, 133, 137
    Mabel Luhan invites DHL to, 133
Terriss, Ellaline, 38
Thirroul, 136
Thornycroft, Rosalind. *See*
    Baynes, Rosalind.
Titus, Edward, 166
'Toby'. *See* Brett, Dorothy.
Tolstoy, Leo, 32, 35
Tregerthen. *See* Higher Tregerthen,
Trier, 68
Tuberculosis (consumption), 154, 124
    DHL's diagnosis of, 147-48
    DHL in danger of developing, 58
    DHL's final illness with, 169
    DHL's treatment for, 169
        suggested inhalation cure, 158
    Gertrude Cooper's diagnosis of, 154
    Katherine Mansfield suffering from,
        116, 124
    preventing DHL from entering
        USA, 149
Tuscany, xii

Ulysses. See James Joyce.
USA. *See* America.

Vence, 2, 170, 172-74
Venice, 127-28

Waldbröl, 66, 68, 70
Walker Street. *See* Eastwood.

War, First World, 93, 97-8, 101, 105,
    109, 116
    Armistice, the, 115
    DHL's call up and medical exams,
        106, 114
    DHL's thoughts on, 93-4, 98-9,
        101, 104
    evidence in London of, 93, 111
    outbreak of, 93
Warren, Dorothy, 167
Warren Gallery, 157, 167
Weber, Alfred, 70
Weekley, Barbara ('Barby'), 65, 82,
    152, 161
    DHL and, 151
    present at DHL's death, 170
    sides with DHL, 153
Weekley, Elsa, 65, 82, 151-53
Weekley, Ernest, 63, 66, 85, 172-73, 73-5,
    81-2, 92
    divorce from Frieda, 67, 69, 79,
        81, 89-90

Frieda separates from, 66
initial relationship with DHL, 63
insults directed at Frieda, 84
isolates children from Frieda, 71, 78-9,
    84, 87, 95
meets and marries Frieda, 64
quarrels with Frieda, 71
Weekley, Maude, 84
Weekley, Montagu ('Monty'), 65-6, 69,
    151, 154
    Frieda attempts to see, 82, 84, 87
    Katherine Mansfield as a messenger for
        Frieda, 85, 87
Wells, H.G., 32, 35-6, 170
Wesleyan. See Chapel.
Woolf, Virginia, 89, 129

Yorke, Dorothy 'Arabella', 163

Zennor, 105